Contemporary American Poetry

Houghton Mifflin Company · Boston

New York   Atlanta   Geneva, Illinois   Dallas   Palo Alto

Contemporary American Poetry

Edited by

A. Poulin, Jr.

St. Francis College

Library of Congress Catalog Card Number: 78–131056
ISBN: 0–395–05063–4

COPYRIGHTS AND ACKNOWLEDGEMENTS

Louis Simpson "American Poetry": Copyright © 1963 by Louis Simpson. Reprinted from *At the End of the Open Road,* by Louis Simpson, by permission of Wesleyan University Press.

John Ashbery "Some Trees" reprinted by permission of International Famous Agency, Inc. "They Dream Only of America," "Leaving the Atocha Station," "Our Youth": Copyright © 1957, 1959, 1961 by John Ashbery. Reprinted from *The Tennis Court Oath,* by John Ashbery, by permission of Wesleyan University Press. "Our Youth" originally appeared in *Poetry.* "Dido": Copyright © 1962 by John Ashbery. From "Two Sonnets" in *The Tennis Court Oath,* by John Ashbery, reprinted by permission of Wesleyan University Press. "These Lacustrine Cities," "Last Month," "Civilization and Its Discontents": From *Rivers and Mountains* by John Ashbery. Copyright © 1962, 1963, 1964, 1966 by John Ashbery. Reprinted by permission of Holt, Rinehart and Winston, Inc.

John Berryman "Dream Songs" 1, 4, 8, 9, 13, 14, 29, 45, 46, 55: Reprinted with the permission of Farrar, Straus & Giroux, Inc. from *77 Dream Songs,* copyright © 1959, 1962, 1963, 1964 by John Berryman. "Dream Songs" 91, 170, 172, 230, 266, 353, 380, 382, 384, 385: From *His Toy, His Dream, His Rest* by John Berryman, copyright © 1964, 1965, 1966, 1967, 1968 by John Berryman.

Robert Bly "Waking from Sleep," "In a Train," "Old Boards," "Snowfall in the Afternoon": Copyright 1962 by Robert Bly; "Surprised by Evening": Copyright 1961 by Robert Bly; "Poem in Three Parts," "Poem Against the Rich": Copyright 1959 by Robert Bly. All reprinted from *Silence in the Snowy Fields* by Robert Bly, Wesleyan University Press, 1962, by permission of Robert Bly. "Come with Me": Copyright © 1964 by Robert Bly; "War and Silence,"

Photo by Arthur Furst

for Basilike and Daphne

AMERICAN POETRY

Whatever it is, it must have
A stomach that can digest
Rubber, coal, uranium, moons, poems.

Like the shark, it contains a shoe.
It must swim for miles through the desert
Uttering cries that are almost human.

Louis Simpson

Contents

Allen Ginsberg

LeRoi Jones

Kenneth Koch

Denise Levertov

John Logan

Robert Lowell

W. S. Merwin

Frank O'Hara

Sylvia Plath

James Wright

Introduction

The high ones die, die. They die. You look up and who's there?

John Berryman

Most of the high ones who straddled American poetry for half a century are indeed dead: Eliot, Frost, Stevens, Williams. Silent and staring, only Pound is still around. However, one thing's certain: with the death of poets as with that of kings the cry's the same: Long live! The life and continuity of poetry, except in the most extraordinary circumstances, cannot tolerate a vacuum. So now we're due for a re-interpretation of what constitutes 'modern poetry'; the Second rather than the First World War presently seems a more exact, more appropriate moment and experience of demarkation. The tenets of New Criticism are undergoing their own revaluations. Critics have started weighing our poets for greatness, grading them like eggs. The left has begun canonization procedures for one or two of its beatific figures not venerated by the Establishment. A new dictator may be mapping his strategy to create the literary situation most suitable for his own poetry; and a future President may be eyeing his one-day unofficial and rustic laureate. For the time being, Henry Pussycat's question may be unanswerable—too much depends on vantage point, the angle of vision, the focus of your telescope. But there's no doubt that a new generation of poets has come into its own. Vibrant and diversified, their work testifies to the continued rich life of American poetry.

This anthology is a cross-section of the work of twenty-two of the more significant American poets who have shaped the contours and direction of contemporary poetry since about 1945. It is also intended to be representative of the vitality and diversity of American poetry written during the past quarter of a century. Because this collection is meant to be selective *and* representative (a most delicate balance), I have been unable to include many, many poets whose work I greatly admire. However, the inclusion of more poets would have necessitated considerably fewer poems by each. I trust the book's controlled scope is more than counterbalanced by its greater intensity of focus and depth.

I have attempted to represent each poet as fully and as equitably as possible, selecting those poems which reflect his or her characteristic subjects, themes and style(s). For the poets whose styles have undergone radical changes in the course of their careers, with few exceptions I've focused on the more recent poems. Although these may be more "difficult," often not obviously constructed according to the expected critical premises of the modern poem, they reflect some of the important innovations in American poetry since 1945 and are more challenging, exciting and historically important.

Various poets in this book share a number of characteristics, and they might have been grouped accordingly. But no contemporary poet belongs to one "school" exclusively; some belong to no "school" at all. And, to date, attempts to categorize poets in such a fashion have resulted in convincing the discriminating reader that so-and-so simply isn't a personal-confessional, Beat, New York or projectivist poet. Moreover, in some instances one must choose between believing the poet or the man; and either choice is necessarily wrong. Besides, such an approach predisposes the uninitiated reader to a given set of anticipations and violates the integrity of the individual poem, the uniqueness of the individual poet, and the spontaneity of the reader's response.

For much the same reason I have placed all critical apparatus at the back of the book, where the reader may turn should he need or feel uncontrollably compelled to do so. For each poet I have supplied a selected bibliography of primary and secondary works and a brief biographical and critical note sketching some of the prominent features of his or her work. In these notes I've taken "schooling" into account now and then, but primarily I've let the poet's work and not any particular set of critical assumptions serve as my point of departure. Occasionally I have also suggested one or two critical points which, in my estimation, have been overlooked and which, whether or not they can withstand greater scrutiny, at least deserve consideration. I have also supplied a more substantial though basic essay in which I've attempted to delineate the major characteristics of contemporary poetry and to view it in a critical and historical perspective, hopefully providing the uninitiated reader of contemporary poetry with a sense of how and why it is both new and a continuation of various American literary traditions. Lastly, I've supplied a selected bibliography of the more substantial works of criticism devoted to the poetry of this generation.

Anthologies of contemporary poetry, like new cars, run the risk of being obsolete within a couple years. My hope is that this one will have the lasting power of a Volkswagen at least. If so, its capacity to survive will be due not only to the power of the poetry but also to the good will and help of many who made this book possible. Thus I want to thank the poets, their agents and publishers for their cooperation, especially those who provided me with manuscripts and page-proofs of new books in order that this collection might be as up-to-date as possible. I am particularly grateful to several individuals whose suggestions and personal interest in this book have been invaluable: Gayatri Spivac, Judson Jerome, Marvin Bell, George Starbuck, Allen Ginsberg, Robert Bly, John Logan and Richard Wilbur. My assistant, Richard Fillion, performed even the most pedestrian tasks with the enthusiasm of a blood-brother, which he is. Thomas Wittenberg honed down my idealism with a professional practicality and good sense that would have threatened Benjamin Franklin—but with friendship. And my wife who offered words, silence and love: this book is her's, too.

A. Poulin, Jr.

Biddeford, Maine

Brigid Polk

John Ashbery

SOME TREES

These are amazing: each
Joining a neighbour, as though speech
Were a still performance.
Arranging by chance

To meet as far this morning
From the world as agreeing
With it, you and I
Are suddenly what the trees try

To tell us we are:
That their merely being there
Means something; that soon
We may touch, love, explain.

And glad not to have invented
Such comeliness, we are surrounded:
A silence already filled with noises,
A canvas on which emerges

A chorus of smiles, a winter morning.
Placed in a puzzling light, and moving,
Our days put on such reticence
These accents seem their own defence.

OUR YOUTH

Of bricks . . . Who built it? Like some crazy balloon
When love leans on us
Its nights . . . The velvety pavement sticks to our feet.
The dead puppies turn us back on love.

Where we are. Sometimes
The brick arches led to a room like a bubble, that broke when you
    entered it
And sometimes to a fallen leaf.
We got crazy with emotion, showing how much we knew.

The Arabs took us. We knew
The dead horses. We were discovering coffee,
How it is to be drunk hot, with bare feet
In Canada. And the immortal music of Chopin

Which we had been discovering for several months
Since we were fourteen years old. And coffee grounds,
And the wonder of hands, and the wonder of the day
When the child discovers her first dead hand.

Do you know it? Hasn't she
Observed you too? Haven't you been observed to her?
My, haven't the flowers been? Is the evil
In't? What window? What did you say there?

Heh? Eh? Our youth is dead.
From the minute we discover it with eyes closed
Advancing into mountain light.
Ouch . . . You will never have that young boy,

That boy with the monocle
Could have been your father
He is passing by. No, that other one,
Upstairs. He is the one who wanted to see you.

He is dead. Green and yellow handkerchiefs cover him.
Perhaps he will never rot, I see
That my clothes are dry. I will go.
The naked girl crosses the street.

Blue hampers . . . Explosions,
Ice . . . The ridiculous
Vases of porphyry. All that our youth
Can't use, that it was created for.

It's true we have not avoided our destiny
By weeding out the old people.
Our faces have filled with smoke. We escape
Down the cloud ladder, but the problem has not been solved.

DIDO

from **Two Sonnets**

The body's products become
Fatal to it. Our spit
Would kill us, but we
Die of our heat.
Though I say the things I wish to say
They are needless, their own flame conceives it.
So I am cheated of perfection.

The iodine bottle sat in the hall
And out over the park where crawled roadsters
The apricot and purple clouds were
And our blood flowed down the grating
Of the cream-colored embassy.
Inside it they had a record of "The St. Louis Blues."

"THEY DREAM ONLY OF AMERICA"

They dream only of America
To be lost among the thirteen million pillars of grass:
"This honey is delicious
Though it burns the throat."

And hiding from darkness in barns
They can be grownups now
And the murderer's ash tray is more easily—
The lake a lilac cube.

He holds a key in his right hand.
"Please," he asked willingly.
He is thirty years old.
That was before

We could drive hundreds of miles
At night through dandelions.
When his headache grew worse we
Stopped at a wire filling station.

Now he cared only about signs.
Was the cigar a sign?
And what about the key?
He went slowly into the bedroom.

"I would not have broken my leg if I had not fallen
Against the living room table. What is it to be back
Beside the bed? There is nothing to do
For our liberation, except wait in the horror of it.

And I am lost without you."

LEAVING THE ATOCHA STATION

The arctic honey blabbed over the report causing darkness
And pulling us out of there experiencing it
he meanwhile . . .   And the fried bats they sell there
dropping from sticks, so that the menace of your prayer folds . . .
Other people . . .   flash
the garden are you boning
and defunct covering . . .   Blind dog expressed royalties . . .
comfort of your perfect tar grams nuclear world bank tulip
Favorable to   near the night pin
loading formaldehyde. the table torn from you
Suddenly   and we are close
Mouthing the root   when you think
generator   homes enjoy leered

The worn stool blazing   pigeons from the roof
                 driving tractor to squash
Leaving the Atocha Station   steel
infected bumps the screws
     everywhere   wells
abolished top ill-lit
scarecrow falls   Time, progress and good sense
strike of shopkeepers dark blood
no forest you can name drunk scrolls
the completely new Italian hair . . .
Baby . . .   ice falling off the port
The centennial   Before we can

                 old   eat
members with their chins
               so high up   rats
     relaxing the cruel discussion
  suds   the painted corners
white   most aerial
     garment crow
                 and when the region took us back

the person left us like birds
   it was fuzz on the passing light
over disgusted heads, far into amnesiac
permanent house depot   amounts he can
      decrepit mayor . . .   exalting flea
for that we turn around
experiencing it is not to go into
the epileptic prank forcing bar
to borrow out onto tide-exposed fells
over her morsel, she chasing you
and the revenge he'd get
establishing the vultural over
rural area cough protection
murdering quintet.   Air pollution terminal
the clean fart genital enthusiastic toe prick album serious evening flames
the lake over your hold   personality
      lightened . . .   roar
You are freed
      including barrels
head of the swan   forestry
the night and stars fork
That is, he said
   and rushing under the hoops of
equations probable
     absolute mush   the right
entity   chain store   sewer opened their books
     The flood dragged you
     I coughed to the window
last month: juice, earlier
like the slacks   to be declining
   the peaches   more
  fist
sprung expecting the cattle
false loam   imports
     next time around

LAST MONTH

No changes of support—only
Patches of gray, here where sunlight fell.
The house seems heavier
Now that they have gone away.
In fact it emptied in record time.
When the flat table used to result
A match recedes, slowly, into the night.
The academy of the future is
Opening its doors and willing
The fruitless sunlight streams into domes
The chairs piled high with books and papers.

The sedate one is this month's skittish one
Confirming the property that,
A timeless value, has changed hands.
And you could have a new automobile
Ping pong set and garage, but the thief
Stole everything like a miracle.
In his book there was a picture of treason only
And in the garden, cries and colors.

THESE LACUSTRINE CITIES

These lacustrine cities grew out of loathing
Into something forgetful, although angry with history.
They are the product of an idea: that man is horrible, for instance,
Though this is only one example.

They emerged until a tower
Controlled the sky, and with artifice dipped back
Into the past for swans and tapering branches,
Burning, until all that hate was transformed into useless love.

Then you are left with an idea of yourself
And the feeling of ascending emptiness of the afternoon
Which must be charged to the embarrassment of others
Who fly by you like beacons.

The night is a sentinel.
Much of your time has been occupied by creative games
Until now, but we have all-inclusive plans for you.
We had thought, for instance, of sending you to the middle of the
    desert,

To a violent sea, or of having the closeness of the others be air
To you, pressing you back into a startled dream
As sea-breezes greet a child's face.
But the past is already here, and you are nursing some private project.

The worst is not over, yet I know
You will be happy here. Because of the logic
Of your situation, which is something no climate can outsmart.
Tender and insouciant by turns, you see.

You have built a mountain of something,
Thoughtfully pouring all your energy into this single monument,
Whose wind is desire starching a petal,
Whose disappointment broke into a rainbow of tears.

CIVILIZATION AND ITS DISCONTENTS

A people chained to aurora
I alone disarming you

Millions of facts of distributed light

Helping myself with some big boxes
Up the steps, then turning to no neighborhood;
The child's psalm, slightly sung
In the hall rushing into the small room.

Such fire! leading away from destruction.
Somewhere in outer ether I glimpsed you
Coming at me, the solo barrier did it this time,
Guessing us staying, true to be at the blue mark
Of the threshold. Tired of planning it again and again,
The cool boy distant, and the soaked-up
Afterthought, like so much rain, or roof.

The miracle took you in beside him.
Leaves rushed the window, there was clear water and the sound of a
  lock.
Now I never see you much any more.
The summers are much colder than they used to be
In that other time, when you and I were young.
I miss the human truth of your smile,
The halfhearted gaze of your palms,
And all things together, but there is no comic reign
Only the facts you put to me. You must not, then,
Be very surprised if I am alone: it is all for you,
The night, and the stars, and the way we used to be.

There is no longer any use in harping on
The incredible principle of daylong silence, the dark sunlight
As only the grass is beginning to know it,
The wreath of the north pole,
Festoons for the late return, the shy pensioners
Agasp on the lamplit air. What is agreeable
Is to hold your hand. The gravel
Underfoot. The time is for coming close. Useless
Verbs shooting the other words far away.
I had already swallowed the poison
And could only gaze into the distance at my life
Like a saint's with each day distinct.
No heaviness in the upland pastures. Nothing
In the forest. Only life under the huge trees
Like a coat that has grown too big, moving far away,
Cutting swamps for men like lapdogs, holding its own,
Performing once again, for you and for me.

Jerry Bauer

John Berryman

DREAM SONGS 1

Huffy Henry hid   the day,
unappeasable Henry sulked.
I see his point,—a trying to put things over.
It was the thought that they thought
they could *do* it made Henry wicked & away.
But he should have come out and talked.

All the world like a woolen lover
once did seem on Henry's side.
Then came a departure.
Thereafter nothing fell out as it might or ought.
I don't see how Henry, pried
open for all the world to see, survived.

What he has now to say is a long
wonder the world can bear & be.
Once in a sycamore I was glad
all at the top, and I sang.
Hard on the land wears the strong sea
and empty grows every bed.

4

Filling her compact & delicious body
with chicken páprika, she glanced at me
twice.

Fainting with interest, I hungered back
and only the fact of her husband & four other people
kept me from springing on her

or falling at her little feet and crying
'You are the hottest one for years of night
Henry's dazed eyes
have enjoyed, Brilliance.' I advanced upon
(despairing) my spumoni. —Sir Bones: is stuffed,
de world, wif feeding girls.

—Black hair, complexion Latin, jewelled eyes
downcast . . . The slob beside her   feasts . . . What wonders is
she sitting on, over there?
The restaurant buzzes. She might as well be on Mars.
Where did it all go wrong? There ought to be a law against Henry.
—Mr. Bones: there is.

8

The weather was fine. They took away his teeth,
white & helpful; bothered his backhand;
halved his green hair.
They blew out his loves, his interests. 'Underneath,'
(they called in iron voices) 'understand,
is nothing. So there.'

The weather was very fine. They lifted off
his covers till he showed, and cringed & pled
to see himself less.
They installed mirrors till he flowed. 'Enough'
(murmured they) 'if you will watch Us instead,
yet you may saved be. Yes.'

The weather fleured. They weakened all his eyes,
and burning thumbs into his ears, and shook
his hand like a notch.

They flung long silent speeches. (Off the hook!)
They sandpapered his plumpest hope. (So capsize.)
They took away his crotch.

9

Deprived of his enemy, shrugged to a standstill
horrible Henry, foaming. Fan their way
toward him who will
in the high wood: the officers, their rest,
with p. a. echoing: his girl comes, say,
conned in to test

if he's still human, see: she love him, see,
therefore she get on the Sheriff's mike & howl
'Come down, come down'.
Therefore he un-budge, furious. He'd flee
but only Heaven hangs over him foul.
At the crossways, downtown,

he dreams the folks are buying parsnips & suds
and paying rent to foes. He slipt & fell.
It's golden here in the snow.
A mild crack: a far rifle. Bogart's duds
truck back to Wardrobe. Fancy the brain from hell
held out so long. Let go.

13

God bless Henry. He lived like a rat,
with a thatch of hair on his head
in the beginning.
Henry was not a coward. Much.
He never deserted anything; instead
he stuck, when things like pity were thinning.

So may be Henry was a human being.
Let's investigate that.
. . . We did; okay.
He is a human American man.
That's true. My lass is braking.
My brass is aching. Come & diminish me, & map my way.

God's Henry's enemy. We're in business . . . Why,
what business must be clear.
A cornering.
I couldn't feel more like it. —Mr. Bones,
as I look on the saffron sky,
you strikes me as ornery.

14

Life, friends, is boring. We must not say so.
After all, the sky flashes, the great sea yearns,
we ourselves flash and yearn,
and moreover my mother told me as a boy
(repeatingly) 'Ever to confess you're bored
mèans you have no

Inner Resources.' I conclude now I have no
inner resources, because I am heavy bored.
Peoples bore me,
literature bores me, especially great literature,
Henry bores me, with his plights & gripes
as bad as achilles,

who loves people and valiant art, which bores me.
And the tranquil hills, & gin, look like a drag
and somehow a dog
has taken itself & its tail considerably away
into mountains or sea or sky, leaving
behind: me, wag.

29

There sat down, once, a thing on Henry's heart
só heavy, if he had a hundred years
& more, & weeping, sleepless, in all them time
Henry could not make good.
Starts again always in Henry's ears
the little cough somewhere, an odour, a chime.

And there is another thing he has in mind
like a grave Sienese face a thousand years
would fail to blur the still profiled reproach of. Ghastly,
with open eyes, he attends, blind.
All the bells say: too late. This is not for tears;
thinking.

But never did Henry, as he thought he did,
end anyone and hacks her body up
and hide the pieces, where they may be found.
He knows: he went over everyone, & nobody's missing.
Often he reckons, in the dawn, them up.
Nobody is ever missing.

45

He stared at ruin. Ruin stared straight back.
He thought they was old friends. He felt on the stair
where her papa found them bare
they became familiar. When the papers were lost
rich with pals' secrets, he thought he had the knack
of ruin. Their paths crossed

and once they crossed in jail; they crossed in bed;
and over an unsigned letter their eyes met,
and in an Asian city

directionless & lurchy at two & three,
or trembling to a telephone's fresh threat,
and when some wired his head

to reach a wrong opinion, 'Epileptic'.
But he noted now that: they were not old friends.
He did not know this one.
This one was a stranger, come to make amends
for all the imposters, and to make it stick.
Henry nodded, un-.

46

I am, outside. Incredible panic rules.
People are blowing and beating each other without mercy.
Drinks are boiling. Iced
drinks are boiling. The worse anyone feels, the worse
treated he is. Fools elect fools.
A harmless man at an intersection said, under his breath: "Christ!"

That word, so spoken, affected the vision
of, when they trod to work next day, shopkeepers
who went & were fitted for glasses.
Enjoyed they then an appearance of love & law.
Millenia whift & waft—one, one-er, er . . .
Their glasses were taken from then, & they saw.

Man has undertaken the top job of all,
son fin. Good luck.
I myself walked at the funeral of tenderness.
Followed other deaths. Among the last,
like the memory of a lovely fuck,
was: *Do, ut des*.

55

Peter's not friendly. He gives me sideways looks.
The architecture is far from reassuring.
I feel uneasy.
A pity,—the interview began so well:
I mentioned fiendish things, he waved them away
and sloshed out a martini

strangely needed. We spoke of indifferent matters—
God's health, the vague hell of the Congo,
John's energy,
anti-matter matter. I felt fine.
Then a change came backward. A chill fell.
Talk slackened,

died, and he began to give me sideways looks.
'Christ,' I thought 'what now?' and would have askt for another
but didn't dare.
I feel my application   failing. It's growing dark,
some other sound is overcoming. His last words are:
'We betrayed me.'

91

Op. posth. no. 14

Noises from underground made gibber some,
others collected & dug Henry up
saying 'You *are* a sight.'
Chilly, he muttered for a double rum
waving the mikes away, putting a stop
to rumours, pushing his fright

off with the now accumulated taxes
accustomed in his way to solitude
and no bills.
Wives came forward, claiming a new Axis,
fearful for their insurance, though, now, glued
to disencumbered Henry's many ills.

A fortnight later, sense a single man
upon the trampled scene at 2 a.m.
insomnia-plagued, with a shovel
digging like mad, Lazarus with a plan
to get his own back, a plan, a stratagem
no newsman will unravel.

170

—I can't read any more of this Rich Critical Prose,
he growled, broke wind, and scratched himself & left
that fragrant area.
When the mind dies it exudes rich critical prose,
especially about Henry, particularly in Spanish, and sends it to him
from Madrid, London, New York.

Now back on down, boys; don't expressed yourself,
begged for their own sake sympathetic Henry,
his spirit full with Mark Twain
and also his memory, lest they might strain
theirselves, to alter the best anecdote
that even he ever invented.

Let the mail demain contain no pro's or con's,
or photographs or prose or sharp translations.
Let one-armed Henry be.
A solitaire of English, free of dons
& journalists, keeping trying in one or two nations
to put his boat back to sea.

172

Your face broods from my table, Suicide.
Your force came on like a torrent toward the end
of agony and wrath.
You were christened in the beginning Sylvia Plath
and changed that name for Mrs Hughes and bred
and went on round the bend

till the oven seemed the proper place for you.
I brood upon your face, the geography of grief,
hooded, till I allow
again your resignation from us now
though the screams of orphaned children fix me anew.
Your torment here was brief,

long falls your exit all repeatingly,
a poor exemplum, one more suicide
to stack upon the others
till stricken Henry with his sisters & brothers
suddenly gone pauses to wonder why he
alone breasts the wronging tide.

230

There are voices, voices. Light's dying. Birds have quit.
He lied about me, months ago. His friendly wit
now slid to apology.
I am sorry that senior genius remembered it.
I am nothing, to occupy his thought
one moment. We

went at his bidding to his cabin, three,
in two bodies; and he spoke like Jove.
I sat there full of love,

salt with attention, while his jokes like nods
pierced for us our most strange history. He
seemed to be in charge of the odds:

hurrah. Three. Three. I must remember that.
I love great men I love. Nobody's great.
I must remember that.
We all fight. Having fought better than the rest,
he sings, & mutters & prophesies in the West
and is our flunked test.

I always come in prostrate; Yeats & Frost.

266

Dinch me, dark God, having smoked me out.
Let Henry's ails fail, pennies on his eyes
never to open more,
the shires are voting him out of time & place,
they'll drop his bundle, drunkard & Boy Scout,
where he was once before:

nowhere, nowhere. Was then the thing all planned?
I mention what I do not understand.
I mention for instance Love:
God loves his creatures when he treats them so?
Surely one grand *exception* here below
his presidency of

the widespread galaxies might once be made
for perishing Henry, whom let not then die.
He can advance no claim,
save that he studied thy Word & grew afraid,
work & fear be the basis for his terrible cry
not to forget his name.

353

These massacres of the superior peoples,
the Armenians, the Jews, the Ibos, all
(cried apoplectic Henry)
serve to remind us that culture was only a phase
through which we threaded, coming out at the other end
to the true light again of savagery.

—You feelin bad, Mr Bones? You don't *look* good.
—Do I looking like a man spent years in Hell?
for that is Henry's case:
and he remembers what he saw, how he felt & smelt,
sharp terror that increases & that stays:
the sufferings of wood

when burned are to our sufferings on the earth
as those are to our sufferings hereafter,
that is, for the Evil:
the otherwise will escape & sleep forever
except for those who in their time gave birth
to the consorts of the Devil

380

From the French Hospital in New York, 901

Wordsworth, thou form almost divine, cried Henry,
'the egotistical sublime' said Keats,
oh ho, you lovely man!
make from the rafters some mere sign to me
whether when after this raving heart which beats
& which to beat began

Long so years since   stops   I may (ah) expect
a fresh version of living or if I stop
wholly.
Oblongs attend my convalescence, wreckt
and now again, by many full propt up,
not irreversible Henry.

Punctured Henry wondered would he die
forever, all his fine body forever lost
and his very useful mind?
Hopeless & violent the man will lie,
on decades' questing, whose crazed hopes have crossed
to wind up here blind.

382

At Henry's bier let some thing fall out well:
enter there none who somewhat has to sell,
the music ancient & gradual,
the voices solemn but the grief subdued,
no hairy jokes but everybody's mood
subdued, subdued,

until the Dancer comes, in a short short dress
hair black & long & loose, dark dark glasses,
uptilted face,
pallor & strangeness, the music changes
to 'Give!' & 'Ow!' and how! the music changes,
she kicks a backward limb

on tiptoe, pirouettes, & she is free
to the knocking music, sails, dips, & suddenly
returns to the terrible gay
occasion hopeless & mad, she weaves, it's hell,
she flings to her head a leg, bobs, all is well,
she dances Henry away.

384

The marker slants, flowerless, day's almost done,
I stand above my father's grave wtih rage,
often, often before
I've made this awful pilgrimage to one
who cannot visit me, who tore his page
out: I come back for more,

I spit upon this dreadful banker's grave
who shot his heart out in a Florida dawn
O ho alas alas
When will indifference come, I moan & rave
I'd like to scrabble till I got right down
away down under the grass

and ax the casket open ha to see
just how he's taking it, which he sought so hard
we'll tear apart
the mouldering grave clothes ha & then Henry
will heft the ax once more, his final card,
and fell it on the start.

385

My daughter's heavier. Light leaves are flying.
Everywhere in enormous numbers turkeys will be dying
and other birds, all their wings.
They never greatly flew. Did they wish to?
I should know. Off away somewhere once I knew
such things.

Or good Ralph Hodgson back then did, or does.
The man is dead whom Eliot praised. My praise
follows and flows too late.

Fall is grievy, brisk. Tears behind the eyes
almost fall. Fall comes to us as a prize
to rouse us toward our fate.

My house is made of wood and it's made well,
unlike us. My house is older than Henry;
that's fairly old.
If there were a middle   ground between things and the soul
or if the sky resembled more the sea,
I wouldn't have to scold

                                        my heavy daughter.

David De Turk

Robert Bly

WAKING FROM SLEEP

Inside the veins there are navies setting forth,
Tiny explosions at the water lines,
And sea gulls weaving in the wind of the salty blood.

It is the morning. The country has slept the whole winter.
Window seats were covered with fur skins, the yard was full
Of stiff dogs, and hands that clumsily held heavy books.

Now we wake, and rise from bed, and eat breakfast!—
Shouts rise from the harbor of the blood,
Mist, and masts rising, the knock of wooden tackle in the sunlight.

Now we sing, and do tiny dances on the kitchen floor.
Our whole body is like a harbor at dawn;
We know that our master has left us for the day.

SURPRISED BY EVENING

There is unknown dust that is near us,
Waves breaking on shores just over the hill,
Trees full of birds that we have never seen,
Nets drawn down with dark fish.

The evening arrives; we look up and it is there,
It has come through the nets of the stars,
Through the tissues of the grass,
Walking quietly over the asylums of the waters.

The day shall never end, we think:
We have hair that seems born for the daylight;
But, at last, the quiet waters of the night will rise,
And our skin shall see far off, as it does under water.

IN A TRAIN

There has been a light snow.
Dark car tracks move in out of the darkness.
I stare at the train window marked with soft dust.
I have awakened at Missoula, Montana, utterly happy.

OLD BOARDS

1.
I love to see boards lying on the ground in early spring:
The ground beneath them is wet, and muddy—
Perhaps covered with chicken tracks—
And they are dry and eternal.

2.
This is the wood one sees on the decks of ocean ships,
Wood that carries us far from land,
With a dryness of something used for simple tasks,
Like a horse's tail.

3.
This wood is like a man who has a simple life,
Living through the spring and winter on the ship of his own desire.
He sits on dry wood surrounded by half-melted snow
As the rooster walks away springily over the dampened hay.

SNOWFALL IN THE AFTERNOON

1.
The grass is half-covered with snow.
It was the sort of snowfall that starts in late afternoon,
And now the little houses of the grass are growing dark.

2.
If I reached my hands down, near the earth,
I could take handfulls of darkness!
A darkness was always there, which we never noticed.

3.
As the snow grows heavier, the cornstalks fade farther away,
And the barn moves nearer to the house.
The barn moves all alone in the growing storm.

4.
The barn is full of corn, and moving toward us now,
Like a hulk blown toward us in a storm at sea;
All the sailors on deck have been blind for many years.

POEM IN THREE PARTS

1.
Oh, on an early morning I think I shall live forever!
I am wrapped in my joyful flesh,
As the grass is wrapped in its clouds of green.

2.
Rising from a bed, where I dreamt
Of long rides past castles and hot coals,
The sun lies happily on my knees;
I have suffered and survived the night
Bathed in dark water, like any blade of grass.

3.
The strong leaves of the box-elder tree,
plunging in the wind, call us to disappear
Into the wilds of the universe,
Where we shall sit at the foot of a plant,
And live forever, like the dust.

POEM AGAINST THE RICH

Each day I live, each day the sea of light
Rises, I seem to see
The tear inside the stone
As if my eyes were gazing beneath the earth.
The rich man in his red hat
Cannot hear
The weaping in the pueblos of the lily,
Or the dark tears in the shacks of the corn.
Each day the sea of light rises
I hear the sad rustle of the darkened armies,
Where each man weeps, and the plaintive
Orisons of the stones.
The stones bow as the saddened armies pass.

WAR AND SILENCE

The bombers spread out, temperature steady
A Negro's ear sleeping in an automobile tire
Pieces of timber float by saying nothing

*

Bishops rush about crying, There is no war,
And bombs fall,
Leaving a dust on the beech trees

*

One leg walks down the road and leaves
The other behind, the eyes part
And fly off in opposite directions

*

Filaments of death grow out.
The sheriff cuts off his black legs
And nails them to a tree

ASIAN PEACE OFFERS REJECTED WITHOUT PUBLICATION

These suggestions by Asians are not taken seriously.
We know Rusk smiles as he passes them to someone.
Men like Rusk are not men:
They are bombs waiting to be loaded in a darkened hangar.
Rusk's assistants eat hurriedly,
Talking of Teilhard de Chardin,
Longing to get back to their offices
So they can cling to the underside of the steel wings shuddering faintly
    in the high altitudes.
They land first, and hand the coffee cup to the drawn pilot.
They start the projector, and show the movie about the mad professor.

Lost angels huddled on a night branch!
The waves crossing
And recrossing beneath,
The sound of the rampaging Missouri,
Bending the reeds again and again—something inside us
Like a ghost train in the Rockies
About to be buried in snow!
Its long hoot
Making the owl in the Douglas fir turn his head . . .

COUNTING SMALL-BONED BODIES

Let's count the bodies over again.

If we could only make the bodies smaller,
The size of skulls,
We could make a whole plain white with skulls in the moonlight!

If we could only make the bodies smaller,
Maybe we could get
A whole year's kill in front of us on a desk!

If we could only make the bodies smaller,
We could fit
A body into a finger-ring, for a keepsake forever.

COME WITH ME

Come with me into those things that have felt this despair for so long—
Those removed Chevrolet wheels that howl with a terrible loneliness,
Lying on their backs in the cindery dirt, like men drunk, and naked,
Staggering off down a hill at night to drown at last in the pond.
Those shredded inner tubes abandoned on the shoulders of thruways,
Black and collapsed bodies, that tried and burst,
And were left behind;
And the curly steel shavings, scattered about on garage benches,
Sometimes still warm, gritty when we hold them,
Who have given up, and blame everything on the government,
And those roads in South Dakota that feel around in the darkness . . .

WHEN THE DUMB SPEAK

There is a joyful night in which we lose
Everything, and drift
Like a radish
Rising and falling, and the ocean
At last throws us into the ocean,
And on the water we are sinking
As if floating on darkness.
The body raging
And driving itself, disappearing in smoke,
Walks in large cities late at night,
Or reading the Bible in Christian Science windows,
Or reading a history of Bougainville.
Then the images appear:
Images of death,
Images of the body shaken in the grave,
And the graves filled with seawater;
Fires in the sea,
The ships smoldering like bodies,
Images of wasted life,
Life lost, imagination ruined,
The house fallen,
The gold sticks broken,
Then shall the talkative be silent,
And the dumb shall speak.

IN DANGER FROM THE OUTER WORLD

This burning in the eyes, as we open doors,
This is only the body burdened down with leaves,
The opaque flesh, heavy as November grass,
Growing stubbornly, triumphant even at midnight.

And another day disappears into the cliff,
And the Eskimos come to greet it with sharp cries—
The black water swells up over the new hole.
The grave moves forward from its ambush,

Moving over the hills on black feet,
Living off the country,
Leaving dogs and sheep murdered where it slept;
Some shining thing, inside, that has served us well

Shakes its bamboo bars—
It may be gone before we wake . . .

Photo by Roy Lewis

Gwendolyn Brooks

from A STREET IN BRONZEVILLE

the mother

Abortions will not let you forget.
You remember the children you got that you did not get,
The damp small pulps with a little or with no hair,
The singers and workers that never handled the air.
You will never neglect or beat
Them, or silence or buy with a sweet.
You will never wind up the sucking-thumb
Or scuttle off ghosts that come.
You will never leave them, controlling your luscious sigh,
Return for a snack of them, with gobbling mother-eye.

I have heard in the voices of the wind the voices of my dim killed
    children.
I have contracted. I have eased
My dim dears at the breasts they could never suck.
I have said, Sweets, if I sinned, if I seized
Your luck
And your lives from your unfinished reach,
If I stole your births and your names,
Your straight baby tears and your games,
Your stilted or lovely loves, your tumults, your marriages, aches, and
    your deaths,
If I poisoned the beginnings of your breaths,
Believe that even in my deliberateness I was not deliberate.
Though why should I whine,
Whine that the crime was other than mine?—
Since anyhow you are dead.

Or rather, or instead,
You were never made.
But that too, I am afraid,
Is faulty: oh, what shall I say, how is the truth to be said?
You were born, you had body, you died.
It is just that you never giggled or planned or cried.

Believe me, I loved you all.
Believe me, I knew you, though faintly, and I loved, I loved you
All.

the ballad of chocolate Mabbie

It was Mabbie without the grammar school gates.
And Mabbie was all of seven.
And Mabbie was cut from a chocolate bar.
And Mabbie thought life was heaven.

The grammar school gates were the pearly gates,
For Willie Boone went to school.
When she sat by him in history class
Was only her eyes were cool.

It was Mabbie without the grammar school gates
Waiting for Willie Boone.
Half hour after the closing bell!
He would surely be coming soon.

Oh, warm is the waiting for joys, my dears!
And it cannot be too long.
Oh, pity the little poor chocolate lips
That carry the bubble of song!

Out came the saucily bold Willie Boone.
It was woe for our Mabbie now.
He wore like a jewel a lemon-hued lynx
With sand-waves loving her brow.

It was Mabbie alone by the grammar school gates.
Yet chocolate companions had she:
Mabbie on Mabbie with hush in the heart.
Mabbie on Mabbie to be.

**of De Witt Williams on his way
to Lincoln Cemetery**

He was born in Alabama.
He was bred in Illinois.
He was nothing but a
Plain black boy.

Swing low swing low sweet sweet chariot.
Nothing but a plain black boy.

Drive him past the Pool Hall.
Drive him past the Show.
Blind within his casket,
But maybe he will know.

Down through Forty-seventh Street:
Underneath the L,
And Northwest Corner, Prairie,
That he loved so well.

Don't forget the Dance Halls—
Warwick and Savoy,
Where he picked his women, where
He drank his liquid joy.

Born in Alabama.
Bred in Illinois.
He was nothing but a
Plain black boy.

Swing low swing low sweet sweet chariot.
Nothing but a plain black boy.

THE BEAN EATERS

They eat beans mostly, this old yellow pair.
Dinner is a casual affair.
Plain chipware on a plain and creaking wood,
Tin flatware.

Two who are Mostly Good.
Two who have lived their day,
But keep on putting on their clothes
And putting things away.

And remembering . . .
Remembering, with twinklings and twinges,
As they lean over the beans in their rented back room that is full of
   beads and receipts and dolls and cloths, tobacco crumbs, vases and
   fringes.

THE LAST QUATRAIN OF THE BALLAD
OF EMMETT TILL

                    after the murder,
                    after the burial

Emmett's mother is a pretty-faced thing;
            the tint of pulled taffy.
She sits in a red room,
            drinking black coffee.
She kisses her killed boy.
            And she is sorry.
Chaos in windy grays
            through a red prairie.

A CATCH OF SHY FISH

garbageman: the man with the orderly mind

What do you think of us in fuzzy endeavor, you whose directions are
       sterling, whose lunge is straight?
Can you make a reason, how can you pardon us who memorize the
       rules and never score?
Who memorize the rules from your own text but never quite transfer
       them to the game,
Who never quite receive the whistling ball, who gawk, begin to absorb
       the crowd's own roar.

Is earnestness enough, may earnestness attract or lead to light;
Is light enough, if hands in clumsy frenzy, flimsy whimsicality, enlist;
Is light enough when this bewilderment crying against the dark shuts
       down the shades?
  Dilute confusion. Find and explode our mist.

sick man looks at flowers

You are sick and old, and there is a closing in—
The eyes gone dead to all that would beguile.
Echoes are dull and the body accepts no touch
Except its pain. Mind is a little isle.

But now invades this impudence of red!
This ripe rebuke, this burgeoning affluence
Mocks me and mocks the desert of my bed.

old people working (garden, car)

Old people working. Making a gift of garden.
Or washing a car, so some one else may ride.
A note of alliance, an eloquence of pride.
A way of greeting or sally to the world.

weaponed woman

Well, life has been a baffled vehicle
And baffling. But she fights, and
Has fought, according to her lights and
The lenience of her whirling-place.

She fights with semi-folded arms,
Her strong bag, and the stiff
Frost of her face (that challenges "When" and "If.")
And altogether she does Rather Well.

old tennis player

Refuses
To refuse the racket, to mutter No to the net.
He leans to life, conspires to give and get
Other serving yet.

a surrealist and Omega

Omega ran to witness him; beseeched;
Brought caution and carnality and cash.
She sauced him brownly, eating him
Under her fancy's finest Worcestershire.

He zigzagged.
He was a knotted hiss.
He was an insane hash
Of rebellious small strengths
And soft-mouthed mumbling weakness.

The art
Would not come right. That smear,
That yellow in the gray corner—
That was not right, he had not reached
The right, the careless flailed-out bleakness.

A god, a child.
He said he was most seriously amiss.

She had no purple or pearl to hang
About the neck of one a-wild.

A bantam beauty
Loving his ownhood for all it was worth.

Spaulding and Francois

There are cloudlets and things of cool silver in our dream, there are all
       of the Things Ethereal.
There is a
Scent of wind cut with pine, a noise of
Wind tangled among bells. There is spiritual laughter
Too hushed to be gay, too high: the happiness
Of angels. And there are angels' eyes, soft,
Heavy with precious compulsion.

But the People
Will not let us alone; will not credit, condone
Art-loves that shun
Them (moderate Christians rotting in the sun.)

Big Bessie throws her son into the street

A day of sunny face and temper.
The winter trees
Are musical.

Bright lameness from my beautiful disease,
You have your destiny to chip and eat.

Be precise.
With something better than candles in the eyes.
(Candles are not enough.)

At the root of the will, a wild inflammable stuff.

New pioneer of days and ways, be gone.
Hunt out your own or make your own alone.

Go down the street.

WE REAL COOL

The Pool Players.
Seven at the Golden Shovel.

We real cool. We
Left school. We

Lurk late. We
Strike straight. We

Sing sin. We
Thin gin. We

Jazz June. We
Die soon.

THE LOVERS OF THE POOR

arrive. The Ladies from the Ladies' Betterment
League
Arrive in the afternoon, the late light slanting
In diluted gold bars across the boulevard brag
Of proud, seamed faces with mercy and murder hinting
Here, there, interrupting, all deep and debonair,
The pink paint on the innocence of fear;
Walk in a gingerly manner up the hall.

Cutting with knives served by their softest care,
Served by their love, so barbarously fair.
Whose mothers taught: You'd better not be cruel!
You had better not throw stones upon the wrens!
Herein they kiss and coddle and assault
Anew and dearly in the innocence
With which they baffle nature. Who are full,
Sleek, tender-clad, fit, fiftyish, a-glow, all
Sweetly abortive, hinting at fat fruit,
Judge it high time that fiftyish fingers felt
Beneath the lovelier planes of enterprise.
To resurrect. To moisten with milky chill.
To be a random hitching-post or plush.
To be, for wet eyes, random and handy hem.
                    Their guild is giving money to the poor.
The worthy poor. The very very worthy
And beautiful poor. Perhaps just not too swarthy?
Perhaps just not too dirty nor too dim
Nor—passionate. In truth, what they could wish
Is—something less than derelict or dull.
Not staunch enough to stab, though, gaze for gaze!
God shield them sharply from the beggar-bold!
The noxious needy ones whose battle's bald
Nonetheless for being voiceless, hits one down.
                    But it's all so bad; and entirely too much for
                        them.
The stench; the urine, cabbage, and dead beans,
Dead porridges of assorted dusty grains,
The old smoke, *heavy* diapers, and, they're told,
Something called chitterlings. The darkness. Drawn
Darkness, or dirty light. The soil that stirs.
The soil that looks the soil of centuries.
And for that matter the *general* oldness. Old
Wood. Old marble. Old tile. Old old old.
Not homekind Oldness! Not Lake Forest, Glencoe.
Nothing is sturdy, nothing is majestic,
There is no quiet drama, no rubbed glaze, no
Unkillable infirmity of such
A tasteful turn as lately they have left,
Glencoe, Lake Forest, and to which their cars

Must presently restore them. When they're done
With dullards and distortions of this fistic
Patience of the poor and put-upon.
        They've never seen such a make-do-ness as
Newspaper rugs before! In this, this "flat,"
Their hostess is gathering up the oozed, the rich
Rugs of the morning (tattered! the bespattered. . . .)
Readies to spread clean rugs for afternoon.
Here is a scene for you. The Ladies look,
In horror, behind a substantial citizeness
Whose trains clank out across her swollen heart.
Who, arms akimbo, almost fills a door.
All tumbling children, quilts dragged to the floor
And tortured thereover, potato peelings, soft-
Eyed kitten, hunched-up, haggard, to-be-hurt.
        Their League is allotting largesse to the Lost.
But to put their clean, their pretty money, to put
Their money collected from delicate rose-fingers
Tipped with their hundred flawless rose-nails seems . . .
        They own Spode, Lowestoft, candelabra,
Mantels, and hostess gowns, and sunburst clocks,
Turtle soup, Chippendale, red satin "hangings,"
Aubussons and Hattie Carnegie. They Winter
In Palm Beach; cross the Water in June; attend,
When suitable, the nice Art Institute;
Buy the right books in the best bindings; saunter
On Michigan, Easter mornings, in sun or wind.
Oh Squalor! This sick four-story hulk, this fibre
With fissures everywhere! Why, what are bringings
Of loathe-love largesse? What shall peril hungers
So old old, what shall flatter the desolate?
Tin can, blocked fire escape and chitterling
And swaggering seeking youth and the puzzled wreckage
Of the middle passage, and urine and stale shames
And, again, the porridges of the underslung
And children children children. Heavens! That
Was a rat, surely, off there, in the shadows? Long
And long-tailed? Gray? The Ladies from the Ladies'
Betterment League agree it will be better
To achieve the outer air that rights and steadies,

To hie to a house that does not holler, to ring
Bells elsetime, better presently to cater
To no more Possibilities, to get
Away. Perhaps the money can be posted.
Perhaps they two may choose another Slum!
Some serious sooty half-unhappy home!—
Where loathe-love likelier may be invested.
                    Keeping their scented bodies in the center
Of the hall as they walk down the hysterical hall,
They allow their lovely skirts to graze no wall,
Are off at what they manage of a canter,
And, resuming all the clues of what they were,
Try to avoid inhaling the laden air.

NEGRO HERO

to suggest Dorie Miller

I had to kick their law into their teeth in order to save them.
However I have heard that sometimes you have to deal
Devilishly with drowning men in order to swim them to shore.
Or they will haul themselves and you to the trash and the fish beneath.
(When I think of this, I do not worry about a few
Chipped teeth.)

It is good I gave glory, it is good I put gold on their name.
Or there would have been spikes in the afterward hands.
But let us speak only of my success and the pictures in the Caucasian
    dailies
As well as the Negro weeklies. For I am a gem.
(They are not concerned that it was hardly The Enemy my fight was
    against
But them.)

It was a tall time. And of course my blood was
Boiling about in my head and straining and howling and singing me on.
Of course I was rolled on wheels of my boy itch to get at the gun.

Of course all the delicate rehearsal shots of my childhood massed in
    mirage before me.
Of course I was child
And my first swallow of the liquor of battle bleeding black air dying
    and demon noise
Made me wild.

It was kinder than that, though, and I showed like a banner my kindness.
I loved. And a man will guard when he loves.
Their white-gowned democracy was my fair lady.
With her knife lying cold, straight, in the softness of her sweet-flowing
    sleeve.
But for the sake of the dear smiling mouth and the stuttered promise I
    toyed with my life.
I threw back!—I would not remember
Entirely the knife.

Still—am I good enough to die for them, is my blood bright enough to
    be spilled,
Was my constant back-question—are they clear
On this? Or do I intrude even now?
Am I clean enough to kill for them, do they wish me to kill
For them or is my place while death licks his lips and strides to them
In the galley still?

(In a southern city a white man said
Indeed, I'd rather be dead;
Indeed, I'd rather be shot in the head
Or ridden to waste on the back of a flood
Than saved by the drop of a black man's blood.)

Naturally, the important thing is, I helped to save them, them and a part
    of their democracy.
Even if I had to kick their law into their teeth in order to do that for
    them.
And I am feeling well and settled in myself because I believe it was a
    good job,
Despite this possible horror: that they might prefer the
Preservation of their law in all its sick dignity and their knives
To the continuation of their creed
And their lives.

RIOT

A riot is the language of the unheard.

Martin Luther King

John Cabot, out of Wilma, once a Wycliffe,
all whitebluerose below his golden hair,
wrapped richly in right linen and right wool,
almost forgot his Jaguar and Lake Bluff;
almost forgot Grandtully (which is The
Best Thing That Ever Happened To Scotch); almost
forgot the sculpture at the Richard Gray
and Distelheim; the kidney pie at Maxim's,
the Grenadine de Boeuf at Maison Henri.

Because the Negroes were coming down the street.

Because the Poor were sweaty and unpretty
(not like Two Dainty Negroes in Winnetka)
and they were coming toward him in rough ranks.
In seas. In windsweep. They were black and loud.
And not detainable. And not discreet.

Gross. Gross. *"Que tu es grossier!"* John Cabot
itched instantly beneath the nourished white
that told his story of glory to the World.
"Don't let It touch me! the blackness! Lord!" he whispered
to any handy angel in the sky.

But, in a thrilling announcement, on It drove
and breathed on him: and touched him. In that breath
the fume of pig foot, chitterling and cheap chili,
malign, mocked John. And, in terrific touch, old
averted doubt jerked forward decently,
cried "Cabot! John! You are a desperate man,
and the desperate die expensively today."

John Cabot went down in the smoke and fire
and broken glass and blood, and he cried "Lord!
Forgive these nigguhs that know not what they do."

AN ASPECT OF LOVE,
ALIVE IN THE ICE AND FIRE

LaBohem Brown

It is the morning of our love.

In a package of minutes there is this We.
How beautiful.
Merry foreigners in our morning,
we laugh, we touch each other,
are responsible props and posts.

A physical light is in the room.

Because the world is at the window
we cannot wonder very long.

You rise. Although
genial, you are in yourself again.
I observe
your direct and respectable stride.
You are direct and self-accepting as a lion
in African velvet. You are level, lean,
remote.

There is a moment in Camaraderie
when interruption is not to be understood.
I cannot bear an interruption.
This is the shining joy;
the time of not-to-end.

On the street we smile.
We go
in different directions
down the imperturbable street.

Robert Creeley

I KNOW A MAN

As I sd to my
friend, because I am
always talking,—John, I

sd, which was not his
name, the darkness sur-
rounds us, what

can we do against
it, or else, shall we &
why not, buy a goddamn big car,

drive, he sd, for
christ's sake, look
out where yr going.

A WICKER BASKET

Comes the time when it's later
and onto your table the headwaiter
puts the bill, and very soon after
rings out the sound of lively laughter—

Picking up change, hands like a walrus,
and a face like a barndoor's,
and a head without any apparent size,
nothing but two eyes—

So that's you, man,
or me. I make it as I can,
I pick up, I go
faster than they know—

Out the door, the street like a night,
any night, and no one in sight,
but then, well, there she is,
old friend Liz—

And she opens the door of her cadillac,
I step in back,
and we're gone.
She turns me on—

There are very huge stars, man, in the sky,
and from somewhere very far off someone hands me a slice of apple pie,
with a gob of white, white ice cream on top of it,
and I eat it—

Slowly. And while certainly
they are laughing at me, and all around me is racket
of these cats not making it, I make it

in my wicker basket.

THE BUSINESS

To be in love is like going out-
side to see what kind of day

it is. Do not
mistake me. If you love

her how prove she
loves also, except that it

occurs, a remote chance on
which you stake

yourself? But barter for
the Indian was a means of sustenance.

There are records.

A FORM OF WOMEN

I have come far enough
from where I was not before
to have seen the things
looking in at me through the open door

and have walked tonight
by myself
to see the moonlight
and see it as trees

and shapes more fearful
because I feared
what I did not know
but have wanted to know.

My face is my own, I thought.
But you have seen it
turn into a thousand years.
I watched you cry.

I could not touch you.
I wanted very much to
touch you
but could not.

If it is dark
when this is given to you,
have care for its content
when the moon shines.

My face is my own.
My hands are my own.
My mouth is my own
but I am not.

Moon, moon,
when you leave me alone
all the darkness is
an utter blackness,

a pit of fear,
a stench,
hands unreasonable
never to touch.

But I love you.
Do you love me.
What to say
when you see me.

THE RAIN

All night the sound had
come back again,
and again falls
this quiet, persistent rain.

What am I to myself
that must be remembered,
insisted upon
so often? Is it

that never the ease,
even the hardness,
of rain falling
will have for me

something other than this,
something not so insistent—
am I to be locked in this
final uneasiness.

Love, if you love me,
lie next to me.
Be for me, like rain,
the getting out

of the tiredness, the fatuousness, the semi-
lust of intentional indifference.
Be wet
with a decent happiness.

THE MEMORY

Like a river she was,
huge roily mass of water
carrying tree trunks
and divers drunks.

Like a Priscilla, a feminine Benjamin,
a whore gone right over
the falls,
she was.

Did you know her.
Did you love her, brother.
Did wonder pour down
on the whole goddamn town.

THE RESCUE

The man sits in a timelessness
with the horse under him in time
to a movement of legs and hooves
upon a timeless sand.

Distance comes in from the foreground
present in the picture as time
he reads outward from
and comes from that beginning.

A wind blows in
and out and all about the man
as the horse ran
and runs to come in time.

A house is burning in the sand.
A man and horse are burning.
The wind is burning
They are running to arrive.

THE FLOWER

I think I grow tensions
like flowers
in a wood where
nobody goes.

Each wound is perfect,
encloses itself in a tiny
imperceptible blossom,
making pain.

Pain is a flower like that one,
like this one,
like that one,
like this one.

THE WINDOW

Position is where you
put it, where it is,
did you, for example, that

large tank there, silvered,
with the white church along-
side, lift

all that, to what
purpose? How
heavy the slow

world is with
everything put
in place. Some

man walks by, a
car beside him on
the dropped

road, a leaf of
yellow color is
going to

fall. It
all drops into
place. My

face is heavy
with the sight. I can
feel my eye breaking.

THE LANGUAGE

Locate *I*
love you some-
where in

teeth and
eyes, bite
it but

take care not
to hurt, you
want so

much so
little. Words
say everything,

I
love you
again,

then what
is emptiness
for. To

fill, fill.
I heard words
and words full

of holes
aching. Speech
is a mouth.

© Rollie McKenna

James Dickey

IN THE MOUNTAIN TENT

I am hearing the shape of the rain
Take the shape of the tent and believe it,
Laying down all around where I lie
A profound, unspeakable law.
I obey, and am free-falling slowly

Through the thought-out leaves of the wood
Into the minds of animals.
I am there in the shining of water
Like dark, like light, out of Heaven.

I am there like the dead, or the beast
Itself, which thinks of a poem—
Green, plausible, living, and holy—
And cannot speak, but hears,
Called forth from the waiting of things,

A vast, proper, reinforced crying
With the sifted, harmonious pause,
The sustained intake of all breath
Before the first word of the Bible.

At midnight water dawns
Upon the held skulls of the foxes
And weasels and tousled hares
On the eastern side of the mountain.
Their light is the image I make

As I wait as if recently killed,
Receptive, fragile, half-smiling,
My brow watermarked with the mark
On the wing of a moth

And the tent taking shape on my body
Like ill-fitting, Heavenly clothes.
From holes in the ground comes my voice
In the God-silenced tongue of the beasts.
"I shall rise from the dead," I am saying.

SPRINGER MOUNTAIN

Four sweaters are woven upon me,
All black, all sweating and waiting,
And a sheepherder's coat's wool hood,
Buttoned strainingly, holds my eyes
With their sight deepfrozen outside them
From their gaze toward a single tree.
I am here where I never have been,
In the limbs of my warmest clothes,
Waiting for light to crawl, weakly
From leaf to dead leaf onto leaf
Down the western side of the mountain.
Deer sleeping in light far above me

Have already woken, and moved,
In step with the sun moving strangely
Down toward the dark knit of my thicket
Where my breath takes shape on the air
Like a white helmet come from the lungs.
The one tree I hope for goes inward
And reaches the limbs of its gold.
My eyesight hangs partly between
Two twigs on the upslanting ground,
Then steps like a god from the dead
Wet of a half-rotted oak log
Steeply into the full of my brow.
My thighbones groaningly break

Upward, releasing my body
To climb, and to find among humus
New insteps made of snapped sticks.
On my back the faggot of arrows
Rattles and scratches its feathers.

I go up over logs slowly
On my painfully reborn legs,
My ears putting out vast hearing
Among the invisible animals,
Passing under thin branches held still,
Kept formed all night as they were
By the thought of predictable light.
The sun comes openly in
To my mouth, and is blown out white,

But no deer is anywhere near me.
I sit down and wait as in darkness.

The sweat goes dead at the roots

Of my hair: a deer is created
Descending, then standing and looking.
The sun stands and waits for his horns

To move. I may be there, also,
Between them, in head bones uplifted
Like a man in an animal tree
Nailed until light comes:
A dream of the unfeared hunter
Who has formed in his brain in the dark
And rose with light into his horns,
Naked, and I have turned younger

At forty than I ever have been.
I hang my longbow on a branch.
The buck leaps away and then stops,
And I step forward, stepping out

Of my shadow and pulling over
My head one dark heavy sweater
After another, my dungarees falling

Till they can be kicked away,
Boots, socks, all that is on me
Off. The world catches fire.
I put an unbearable light
Into breath skinned alive of its garments:
I think, beginning with laurel,

Like a beast loving
With the whole god bone of his horns:
The green of excess is upon me
Like deer in fir thickets in winter
Stamping and dreaming of men
Who will kneel with them naked to break
The ice from streams with their faces
And drink from the lifespring of beasts.
He is moving. I am with him

Down the shuddering hillside moving
Through trees and around, inside
And out of stumps and groves
Of laurel and slash pine,
Through hip-searing branches and thorn
Brakes, unprotected and sure,
Winding down to the waters of life
Where they stand petrified in a creek bed
Yet melt and flow from the hills
At the touch of an animal visage,

Rejoicing wherever I come to
With the gold of my breast unwrapped,
My crazed laughter pure as good church-cloth,
My brain dazed and pointed with trying
To grow horns, glad that it cannot,
For a few steps deep in the dance
Of what I most am and should be
And can be only once in this life.
He is gone below, and I limp
To look for my clothes in the world,

A middle-aged, softening man
Grinning and shaking his head
In amazement to last him forever.

I put on the warm-bodied wool,
The four sweaters inside out,
The bootlaces dangling and tripping,
Then pick my tense bow off the limb
And turn with the unwinding hooftracks,
In my good, tricked clothes,
To hunt, under Springer Mountain,
Deer for the first and last time.

ENCOUNTER IN THE CAGE COUNTRY

What I was would not work
For them all, for I had not caught
The lion's eye. I was walking down

The cellblock in green glasses   and came
At last to the place where someone was hiding
His spots in his black hide.

Unchangeably they were there,
Driven in as by eyes
Like mine, his darkness ablaze

In the stinking sun of the beast house.
Among the crowd, he found me
Out   and dropped his bloody snack

And came to the perilous edge
Of the cage, where the great bars tremble
Like wire. All Sunday ambling stopped,

The curved cells tightened around
Us all   as we saw he was watching only
Me. I knew the stage was set, and I began

To perform   first saunt'ring   then stalking
Back and forth like a sentry   faked
As if to run   and at one brilliant move

I made as though drawing a gun from my hip-
bone, the bite-sized children broke
Up   changing their concept of laughter,

But none of this changed his eyes, or changed
My green glasses. Alert, attentive,
He waited for what I could give him:

My moves   my throat   my wildest love,
The eyes behind my eyes. Instead, I left
Him, though he followed me right to the end

Of concrete. I wiped my face, and lifted off
My glasses. Light blasted the world of shade
Back under every park bush   the crowd

Quailed from me   I was inside and out
Of myself   and something was given a life-
mission to say to me hungrily over

And over and over   *your moves are exactly right*
For a few things in this world: we know you
When you come, Green Eyes, Green Eyes.

THE SHEEP CHILD

Farm boys wild to couple
With anything   with soft-wooded trees
With mounds of earth   mounds
Of pinestraw   will keep themselves off
Animals by legends of their own:
In the hay-tunnel dark
And dung of barns, they will
Say   I have heard tell

That in a museum in Atlanta
Way back in a corner somewhere
There's this thing that's only half

Sheep   like a woolly baby
Pickled in alcohol   because
Those things can't live   his eyes
Are open   but you can't stand to look
I heard from somebody who . . .

But this is now almost all
Gone. The boys have taken
Their own true wives in the city,
The sheep are safe in the west hill
Pasture   but we who were born there
Still are not sure. Are we,
Because we remember, remembered
In the terrible dust of museums?

Merely with his eyes, the sheep-child may

Be saying   saying

> *I am here, in my father's house.*
> *I who am half of your world, came deeply*
> *To my mother in the long grass*
> *Of the west pasture, where she stood like moonlight*
> *Listening for foxes. It was something like love*
> *From another world that seized her*
> *From behind, and she gave, not lifting her head*
> *Out of dew, without ever looking, her best*
> *Self to that great need. Turned loose, she dipped her face*
> *Farther into the chill of the earth, and in a sound*
> *Of sobbing   of something stumbling*
> *Away, began, as she must do,*
> *To carry me. I woke, dying,*
>
> *In the summer sun of the hillside, with my eyes*
> *Far more than human. I saw for a blazing moment*
> *The great grassy world from both sides,*
> *Man and beast in the round of their need,*
> *And the hill wind stirred in my wool,*
> *My hoof and my hand clasped each other,*
> *I ate my one meal*
> *Of milk, and died*
> *Staring. From dark grass I came straight*

To my father's house, whose dust
Whirls up in the halls for no reason
When no one comes   piling deep in a hellish mild corner,
And, through my immortal waters,
I meet the sun's grains eye
To eye, and they fail at my closet of glass.
Dead, I am most surely living
In the minds of farm boys: I am he who drives
Them like wolves from the hound bitch and calf
And from the chaste ewe in the wind.
They go into woods   into bean fields   they go
Deep into their known right hands. Dreaming of me,
They groan   they wait   they suffer
Themselves, they marry, they raise their kind.

THE HEAVEN OF ANIMALS

Here they are. The soft eyes open.
If they have lived in a wood
It is a wood.
If they have lived on plains
It is grass rolling
Under their feet forever.

Having no souls, they have come,
Anyway, beyond their knowing.
Their instincts wholly bloom
And they rise.
The soft eyes open.

To match them, the landscape flowers,
Outdoing, desperately
Outdoing what is required:
The richest wood,
The deepest field.

For some of these,
It could not be the place
It is, without blood.
These hunt, as they have done,
But with claws and teeth grown perfect,

More deadly than they can believe.
They stalk more silently,
And crouch on the limbs of trees,
And their descent
Upon the bright backs of their prey

May take years
In a sovereign floating of joy.
And those that are hunted
Know this as their life,
Their reward: to walk

Under such trees in full knowledge
Of what is in glory above them,
And to feel no fear,
But acceptance, compliance.
Fulfilling themselves without pain

At the cycle's center,
They tremble, they walk
Under the tree,
They fall, they are torn,
They rise, they walk again.

ADULTERY

We have all been in rooms
We cannot die in, and they are odd places, and sad.
Often Indians are standing eagle-armed on hills

In the sunrise   open wide to the Great Spirit
Or gliding in canoes   or cattle are browsing on the walls
Far away   gazing down with the eyes of our children

Not far away   or there are men driving
The last railspike, which has turned
Gold in their hands. Gigantic forepleasure lives

Among such scenes, and we are alone with it
At last. There is always some weeping
Between us   and someone is always checking

A wrist watch by the bed to see how much
Longer we have left. Nothing can come
Of this   nothing can come

Of us: of me with my grim techniques
Or you who have sealed your womb
With a ring of convulsive rubber:

Although we come together,
Nothing will come of us. But we would not give
It up, for death is beaten

By praying Indians   by distant cows   historical
Hammers   by hazardous meetings that bridge
A continent. One could never die here

Never die   never die
While crying. My lover, my dear one
I will see you next week

When I'm in town. I will call you
If I can. Please get hold of   please don't
Oh God, Please don't any more I can't bear . . . Listen:

We have done it again   we are
Still living. Sit up and smile,
God bless you. Guilt is magical.

SUN

O Lord, it was all night
Consuming me   skin crawling tighter than any
Skin of my teeth. Bleary with ointments, dazzling
Through the dark house   man red as iron   glowing
Blazing up anew with each bad
Breath from the bellowing curtains

I had held the sun longer
Than it could stay   and in the dark it turned
My face on, infra-red: there were cracks circling
My eyes where I had squinted
Up from stone-blind sand, and seen
Eternal fire   coronas   huge

Vertical banners of flame
Leap scrollingly from the sun and tatter
To nothing in blue-veined space
On the smoked-crimson glass of my lids.
When the sun fell, I slit my eyeskins
In the dazed ruddy muddle of twilight

And in the mirror saw whiteness
Run from my eyes like tears   going upward
And sideways   slanting   as well as falling,
All in straight lines like rays
Shining   and behind me, careful not
To touch without giving me a chance

To brace myself   a smeared
Suffering woman came merging her flame-shaken
Body halo with mine   her nose still clownish
With oxides: walked to me sweating
Blood, and turned around. I peeled off
Her bathing suit like her skin   her colors

Wincing   she silently biting
Her tongue off   her back crisscrossed with stripes
Where winter had caught her and whipped her.
We stumbled together, and in the double heat
The last of my blond hair blazed up,
Burned off me forever   as we dived

For the cool of the bed
In agony even at holding hands   the blisters
On our shoulders shifting   crackling
Releasing boiling water on the sheets. *O Lord*
Who can turn out the sun, turn out that neighbor's
One bulb on his badminton court

For we are dying
Of light   searing each other   not able
To stop   to get away   she screaming O Lord
Apollo or *Water, Water*   as the moonlight drove
Us down on the tangled grid
Where in the end we lay

Suffering equally   in the sun
Backlashed from the moon's brutal stone
And meeting itself where we had stored it up
All afternoon in pain   in the gentlest touch
As we lay, O Lord,
In Hell, in love.

SLAVE QUARTERS

In the great place the great house is gone from   in the sun
Room, near the kitchen of air   I look across at low walls
Of slave quarters, and feel my imagining loins

Rise with the madness of Owners
To take off the Master's white clothes
And slide all the way into moonlight
Two hundred years old with this moon.
Let me go,

Ablaze with my old me-
scent, in moonlight made by the mind
From the dusk sun, in the yard where my dogs would smell
For once what I totally am,
Flaming up in their brains as the Master
They but dimly had sensed through my clothes:
Let me stand as though moving

At midnight, now at the instant of sundown
When the wind turns

From sea wind to land, and the marsh grass
Hovers, changing direction:
                                    there was this house
That fell before I got out. I can pull
It over me where I stand, up from the earth,
Back out of the shells
Of the sea:
                    become with the change of this air
A coastal islander, proud of his grounds,
His dogs, his spinet
From Savannah, his pale daughters,
His war with the sawgrass, pushed back into
The sea it crawled from. Nearer dark, unseen,
I can begin to dance
Inside my gabardine suit
As though I had left my silk nightshirt

In the hall of mahogany, and crept
To slave quarters to live out
The secret legend of Owners. Ah, stand up,
Blond loins, another
Love is possible! My thin wife would be sleeping
Or would not mention my absence:

                                    the moonlight

On these rocks can be picked like cotton
By a crazed Owner dancing-mad
With the secret repossession of his body

Phosphorescent and mindless, shedding
Blond-headed shadow on the sand,
Hounds pressing in their sleep
Around him, smelling his footblood
On the strange ground that lies between skins
With the roof blowing off slave quarters
To let the moon in burning
The years away
In just that corner where crabgrass proves it lives
Outside of time.
Who seeks the other color of his body,
His loins giving off a frail light
On the dark lively shipwreck of grass   sees
Water live where
The half-moon touches,
The moon made whole in one wave
Very far from the silent piano   the copy of Walter Scott
Closed on its thin-papered battles
Where his daughter practiced, decorum preventing the one
Bead of sweat in all that lace   collected at her throat
From breaking and humanly running
Over Mozart's unmortal keys—

                  I come past
A sand crab pacing sideways   his eyes out
On stalks   the bug-eyed vision of fiddler
Crabs sneaking a light on the run
From the split moon   holding in it a white man stepping
Down the road of clamshells and cotton   his eyes out
On stems   the tops of the sugar
Cane soaring   the sawgrass walking:
                     I come past
The stale pools left
Over from the high tide   where the crab in the night sand
Is basting himself with his claws   moving ripples outward
Feasting on brightness
           and above
A gull also crabs slowly,
Tacks, jibes   then turning the corner
Of wind, receives himself like a brother
As he glides down upon his reflection:

My body has a color not yet freed:
In that ruined house let me throw
Obsessive gentility off;
Let Africa rise upon me like a man
Whose instincts are delivered from their chains
Where they lay close-packed and wide-eyed
In muslin sheets
As though in the miserly holding
Of too many breaths by one ship.   Now

Worked in silver   their work lies all
Around me   the fields dissolving
Into the sea   and   not on a horse
I stoop to the soil   working
Gathering   moving to the rhythm of a music
That has crossed the ocean in chains

In the grass the great singing void of slave

Labor about me   the moonlight bringing
Sweat out of my back as though the sun
Changed skins upon me   some other
Man moving near me on horseback   whom I look in the eyes
Once a day:
                    there in that corner

Her bed turned to grass. Unsheltered by these walls
The outside fields form slowly
Anew, in a kind of barrelling blowing,
Bend in all the right places   as faintly Michael rows
The boat ashore   his spiritual lungs
Entirely filling the sail.   How take on the guilt

Of slavers? How shudder like one who made
Money from buying a people
To work as ghosts
In this blowing solitude?
I only stand here upon shells   dressed poorly
For nakedness   poorly
For the dark wrecked hovel of rebirth

Picking my way in thought
To the black room
Where starlight blows off the roof
And the great beasts that came in the minds
Of the first slaves, stand at the door, asking
For death, asking to be
Forgotten: the sadness of elephants
The visionary pain in the heads
Of incredibly poisonous snakes
Lion   wildebeest   giraffe   all purchased also
When one wished only
Labor
          those beasts becoming
For the white man the animals of Eden
Emblems of sexual treasure   all beasts attending
Me now   my dreamed dogs snarling at the shades
Of eland and cheetah
On the dispossessed ground where I dance
In my clothes beyond movement:

In nine months she would lie
With a knife between her teeth to cut the pain
Of bearing
A child who belongs in no world   my hair in that boy
Turned black   my skin
Darkened by half   his, lightened
By that half exactly   the beasts of Africa reduced
To cave shadows flickering on his brow
As I think of Him: a child would rise from that place
With half my skin. He could for an instant
Of every day   when the wind turns   look
Me in the eyes.   What do you feel when passing

Your blood beyond death
To another in secret: into
Another who takes your features   and adds
A misplaced Africa to them,
Changing them forever
As they must live? What happens
To you, when such a one bears

You after your death into rings
Of battling light   a heavyweight champion
Through the swirling glass of four doors,
In epauletted coats   into places
Where you learn to wait
On tables   into sitting in all-night cages
Of parking lots   into raising
A sun-sided hammer in a gang
Of men on a tar road working
Until the crickets give up?
What happens when the sun goes down

And the white man's loins still stir
In a house of air   still draw him toward
Slave quarters? When Michael's voice is heard
Bending the sail like grass,
The real moon begins to come
Apart on the water
And two hundred years are turned back
On with the headlights of a car?
When you learn that there is no hatred
Like love in the eyes
Of a wholly owned face?   When you think of what
It would be like   what it has been
What it is to look once a day
Into an only
Son's brown, waiting, wholly possessed
Amazing eyes, and not
Acknowledge, but own?

THE FIREBOMBING

Denke daran, dass nach den grossen Zerstörungen
Jedermann beweisen wird, dass er unshuldig war.

Günther Eich

Or hast thou an arm like God?

The Book of Job

Homeowners unite.

All families lie together, though some are burned alive.
The others try to feel
For them. Some can, it is often said.

Starve and take off

Twenty years in the suburbs, and the palm trees willingly leap
Into the flashlights,
And there is beneath them also
A booted crackling of snailshells and coral sticks.
There are cowl flaps and the tilt cross of propellers,
The shovel-marked clouds' far sides against the moon,
The enemy filling up the hills
With ceremonial graves. At my somewhere among these,

Snap, a bulb is tricked on in the cockpit

And some technical-minded stranger with my hands
Is sitting in a glass treasure-hole of blue light,
Having potential fire under the undeodorized arms
Of his wings, on thin bomb-shackles,
The "tear-drop-shaped" 300-gallon drop-tanks
Filled with napalm and gasoline.

Thinking forward ten minutes
From that, there is also the burst straight out
Of the overcast into the moon; there is now
The moon-metal-shine of propellers, the quarter-
moonstone, aimed at the waves,
Stopped on the cumulus.

There is then this re-entry
Into cloud, for the engines to ponder their sound.
In white dark the aircraft shrinks; Japan

Dilates around it like a thought.
Coming out, the one who is here is over
Land, passing over the all-night grainfields,
In dark paint over
The woods with one silver side,
Rice-water calm at all levels
Of the terraced hill.
                        Enemy rivers and trees
Sliding off me like snakeskin,
Strips of vapor spooled from the wingtips
Going   invisible   passing   over   on
Over   bridges   roads for nightwalkers
Sunday night in the enemy's country   absolute
Calm   the moon's face   coming   slowly
About
        the inland sea
Slants   is woven with wire thread
Levels out   holds together like a quilt
Off the starboard wing   cloud flickers
At my glassed-off forehead   the moon's now and again
Uninterrupted face going forward
Over the waves in a glide-path
Lost into land.

Going: going with it

Combat booze by my side in a cratered canteen,
Bourbon frighteningly mixed
With GI pineapple juice,
Dogs trembling under me for hundreds of miles, on many
Islands, sleep-smelling that ungodly mixture
Of napalm and high-octane fuel,
Good bourbon and GI juice.

Rivers circling behind me around
Come to the fore, and bring
A town with everyone darkened.

Five thousand people are sleeping off
An all-day American drone.
Twenty years in the suburbs have not shown me
Which ones were hit and which not.

Haul on the wheel   racking slowly
The aircraft blackly around
In a dark dream   that   that is
That is like flying inside someone's head

Think of this   think of this

I did not think of my house
But think of my house now

Where the lawn mower rests on its laurels
Where the diet exists
For my own good   where I try to drop
Twenty years, eating figs in the pantry
Blinded by each and all
Of the eye-catching cans that gladly have caught my wife's eye
Until I cannot say
Where the screwdriver is   where the children
Get off the bus   where the new
Scoutmaster lives   where the fly
Hones his front legs   where the hammock folds
Its erotic daydreams   where the Sunday
School text for the day has been put   where the fire
Wood is   where the payments
For everything under the sun
Pile peacefully up,

But in this half-paid-for pantry
Among the red lids that screw off
With an easy half-twist to the left
And the long drawers crammed with dim spoons,
I still have charge—secret charge—
Of the fire developed to cling
To everything: to golf carts and fingernail
Scissors as yet unborn   tennis shoes

Grocery baskets   toy fire engines
New Buicks stalled by the half-moon
Shining at midnight on crossroads   green paint
Of jolly garden tools   red Christmas ribbons:

Not atoms, these, but glue inspired
By love of country to burn,
The apotheosis of gelatin.

Behind me having risen the Southern Cross
Set up by chaplains in the Ryukyus—
Orion, Scorpio, the immortal silver
Like the myths of king-
insects at swarming time—
One mosquito, dead drunk
On altitude, drones on, far under the engines,
And bites between
The oxygen mask and the eye.
The enemy-colored skin of families
Determines to hold its color
In sleep, as my hand turns whiter
Than ever, clutching the toggle—
The ship shakes   bucks
Fire hangs   not yet fire
In the air above Beppu
For I am fulfilling

An "anti-morale" raid upon it.
All leashes of dogs
Break under the first bomb, around those
In bed, or late in the public baths: around those
Who inch forward on their hands
Into medicinal waters.
Their heads come up with a roar
Of Chicago fire:
Come up with the carp pond showing
The bathhouse upside down,
Standing stiller to show it more
As I sail artistically over
The resort town followed by farms,

Singing and twisting
All the handles in heaven   kicking
The small cattle off their feet
In a red costly blast
Flinging jelly over the walls
As in a chemical war-
fare field demonstration.
With fire of mine like a cat

Holding onto another man's walls,
My hat should crawl on my head
In streetcars, thinking of it,
The fat on my body should pale.

Gun down
The engines, the eight blades sighing
For the moment when the roofs will connect
Their flames, and make a town burning with all
American fire.
           Reflections of houses catch;
Fire shuttles from pond to pond
In every direction, till hundreds flash with one death.
With this in the dark of the mind,
Death will not be what it should;
Will not, even now, even when
My exhaled face in the mirror
Of bars, dilates in a cloud like Japan.
The death of children is ponds
Shutter-flashing; responding mirrors; it climbs
The terraces of hills
Smaller and smaller, a mote of red dust
At a hundred feet; at a hundred and one it goes out.
That is what should have got in
To my eye
And shown the insides of houses, the low tables
Catch fire from the floor mats,
Blaze up in gas around their heads
Like a dream of suddenly growing
Too intense for war. Ah, under one's dark arms
Something strange-scented falls—when those on earth

Die, there is not even sound;
One is cool and enthralled in the cockpit,
Turned blue by the power of beauty,
In a pale treasure-hole of soft light
Deep in aesthetic contemplation,
Seeing the ponds catch fire
And cast it through ring after ring
Of land: O death in the middle
Of acres of inch-deep water!   Useless

Firing   small arms
Speckles   from the river
Bank   one ninety-millimeter
Misses   far down   wrong petals   gone

It is this detachment,
The honored aesthetic evil,
The greatest sense of power in one's life,
That must be shed in bars, or by whatever
Means, by starvation
Visions in well-stocked pantries:
The moment when the moon sails in between
The tail-booms   the rudders nod   I swing
Over   directly over the heart
The *heart* of the fire. A mosquito burns out on my cheek
With the cold of my face   there are the eyes
In blue light   bar light
All masked but them   the moon
Crossing from left to right   in the streams below
Oriental fish form quickly
In the chemical shine,
In their eyes one tiny seed
Of deranged, Old Testament light.

Letting go   letting go
The plane rises gently   dark forms
Glide off me   long water   pales
In safe zones   a new cry enters
The voice box of chained family dogs

We buck   leap over something
Not there   settle back
Leave it   leave it clinging and crying
It consumes them in a hot
Body-flash, old age or menopause
Of children, clings and burns
                          eating through
And when a reed mat catches fire
From me, it explodes through field after field
Bearing its sleeper   another

Bomb finds a home
And clings to it like a child. And so

Goodbye to the grassy mountains
To cloud streaming from the night engines
Flags   pennons   curved silks
Of air   myself streaming also
My body covered
With flags, the air of flags
Between the engines.
Forever I do sleep in that position,
Forever in a turn
For home that breaks out streaming banners
From my wingtips,
Wholly in position to admire.

O then I knock it off
And turn for home over the black complex thread worked through
The silver night-sea,
Following the huge, moon-washed steppingstones
Of the Ryukyus south,
The nightgrass of mountains billowing softly
In my rising heat.
                        Turn and tread down
The yellow stones of the islands
To where Okinawa burns,
Pure gold, on the radar screen,
Beholding, beneath, the actual island form

In the vast water-silver poured just above solid ground,
An inch of water extending for thousands of miles
Above flat ploughland. Say "down," and it is done.

All this, and I am still hungry,
Still twenty years overweight, still unable
To get down there or see
What really happened.
                             But it may be that I could not,
If I tried, say to any
Who lived there, deep in my flames: say, in cold
Grinning sweat, as to another
As these homeowners who are always curving
Near me down the different-grassed street: say
As though to the neighbor
I borrowed the hedge-clippers from
On the darker-grassed side of the two,
Come in, my house is yours, come in
If you can, if you
Can pass this unfired door. It is that I can imagine
At the threshold nothing
With its ears crackling off
Like powdery leaves,
Nothing with children of ashes, nothing not
Amiable, gentle, well-meaning,
A little nervous for no
Reason   a little worried   a little too loud
Or too easygoing   nothing I haven't lived with
For twenty years, still nothing not as
American as I am, and proud of it.

Absolution? Sentence? No matter;
The thing itself is in that.

REINCARNATION (II)

—the white thing was so white, its wings
so wide, and in those for ever exiled waters

Melville

As apparitional as sails that cross
Some page of figures to be filed away

Hart Crane

One can do   one begins to   one can only

Circle   eyes wide with fearing the spirit

Of weight   as though to be born   to awaken to what one is
Were to be carried   passed out
With enormous cushions of air under the arms
Straight up   the head growing stranger
And released between wings near an iceberg

It is too much to ask   to ask
For   under the white mild sun
On that huge frozen point to move

As one is so easily doing

Boring into it with one's new
born excessive eye   after a long
Half-sleeping self-doubting voyage   until
The unbased mountain falters
Turns over like a whale   one screams for the first time

With a wordless voice   swings over
The berg's last treasured bubble
Straightens   wings trembling   RIDING!
Rises into a new South

Sensitive current   checks each wing
It is living there
                              and starts out.

There is then this night
Crawling slowly in under one wing
This night of all nights
Aloft   a night five thousand feet up
Where he soars among the as-yet-unnamed
The billion unmentionable stars
Each in its right relation
To his course   he shivers   changes his heading
Slightly   feels the heavenly bodies
Shake   alter   line up in the right conjunction
For mating   for the plunge
Toward the egg   he soars   borne toward his offspring

By the Dragon balanced exactly
Again the Lion   the sense of the galaxies
Right from moment to moment
Drawing slowly for him a Great
Circle   all the stars in the sky
Embued with the miracle of
The single human Christmas one
Conjoining to stand now over
A rocky island ten thousand
Miles of water away.
                    With a cold new heart
With celestial feathered crutches
A "new start" like a Freudian dream
Of a new start   he hurtles as if motionless
All the air in the upper world
Splitting apart on his lips.

Sleep   *wingless* —NO!
The stars appear, rimmed with red
Space under his breastbone maintains
Itself   he sighs like a man
Between his cambered wings
Letting down now   curving around
Into the wind   slowly toward
Any wave   that—
That one.   He folds his wings and moves
With the mid-Pacific

Carried for miles in no particular direction
On a single wave   a wandering hill
Surging softly along in a powerful
Long-lost phosphorous seethe   folded in those wings
Those ultimate wings   home is like   home is
A folding of wings   Mother
Something whispers   one eye opens   a star shifts
Does not fall   from the eye of the Swan   he dreams

He sees the Southern Cross
Painfully over the horizon   drawing itself
Together   inching
Higher each night of the world   thorn
Points   tilted   he watches   not to be taken in
By the False Cross   as in   in
Another life   not taken

Knowing the true south rises
In a better make of cross   smaller   compact
And where its lights must appear.
Just after midnight he rises
And goes for it   joy with him
Springing out of the water
Disguised as wind   he checks each feather
As the stars burn out   waiting
Taking his course on faith until
The east begins
To pulse with unstoppable light.
Now darkness and dawn melt exactly
Together on one indifferent rill
Which sinks and is
Another   he lives

In renewed light, utterly alone!
In five days there is one ship
Dragging its small chewed off-white
Of ship-water   one candle in a too-human cabin
One vessel moving embedded
In its blue endurable country

Water warms   thereafter it is not
That the sea begins to tinge
Like a vast, laid smoke
But that he closes his eyes and feels himself
Turning whiter and whiter   upheld

At his whitest it is

Midnight   the equator   the center of the world
He sneaks across   afire
With himself   the stars change all their figures
Reach toward him   closer
And now begin to flow
Into his cracked-open mouth   down his throat
A string of lights   emblems   patterns of fire   all
Directions   myths   Hydras
Centaurs   Wolves   Virgins
Eating them all   eating
The void   possessing
Music   order   repose
Hovering   moving on his armbones   crawling
On warm air   covering the whole ocean   the sea deadens
He dulls   new constellations pale off
Him   unmapped roads open out of his breast
Beyond the sick feeling
Of those whose arms drag at treasures   it is like

Roosting   like holding one's arms out
In a clean nightshirt   a good dream   it is all
Instinct   he thinks   I have been born
This way.
                Goes on
His small head holding
It all   the continents firmly fixed
By his gaze   five new ships turned
Rusty by his rich shadow.
His seamless shoulders of dawn-gold
Open   he opens
Them wider   an inch wider and he would

Trees voices white garments meadows
Fail under him again are
Mullet believing their freedom
Is to go anywhere they like in their collected shape
The form of an unthrown net
With no net anywhere near them.
Of these he eats.
        Taking off again
He rocks forward three more days
Twenty-fours hours a day
Balancing without thinking—
In doubt, he opens his bill
And vastness adjusts him
He trims his shoulders and planes up

Up   stalls

In midocean falls off
Comes down in a long, unbeheld
Curve that draws him deep into
         evening

Incredible pasture.

The Cross is up. Looking in through its four panes
He sees something a clean desk-top
Papers shuffled hears
Something a bird word
A too-human word a word
That should have been somewhere spoken
That now can be frankly said
With long stiff lips into
The center of the Southern Cross
A word enabling one to fly
Out the window of office buildings
Lifts up on wings of its own
To say itself over and over sails on
Under the unowned stars sails as if walking

Out the window
That is what I said
That is what I should   that is

Dawn.   Panic   one moment of thinking
Himself in the hell of thumbs   once more   a man
Disguised in these wings   alone   No   again
He thinks   I am here   I have been born
This way   raised up from   raised up in
Myself   my soul
Undivided at last   thrown slowly forward
Toward an unmanned island.

Day overcomes   night comes over
Day with day already

Coming behind it   the sun halved in the east
The moon pressing feathers together.
Who thinks his bones are light
Enough, should try it   it is for everyone
He thinks   the world is for everything born—
I always had
These wings   buried deep in my back:
There is a wing-growing motion
Half-alive in every creature.

Comes down   skims for fifty miles
All afternoon lies skimming
His white shadow burning his breast
The flying-fish darting before him
In and out of the ash-film glaze

Or "because it is there"   into almighty cloud

In rain crying hoarsely
No place to go except
Forward into water in the eyes
Tons of water falling on the back
For hours   no sight   no insight

Beating up   trying
To rise above it   not knowing which way
Is up   no stars   crying
Home   fire   windows   for God
Sake   beating down   up   up-down
No help   streaming   another
Death   vertigo   falling
Upward   mother   God   country
Then seizing one grain of water in his mouth
Glides forward   heavy with cloud
Enveloped   gigantic   blazing with St. Elmo's
Fire   alone at the heart
Of rain   pure bird   heaving up   going

Up from that
                       and from that

Finally breaking

Out   where the sun is violently shining

On the useless enormous ploughland
Of cloud   then up
From just above it   up
Reducing the clouds more and more
To the color of their own defeat
The beauty of history   forgotten bird-
kingdoms packed in batting
The soft country   the endless fields
Raining away beneath him   to be dead
In one life is to enter
Another   to break out   to rise above   the clouds
Fail   pull back their rain

Dissolve.   All the basic blue beneath
Comes back, tattering through. He cries out
As at sight of home   a last human face
In a mirror dazzles   he reaches
Glides off on one wing   stretching himself wider
Floats into night   dark follows

At his pace
        the stars' threads all connect
On him   and, each in its place, the islands
Rise   small form of beaches

Treeless   tons of guano   eggshells
Of generations
        down
          circling

Mistrusting

The land   coming in
Wings ultra-sensitive
To solids   the ground not reflecting his breast
Feet tentatively out
Creaking   close   closer
Earth blurring   tilt back and brace
Against the wind   closest   touch

Sprawl.   In ridiculous wings, he flounders,
He waddles   he goes to sleep
In a stillness of body not otherwhere to be found
Upheld for one night
With his wings closed   the stiff land failing to rock him.

Here mating   the new life
Shall not be lost   wings tangle
Over the beaches   over the pale
Sketches of coral reefs   treading the air
The father moving almost
At once out the vast blue door
He feels it swing open
The island fall off him   the sun

Rise in the shape of an egg   enormous
Over the islands
        passing out
Over the cliffs   scudding
Fifteen feet from the poor skinned sod

Dazing with purity the eyes of turtles
Lizards then feeling the world at once
Sheerly restore the sea the island not
Glanced back at where the egg
Fills with almighty feathers
The dead rise, wrapped in their wings
The last thread of white
Is drawn from the foot of the cliffs
As the great sea takes itself back
From around the island

And he sails out heads north
His eyes already on icebergs
Ten thousand miles off already feeling
The shiver of the equator as it crosses
His body at its absolute
Midnight whiteness
     and death also
Stands waiting years away
In midair beats
Balanced on starpoints
Latitude and longitude correct
Oriented by instinct by stars
By the sun in one eye the moon
In the other bird-death

Hovers for years on its wings
With a time sense that cannot fail
Waits to change
Him again circles abides no feather
Falling conceived by stars and the void
Is born perpetually
In midair where it shall be
Where it is.

© Rollie McKenna

Alan Dugan

LOVE SONG: I AND THOU

Nothing is plumb, level or square:
   the studs are bowed, the joists
are shaky by nature, no piece fits
   any other piece without a gap
or pinch, and bent nails
   dance all over the surfacing
like maggots. By Christ
   I am no carpenter. I built
the roof for myself, the walls
   for myself, the floors
for myself, and got
   hung up in it myself. I
danced with a purple thumb
   at this house-warming, drunk
with my prime whiskey: rage.
   Oh I spat rage's nails
into the frame-up of my work:
   it held. It settled plumb,
level, solid, square and true
   for that great moment. Then
it screamed and went on through,
   skewing as wrong the other way.
God damned it. This is hell,
   but I planned it, I sawed it,
I nailed it, and I
   will live in it until it kills me.
I can nail my left palm
   to the left-hand cross-piece but

I can't do everything myself.
　　I need a hand to nail the right,
a help, a love, a you, a wife.

STUTTERER

Courage: your tongue has left
its natural position in the cheek
where eddies of the breath
are navigable calms. Now
it locks against the glottis or
is snapped at by the teeth,
in mid-stream: it must be work
to get out what you mean:
the rapids of the breath
are furious with belief
and want the tongue, as blood
and animal of speech,
to stop it, block it or come clean
over the rocks of teeth
and down the races of the air,
tumbled and bruised to death.
Relax it into acting, be
the air's straw-hat
canoeist with a mandolin
yodeling over the falls.
This is the sound advice
of experts and a true despair:
it is the toll to pass the locks
down to the old mill stream
where lies of love are fair.

TRIBUTE TO KAFKA
FOR SOMEONE TAKEN

The party is going strong.
The doorbell rings. It's
for someone named me.
I'm coming. I take
a last drink, a last
puff on a cigarette,
a last kiss at a girl,
and step into the hall,
                              bang,
shutting out the laughter. "Is
your name you?" "Yes."
"Well come along then."
"See here. See here. See here."

ELEGY

I know but will not tell
you, Aunt Irene, why there
are soap-suds in the whiskey:
Uncle Robert had to have
a drink while shaving. May
there be no bloodshed in your house
this morning of my father's death
and no unkept appearance
in the living, since he has
to wear the rouge and lipstick
of your ceremony, mother,
for the first and last time:
father, hello and goodbye.

TO A RED-HEADED DO-GOOD WAITRESS

Every morning I went to her charity and learned
to face the music of her white smile so well
that it infected my black teeth as I escaped,
and those who saw me smiled too and went in
the White Castle, where she is the inviolable lady.

There cripples must be bright and starvers noble:
no tears, no stomach-cries, but pain made art
to move her powerful red pity toward philanthropy.
So I must wear my objectively stinking poverty
like a millionaire clown's rags and sing. "Oh I

got plenty o' nuttin'," as if I made
a hundred grand a year like Gershwin, while
I get a breakfast every day from her for two
weeks and nothing else but truth: she has
a policeman and a wrong sonnet in fifteen lines.

FOR MASTURBATION

I have allowed myself
this corner and am God.
Here in the must
beneath their stoop
I will do as I will,
either as act as act,
or dream for the sake of dreams,
and if they find me out
in rocket ships or jets
working to get away,

then let my left great-toe-
nail grow into the inside knob
of my right ankle-bone and let

my fingernails make eight new moons
temporarily in the cold salt marshes of my palms!
THIS IS THE WAY IT IS, and if
it is "a terrible disgrace"
it is as I must will,
because I am not them
though I am theirs to kill.

POEM

What's the balm
for a dying life,
dope, drink, or Christ,
is there one?

I puke and choke
with it and find
no peace of mind
in flesh, and no hope.

It flows away
in mucous juice.
Nothing I can do
can make it stay,

so I give out
and water the garden: it
is all shit
for the flowers anyhow.

ADULTERY

What do a few crimes
matter in a good life?
Adultery is not so bad.

You think yourself too old
for loving, gone in the guts
and charms, but a woman says,
"I love you," a drunken lie,
and down you go on the grass
outside the party. You rejoin
the wife, delighted and renewed!
She's grateful but goes out
with a bruiser. Blood
passions arise and die
in lawyers' smiles, a few
children suffer for life,
and that's all. But: One
memo from that McNamara and his band
can kill a city of lives
and the life of cities, too,
while L. B. "Killer" Johnson And His Napalm Boys
sit singing by their fire:
The Goldberg Variations.
So, what do a few crimes
matter in a neutral life?
They pray the insignificance
of most private behavior.

AMERICAN AGAINST SOLITUDE

Ah to be alone and uninhibited!
To make mistakes in private, then
to show a good thing! But that's
not possible: it's in the Close of life
that towering Virtù happens. Why
be absent from the wheeling world?
It is an education! Act by act,
Futures materialize! So, go deal,
old bones, enjoy it while you may!:
eat, drink, think, and love; oh even work!,
as if all horrors are mistakes,

and make the social product: new
invisible skies arriving! full
of life, death, insanity, and grace!

ELEGY FOR A PURITAN CONSCIENCE

I closed my ears with stinging bugs
and sewed my eyelids shut
but heard a sucking at the dugs
and saw my parents rut.

I locked my jaw with rusty nails
and cured my tongue in lime
but ate and drank in garbage pails
and said these words of crime.

I crushed my scrotum with two stones
and drew my penis in
but felt your wound expect its own
and fell in love with sin.

Beth Bagby

Lawrence Ferlinghetti

'CONSTANTLY RISKING ABSURDITY'

Constantly risking absurdity
                              and death
            whenever he performs
                              above the heads
                                    of his audience
    the poet like an acrobat
                    climbs on rime
                        to a high wire of his own making
and balancing on eyebeams
                        above a sea of faces
            paces his way
                    to the other side of day
    performing entrechats
                    and sleight-of-foot tricks
and other high theatrics
                    and all without mistaking
            any thing
                    for what it may not be

    For he's the super realist
                        who must perforce perceive
            taut truth
                    before the taking of each stance or step
in his supposed advance
                        toward that still higher perch
where Beauty stands and waits
                        with gravity
                              to start her death-defying leap

And he
      a little charleychaplin man
                  who may or may not catch
      her fair eternal form
             spreadeagled in the empty air
    of existence

'THE WORLD IS A BEAUTIFUL PLACE'

      The world is a beautiful place
                  to be born into
if you don't mind happiness
              not always being
                    so very much fun
   if you don't mind a touch of hell
              now and then
     just when everything is fine
                because even in heaven
        they don't sing
          all the time

      The world is a beautiful place
                  to be born into
if you don't mind some people dying
               all the time
    or maybe only starving
             some of the time
    which isn't half so bad
          if it isn't you

   Oh the world is a beautiful place
                to be born into
    if you don't much mind
           a few dead minds
    in the higher places
         or a bomb or two
      now and then

in your upturned faces
or such other improprieties
as our Name Brand society
is prey to
with its men of distinction
and its men of extinction
and its priests
and other patrolmen
and its various segregations
and congressional investigations
and other constipations
that our fool flesh
is heir to

Yes the world is the best place of all
for a lot of such things as
making the fun scene
and making the love scene
and making the sad scene
and singing low songs and having inspirations
and walking around
looking at everything
and smelling flowers
and goosing statues
and even thinking
and kissing people and
making babies and wearing pants
and waving hats and
dancing
and going swimming in rivers
on picnics
in the middle of summer
and just generally
'living it up'

Yes
but then right in the middle of it
comes the smiling
mortician

'WHAT COULD SHE SAY TO THE FANTASTIC FOOLYBEAR'

What could she say to the fantastic foolybear
and what could she say to brother
and what could she say
                              to the cat with future feet
and what could she say to mother
after that time that she lay lush
                              among the lolly flowers
      on that hot riverbank
            where ferns fell away in the broken air
                  of the breath of her lover
      and birds went mad
                              and threw themselves from trees
to taste still hot upon the ground
                              the spilled sperm seed

'THE PENNYCANDYSTORE BEYOND THE EL'

The pennycandystore beyond the El
is where I first
            fell in love
                        with unreality
Jellybeans glowed in the semi-gloom
of that september afternoon
A cat upon the counter moved among
                              the licorice sticks
            and tootsie rolls
      and Oh Boy Gum

Outside the leaves were falling as they died

A wind had blown away the sun

A girl ran in
Her hair was rainy
Her breasts were breathless in the little room

Outside the leaves were falling
                    and they cried
                            Too soon! too soon!

'SOMETIME DURING ETERNITY'

            Sometime during eternity
                            some guys show up
and one of them
                who shows up real late
                                is a kind of carpenter
        from some square-type place
                            like Galilee
            and he starts wailing
                        and claiming he is hep
            to who made heaven
                            and earth
                                and that the cat
            who really laid it on us
                            is his Dad

        And moreover
            he adds
                It's all writ down
                        on some scroll-type parchments
            which some henchmen
                        leave lying around the Dead Sea somewheres
            a long time ago
                        and which you won't even find
for a coupla thousand years or so
                            or at least for
        nineteen hundred and fortyseven
                            of them

                    to be exact
                              and even then
         nobody really believes them
                              or me
                                   for that matter

         You're hot
                    they tell him

         And they cool him

         They stretch him on the Tree to cool

            And everybody after that
                                   is always making models
                    of this Tree
                              with Him hung up
         and always crooning His name
                                   and calling Him to come down
                    and sit in
                              on their combo
                as if he is the king cat
                              who's got to blow
         or they can't quite make it

         Only he don't come down
                              from His Tree

         Him just hang there
                    on His Tree
                              looking real Petered out
                    and real cool
                              and also
                according to a roundup
                              of late world news
         from the usual unreliable sources
                              real dead

STARTING FROM SAN FRANCISCO

Here I go again
crossing the country in coach trains
(back to my old
lone wandering)
All night Eastward . . . Upward
over the Great Divide and on
into Utah
over Great Salt Plain
and onward, rocking,
the white dawn burst
across mesas,
table-lands,
all flat, all laid away.
Great glary sun—
wood bridge over water. . . .
Later in still light, we still reel onward—
Onward?
Back and forth, across the Continent,
bang bang
by any wheel or horse,
any rail,
by car
by buggy
by stagecoach,
walking,
riding,
hooves pounding the Great Plains,
caravans into the night. Forever.
Into Wyoming.
All that day and night, rocking through it,
snow on steppes and plains of November,
roads lost in it—or never existent—
back in the beginning again, no People yet,
no ruts Westward yet
under the snow. . . .
Still more huge spaces we bowl through,

still untouched dark land—
Indomitable.
Horizons of mesas
like plains of Spain high up
in Don Quixote country—
sharp eroded towers of bluffs
like windmills tilted,
"los molinos" of earth, abandoned—
Great long rectangular stone islands
sticking up on far plains, like forts
or immense light cargo ships
high on plains of water,
becalmed and rudderless,
props thrashing wheat,
stranded forever,
no one on those bridges. . . .
Later again, much later,
one small halfass town,
followed by one telephone wire
and one straight single iron road
hung to the tracks as by magnets
attached to a single endless fence,
past solitary pumping stations,
each with a tank, a car, a small house, a dog,
no people anywhere—
All hiding?
White Man gone home?
Must be a cowboy someplace . . .
Birds flap from fences, trestles,
caw and caw their nothingness.
Stone church sticks up
quote Out of Nowhere unquote
This must be Interzone
between Heaven and Brooklyn.
Do they have a Classified Section
as in phonebooks
in the back of the Bibles here?
Otherwise they'd never find Anything.
Try Instant Zen. . . .
Still later again,
sunset and strange clouds like udders

rayed with light from below—
some God's hand sticks through,
black trees stand out.
The world is a winter farm—
Cradle we rocked out of—
prairie schooners into Pullmans,
their bright saloons sheeted in oblivion—
Wagon-lits—bedwagons over the prairies,
bodies nested in them,
hurtled through night,
inscrutable. . . .
Onward still . . . or Backward . . .
huge snow fields still, on and on,
still no one,
Indians all gone to Florida
or Cuba!
Train hoots at something
in the nowhere we still rock through,
Dingding crossroads flicker by,
Mining towns, once roaring,
now shrunk to the railhead,
streetlights stoned with loneliness
or lit with leftover sun
they drank too much of during the day. . . .
And at long last now
this world shrunk
to one lone brakeman's face
stuck out of darkness—
long white forehead
like bleached skull of cow—
huge black sad eyes—
high-peaked cloth cap, grey-striped—
swings his railroad lantern high, close up,
as our window whizzes by—
his figure splashed upon it,
slanted, muezzin-like,
very grave, very tall,
strange skeleton—
Who stole America?

Myself I saw in the window reflected.

I AM WAITING

I am waiting for my case to come up
and I am waiting
for a rebirth of wonder
and I am waiting for someone
to really discover America
and wail
and I am waiting
for the discovery
of a new symbolic western frontier
and I am waiting
for the American Eagle
to really spread its wings
and straighten up and fly right
and I am waiting
for the Age of Anxiety
to drop dead
and I am waiting
for the war to be fought
which will make the world safe
for anarchy
and I am waiting
for the final withering away
of all governments
and I am perpetually awaiting
a rebirth of wonder

I am waiting for the Second Coming
and I am waiting
for a religious revival
to sweep thru the state of Arizona
and I am waiting
for the Grapes of Wrath to be stored
and I am waiting
for them to prove
that God is really American
and I am seriously waiting

for Billy Graham and Elvis Presley
to exchange roles seriously
and I am waiting
to see God on television
piped onto church altars
if only they can find
the right channel
to tune in on
and I am waiting
for the Last Supper to be served again
with a strange new appetizer
and I am perpetually awaiting
a rebirth of wonder

I am waiting for my number to be called
and I am waiting
for the living end
and I am waiting
for dad to come home
his pockets full
of irradiated silver dollars
and I am waiting
for the atomic tests to end
and I am waiting happily
for things to get much worse
before they·improve
and I am waiting
for the Salvation Army to take over
and I am waiting
for the human crowd
to wander off a cliff somewhere
clutching its atomic umbrella
and I am waiting
for Ike to act
and I am waiting
for the meek to be blessed
and inherit the earth
without taxes
and I am waiting
for forests and animals

to reclaim the earth as theirs
and I am waiting
for a way to be devised
to destroy all nationalisms
without killing anybody
and I am waiting
for linnets and planets to fall like rain
and I am waiting for lovers and weepers
to lie down together again
in a new rebirth of wonder

I am waiting for the Great Divide to be crossed
and I am anxiously waiting
for the secret of eternal life to be discovered
by an obscure general practitioner
and save me forever from certain death
and I am waiting
for life to begin
and I am waiting
for the storms of life
to be over
and I am waiting
to set sail for happiness
and I am waiting
for a reconstructed Mayflower
to reach America
with its picture story and tv rights
sold in advance to the natives
and I am waiting
for the lost music to sound again
in the Lost Continent
in a new rebirth of wonder

I am waiting for the day
that maketh all things clear
and I am waiting
for Ole Man River
to just stop rolling along
past the country club

and I am waiting
for the deepest South
to just stop Reconstructing itself
in its own image
and I am waiting
for a sweet desegregated chariot
to swing low
and carry me back to Ole Virginie
and I am waiting
for Ole Virginie to discover
just why Darkies are born
and I am waiting
for God to lookout
from Lookout Mountain
and see the *Ode to the Confederate Dead*
as a real farce
and I am awaiting retribution
for what America did
to Tom Sawyer
and I am perpetually awaiting
a rebirth of wonder

I am waiting for Tom Swift to grow up
and I am waiting
for the American Boy
to take off Beauty's clothes
and get on top of her
and I am waiting
for Alice in Wonderland
to retransmit to me
her total dream of innocence
and I am waiting
for Childe Roland to come
to the final darkest tower
and I am waiting
for Aphrodite
to grow live arms
at a final disarmament conference
in a new rebirth of wonder

I am waiting
to get some intimations
of immortality
by recollecting my early childhood
and I am waiting
for the green mornings to come again
youth's dumb green fields come back again
and I am waiting
for some strains of unpremeditated art
to shake my typewriter
and I am waiting to write
the great indelible poem
and I am waiting
for the last long careless rapture
and I am perpetually waiting
for the fleeing lovers on the Grecian Urn
to catch each other up at last
and embrace
and I am awaiting
perpetually and forever
a renaissance of wonder

ASSASSINATION RAGA

Tune in to a raga
on the stereo
and turn on Death TV
without its sound
Outside the plums are growing in a tree
'The force that through the green fuse
drives the flower'
drives Death TV
'A grief ago'
They lower the body soundlessly
into a huge plane in Dallas
into a huge plane in Los Angeles
marked 'United States of America'

and soundlessly
the 'United States of America'
takes off
& wings away with that Body
Tune out the TV sound
& listen soundlessly
to the blind mouths of its motors
& a sitar speaking on the stereo
a raga in a rage
at all that black death
and all that bad karma
La illaha el lill Allah
There is no god but God
The force that through the red fuze
drives the bullet
drives the needle in its dharma groove
and man the needle
drives that plane
of the 'United States of America'
through its sky full of shit & death
and the sky never ends
as it wings soundlessly
from those fucked-up cities
whose names we'd rather not remember
Inside the plane
inside the plane a wife
lies soundlessly
against the coffin
Engine whines as sitar sings outrageously
La illaha el lill Allah
There is no god but God?
There is no god but Death
The plums are falling through the tree
The force that drives the bullet
through the gun
drives everyone
as the 'United States of America'
flies on sightlessly
through the swift fierce years
with the dead weight of its Body

which they keep flying from Dallas
which they keep flying from Los Angeles
And the plane lands
without folding its wings
its shadow in mourning for itself
withdraws into itself
in death's draggy dominion
La illaha el lill Allah
There is no god but Death
The force that through the green fuze
drove his life
drives everyone
La illaha el lill Allah
And they are driving the Body
they are driving the Body
up Fifth Avenue
past a million people in line
'We are going to be here a long time'
says Death TV's spielman
The cortège passes soundlessly
'Goodbye! Goodbye!' some people cry
The traffic flows around & on
The force that drives the cars
combusts our karma
La illaha el lill Allah
There is no god but Death
The force that drives our life to death
drives sitar too
so soundlessly
La illaha el lill Allah
And they lift the Body
They lift the Body
of the United States of America
and carry it into a cathedral
singing Hallelujah He Shall Live
For ever & ever
And then the Body moves again
down Fifth Avenue
Fifty-seven black sedans after it
There are people with roses

behind the barricades
in bargain-basement dresses
And sitar sings & sings nonviolence
sitar sounds in us its images of ecstasy
its depth of ecstasy
against old dung & death
La illaha el lill Allah
La illaha el lill Allah
The force that strikes its strings
strikes us
And the funeral train
the silver train
starts up soundlessly
at a dead speed
over the hot land
an armed helicopter over it
They are clearing the tracks ahead of assassins
The tracks are lined with bare faces
A highschool band in New Brunswick plays
The Battle Hymn of the Republic
They have shot it down again
They have shot him down again
& will shoot him down again
& take him on a train
& lower him again
into a grave in Washington
La illaha el lill Allah
Day & night journeys the coffin
through the dark land
too dark now to see the dark faces
La illaha el lill Allah
Plums & planes are falling through the air
La illaha el lill Allah
as sitar sings the only answer
sitar sings its only answer
sitar sounds the only sound
that still can still all violence
La illaha el lill Allah
There is no god but Life
Sitar says it Sitar sounds it

Sitar sounds on us to love love & hate hate
Sitar breathes its Atman breath in us
sounds & sounds in us its lovely *om om*
La illaha el lill Allah
At every step the pure wind rises
La illaha el lill Allah
People with roses
behind the barricades!

*First read, to a loud evening raga, at "The Incredible
Poetry Reading," Nourse Auditorium, San Francisco,
June 8, 1968, the day Robert Kennedy was buried.*

*"Death TV": the phrase comes from "So Who Owns
Death TV" by William Burroughs, Claude Pélieu &
Carl Weissner.*

*"The force that through the green fuse drives the
flower" & "A grief ago": from Dylan Thomas.*

"La illaha el lill Allah": variation of a Sufi ecstatic chant.

*"the swift fierce years": from a phrase in Eldridge
Cleaver's "Soul on Ice."*

Atman: breath, soul, life principle.

*Om: originally a syllable denoting assent—the "ideal,
inaudible sound" of the universe. . . .*

AFTER THE CRIES OF THE BIRDS

Hurrying thru eternity
      after the cries of the birds has stopped
I see the "future of the world"
      in a new visionary society
     now only dimly recognizable
      in folk-rock ballrooms
     free-form dancers in ecstatic clothing
      their hearts their gurus
      every man his own myth
      butterflies in amber
        caught fucking life

hurrying thru eternity
                                    to a new pastoral era
I see the shadows of that future
            in that white island
                            which is San Francisco
            floating in its foreign sea
                                seen high on a hill
                        in the Berkeley Rose Garden
            looking West at sunset to the Golden Gate
            adrift in its Japanese landscape
                under Mt. Tamal-Fuji
                with its grazing bulls
                                hurrying thru heaven
            the city with its white buildings
                "a temple to some unknown god"
                    (as Voznesensky said)
after the cries of the birds has stopped
            I see the sea come in
                            over South San Francisco
        and the island of the city
                                truly floated free at last
            never really a part of America
            East East and West West
                and the twain met long ago
        in "the wish to pursue what lies beyond
                                    the mind"
            and with no place to go but In
                    after Columbus recovered America
        and the West Coast captured by some
                                Spanish Catholics
            cagily getting the jump by sea
                coveredwagons crawling over lost plains
                            hung up in Oklahoma
                Prairie schooners into Pullmans
while whole tribes of Indians
                    shake hopeless feather lances
            and disappear over the horizon
        to reappear centuries later
                        feet up and smoking wild cigars
            at the corner of Hollywood & Vine

hurrying thru eternity
      must we wait for the cries of the birds
                    to be stopped
             before we dig In
   after centuries of running
          up & down the Coast of West
  looking for the right place to jump off
              further Westward
    the Gutenberg Galaxy casts its light no further
     the "Westward march of civilization"
    comes to a dead stop on the shores of
      Big Sur Portland & Santa Monica
      and turns upon itself at last
        after the cries of the birds has stopped
must we wait for that
           to dig a new model
           of the universe
           with instant communication
           a world village
     in which every human being is a part of us
    though we be still throw-aways
            in an evolutionary progression
as Spengler reverses himself
      Mark Twain meets Jack London
     and turns back to Mississippi
     shaking his head
  and the Last Frontier
        having no place to go but In
   can't face it
      and buries its head
Western civilization gone too far West
          might suffer a sea-change
    into Something Else Eastern
           and that won't do
The Chinese are coming anyway
         time we prepared their tea
   Gunga Din still with us
     Kipling nods & cries *I told you so!*
     the French King hollers *Merde!*
    and abandons his Vietnam bordel

but not us
        we love them too much for that
though the Mayflower turned around sets sail again
  back to Plymouth England (and the
                          Piltdown letdown)
    misjudging the coast & landing in Loverpool
    American poets capture Royal Albert Hall
     The Jefferson Airplane takes off
                  and circles heaven
  It all figures
         in a new litany
               probably pastoral
after the cries of the birds has stopped
    Rose petals fall
          in the Berkeley Rose Garden
where I sit trying to remember
        the lines about rose leaves
in the *Four Quartets*
       Stella kisses her lover in the sunset
        under an arbor
  A Los Angeles actor nearby goes *Zap! Zap!*
       at the setting sun
It is the end
    I drop downhill
  into a reception for Anaïs Nin
   with a paperbag full of rose leaves
She is autographing her Book
   I empty the bag over her head from behind
Her gold lacquered hair sheds the petals
  They tumble red & yellow on her
           signed book
  Girl again she presses them
      between the leaves
    delightedly
      like fallen friends
  Her words
     flame in my heart
   Virginia Woolf under water
     she drifts away on the book

a leaf herself blowing skittered
                                over the horizon
The wish to pursue what lies beyond the mind
                    lies just beyond
            Ask a flower what it does
                    to move beyond the senses
        Our cells hate metal
                            The tide turns
            We shoot holes in the clouds' trousers
                    and napalm sears the hillsides
            skips a bridge
            narrows to a grass hut full of charred bodies
    and is later reported looking like
                    "The eternal flame at Kennedy's grave"
            A tree flowers red It can't run

Shall we now advance into the 21st century?
        I see the lyric future of the world
            on the beaches of Big Sur
                gurus at Jack's Flats
            nude swart maidens swimming
            in pools of sunlight
                Kali on the beach
        guitarists with one earring
lovely birds in long dresses and Indian headbands

                    What does this have to do with Lenin?
                Plenty!
Die-hard Maoists lie down together crosswise
                            and out comes a string
                        of Chinese firecrackers
                    and after the cries of the birds
                                has stopped
            Chinese junks show up suddenly
            off the coast of Big Sur
filled with more than Chinese philosophers
                        dreaming they are butterflies
How shall we greet them? Are we ready
                        to receive them?

Shall we put out koan steppingstones
                              scrolls & bowls
          greet them with *agape*
       Tu Fu and bamboo flutes at midnight?
          Big Sur junk meet
             Chinese junk?
Will they ride the breakers into Bixby Cove?
   Will they bring their women with them
       Will we take them on the beach
    like Ron Boise's lovers in Kama Sutra
       face them with Zen zazen & tea
      made from the dust of the wings
           of butterflies dreaming
                     they're philosophers?
   Or meet them with last war's tanks
      roaring out of Fort Ord
          down the highways & canyons
          shooting as they come
    flame-throwers flaming jelly
                     into the Chinese rushes
                     under the bridge at Bixby?
The U.S. owns the highway but is Big Sur
                        in the USA?

       San Francisco floats away
       beyond the three-mile limit
    of the District of Eternal Revenue
       No need to pay your taxes
       The seas come in to cover us
    Agape we are & agape we'll be

Jim Johnson—Pix

Allen Ginsberg

HOWL

For Carl Solomon

1.
I saw the best minds of my generation destroyed by madness, starving
  hysterical naked,
dragging themselves through the negro streets at dawn looking for an
  angry fix,
angelheaded hipsters burning for the ancient heavenly connection to
  the starry dynamo in the machinery of night,
who poverty and tatters and hollow-eyed and high sat up smoking in
  the supernatural darkness of cold-water flats floating across the tops
  of cities contemplating jazz,
who bared their brains to Heaven under the El and saw Mohammedan
  angels staggering on tenement roofs illuminated,
who passed through universities with radiant cool eyes hallucinating
  Arkansas and Blake-light tragedy among the scholars of war,
who were expelled from the academies for crazy & publishing obscene
  odes on the windows of the skull,
who cowered in unshaven rooms in underwear, burning their money
  in wastebaskets and listening to the Terror through the wall,
who got busted in their pubic beards returning through Laredo with a
  belt of marijuana for New York,
who ate fire in paint hotels or drank turpentine in Paradise Alley, death,
  or purgatoried their torsos night after night
with dreams, with drugs, with waking nightmares, alcohol and cock and
  endless balls,
incomparable blind streets of shuddering cloud and lightning in the
  mind leaping toward poles of Canada & Paterson, illuminating all
  the motionless world of Time between,

Peyote solidities of halls, backyard green tree cemetery dawns, wine
    drunkenness over the rooftops, storefront boroughs of teahead joy-
    ride neon blinking traffic light, sun and moon and tree vibrations in
    the roaring winter dusks of Brooklyn, ashcan rantings and kind king
    light of mind,
who chained themselves to subways for the endless ride from Battery to
    holy Bronx on benzedrine until the noise of wheels and children
    brought them down shuddering mouth-wracked and battered bleak
    of brain all drained of brilliance in the drear light of Zoo,
who sank all night in submarine light of Bickford's floated out and sat
    through the stale beer afternoon in desolate Fugazzi's, listening to
    the crack of doom on the hydrogen jukebox,
who talked continuously seventy hours from park to pad to bar to
    Bellevue to museum to the Brooklyn Bridge,
a lost battalion of platonic conversationalists jumping down the stoops
    off fire escapes off windowsills off Empire State out of the moon,
yacketayakking screaming vomiting whispering facts and memories and
    anecdotes and eyeball kicks and shocks of hospitals and jails and
    wars,
whole intellects disgorged in total recall for seven days and nights with
    brilliant eyes, meat for the Synagogue cast on the pavement,
who vanished into nowhere Zen New Jersey leaving a trail of ambiguous
    picture postcards of Atlantic City Hall,
suffering Eastern sweats and Tangerian bone-grindings and migraines of
    China under junk-withdrawal in Newark's bleak furnished room,
who wandered around and around at midnight in the railroad yard
    wondering where to go, and went, leaving no broken hearts,
who lit cigarettes in boxcars boxcars boxcars racketing through snow
    toward lonesome farms in grandfather night,
who studied Plotinus Poe St. John of the Cross telepathy and bop ka-
    balla because the cosmos instinctively vibrated at their feet in Kansas,
who loned it through the streets of Idaho seeking visionary indian
    angels who were visionary indian angels,
who thought they were only mad when Baltimore gleamed in super-
    natural ecstasy,
who jumped in limousines with the Chinaman of Oklahoma on the
    impulse of winter midnight streetlight small town rain,
who lounged hungry and lonesome through Houston seeking jazz or
    sex or soup, and followed the brilliant Spaniard to converse about
    America and Eternity, a hopeless task, and so took ship to Africa,

who disappeared into the volcanoes of Mexico leaving behind nothing but the shadow of dungarees and the lava and ash of poetry scattered in fireplace Chicago,

who reappeared on the West Coast investigating the F.B.I. in beards and shorts with big pacifist eyes sexy in their dark skin passing out incomprehensible leaflets,

who burned cigarette holes in their arms protesting the narcotic tobacco haze of Capitalism,

who distributed Supercommunist pamphlets in Union Square weeping and undressing while the sirens of Los Alamos wailed them down, and wailed down Wall, and the Staten Island ferry also wailed,

who broke down crying in white gymnasiums naked and trembling before the machinery of other skeletons,

who bit detectives in the neck and shrieked with delight in policecars for committing no crime but their own wild cooking pederasty and intoxication,

who howled on their knees in the subway and were dragged off the roof waving genitals and manuscripts,

who let themselves be fucked in the ass by saintly motorcyclists, and screamed with joy,

who blew and were blown by those human seraphim, the sailors, caresses of Atlantic and Caribbean love,

who balled in the morning in the evenings in rosegardens and the grass of public parks and cemeteries scattering their semen freely to whomever come who may,

who hiccupped endlessly trying to giggle but wound up with a sob behind a partition in a Turkish Bath when the blonde & naked angel came to pierce them with a sword,

who lost their loveboys to the three old shrews of fate the one eyed shrew of the heterosexual dollar the one eyed shrew that winks out of the womb and the one eyed shrew that does nothing but sit on her ass and snip the intellectual golden threads of the craftsman's loom,

who copulated ecstatic and insatiate with a bottle of beer a sweetheart a package of cigarettes a candle and fell off the bed, and continued along the floor and down the hall and ended fainting on the wall with a vision of ultimate cunt and come eluding the last gyzym of consciousness,

who sweetened the snatches of a million girls trembling in the sunset, and were red eyed in the morning but prepared to sweeten the snatch of the sunrise, flashing buttocks under barns and naked in the lake,

who went out whoring through Colorado in myriad stolen night-cars,
N.C., secret hero of these poems, cocksman and Adonis of Denver—
joy to the memory of his innumerable lays of girls in empty lots &
diner backyards, moviehouses' rickety rows, on mountaintops in caves
or with gaunt waitresses in familiar roadside lonely petticoat upliftings
& especially secret gas-station solipisisms of johns, & hometown alleys
too,

who faded out in vast sordid movies, were shifted in dreams, woke on
a sudden Manhattan, and picked themselves up out of basements
hungover with heartless Tokay and horrors of Third Avenue iron
dreams & stumbled to unemployment offices,

who walked all night with their shoes full of blood on the snowbank
docks waiting for a door in the East River to open to a room full of
steamheat and opium,

who created great suicidal dramas on the apartment cliff-banks of the
Hudson under the wartime blue floodlight of the moon & their heads
shall be crowned with laurel in oblivion,

who ate the lamb stew of the imagination or digested the crab at the
muddy bottom of the rivers of Bowery,

who wept at the romance of the streets with their pushcarts full of
onions and bad music,

who sat in boxes breathing in the darkness under the bridge, and rose
up to build harpsichords in their lofts,

who coughed on the sixth floor of Harlem crowned with flame under
the tubercular sky surrounded by orange crates of theology,

who scribbled all night rocking and rolling over lofty incantations which
in the yellow morning were stanzas of gibberish,

who cooked rotten animals lung heart feet tail borsht & tortillas dream-
ing of the pure vegetable kingdom,

who plunged themselves under meat trucks looking for an egg,

who threw their watches off the roof to cast their ballot for Eternity
outside of Time, & alarm clocks fell on their heads every day for the
next decade,

who cut their wrists three times successively unsuccessfully, gave up
and were forced to open antique stores where they thought they
were growing old and cried,

who were burned alive in their innocent flannel suits on Madison
Avenue amid blasts of leaden verse & the tanked-up clatter of the
iron regiments of fashion & the nitroglycerine shrieks of the fairies of
advertising & the mustard gas of sinister intelligent editors, or were
run down by the drunken taxicabs of Absolute Reality,

who jumped off the Brooklyn Bridge this actually happened and walked
away unknown and forgotten into the ghostly daze of Chinatown
soup alleyways & firetrucks, not even one free beer,

who sang out of their windows in despair, fell out of the subway win-
dow, jumped in the filthy Passaic, leaped on negroes, cried all over
the street, danced on broken wineglasses barefoot smashed phono-
graph records of nostalgic European 1930's German jazz finished the
whiskey and threw up groaning into the bloody toilet, moans in their
ears and the blast of colossal steamwhistles,

who barreled down the highways of the past journeying to each other's
hotrod-Golgotha jail-solitude watch or Birmingham jazz incarnation,

who drove crosscountry seventytwo hours to find out if I had a vision
or you had a vision or he had a vision to find out Eternity,

who journeyed to Denver, who died in Denver, who came back to Den-
ver & waited in vain, who watched over Denver & brooded & loned
in Denver and finally went away to find out the Time, & now Denver
is lonely for her heroes,

who fell on their knees in hopeless cathedrals praying for each other's
salvation and light and breasts, until the soul illuminated its hair for a
second,

who crashed through their minds in jail waiting for impossible criminals
with golden heads and the charm of reality in their hearts who sang
sweet blues to Alcatraz,

who retired to Mexico to cultivate a habit, or Rocky Mount to tender
Buddha or Tangiers to boys or Southern Pacific to the black loco-
motive or Harvard to Narcissus to Woodlawn to the daisychain or
grave,

who demanded sanity trials accusing the radio of hypnotism & were left
with their insanity & their hands & a hung jury,

who threw potato salad at CCNY lecturers on Dadaism and subsequently
presented themselves on the granite steps of the madhouse with
shaven heads and harlequin speech of suicide, demanding instanta-
neous lobotomy,

and who were given instead the concrete void of insulin metrasol elec-
tricity hydrotherapy psychotherapy occupational therapy pingpong
& amnesia,

who in humorless protest overturned only one symbolic pingpong table,
resting briefly in catatonia,

returning years later truly bald except for a wig of blood, and tears and
fingers, to the visible madman doom of the wards of the madtowns
of the East,

Pilgrim State's Rockland's and Greystone's foetid halls, bickering with the echoes of the soul, rocking and rolling in the midnight solitude-bench dolmen-realms of love, dream of life a nightmare, bodies turned to stone as heavy as the moon,

with mother finally * * * * * *, and the last fantastic book flung out of the tenement window, and the last door closed at 4 AM and the last telephone slammed at the wall in reply and the last furnished room emptied down to the last piece of mental furniture, a yellow paper rose twisted on a wire hanger in the closet, and even that imaginary, nothing but a hopeful little bit of hallucination—

ah, Carl, while you are not safe I am not safe, and now you're really in the total animal soup of time—

and who therefore ran through the icy streets obsessed with a sudden flash of the alchemy of the use of the ellipse the catalog the meter & the vibrating plane,

who dreamt and made incarnate gaps in Time & Space through images juxtaposed, and trapped the archangel of the soul between 2 visual images and joined the elemental verbs and set the noun and dash of consciousness together jumping with sensation of Pater Omnipotens Aeterna Deus

to recreate the syntax and measure of poor human prose and stand before you speechless and intelligent and shaking with shame, re-jected yet confessing out the soul to conform to the rhythm of thought in his naked and endless head,

the madman bum and angel beat in Time, unknown, yet putting down here what might be left to say in time come after death,

and rose reincarnate in the ghostly clothes of jazz in the goldhorn shadow of the band and blew the suffering of America's naked mind for love into an eli eli lamma lamma sabacthani saxophone cry that shivered the cities down to the last radio

with the absolute heart of the poem of life butchered out of their own bodies good to eat a thousand years.

2.

What sphinx of cement and aluminum bashed open their skulls and ate up their brains and imagination?

Moloch! Solitude! Filth! Ugliness! Ashcans and unobtainable dollars! Children screaming under the stairways! Boys sobbing in armies! Old men weeping in the parks!

Moloch! Moloch! Nightmare of Moloch! Moloch the loveless! Mental Moloch! Moloch the heavy judger of men!

Moloch the incomprehensible prison! Moloch the crossbone soulless jailhouse and Congress of sorrows! Moloch whose buildings are judgement! Moloch the vast stone of war! Moloch the stunned governments!

Moloch whose mind is pure machinery! Moloch whose blood is running money! Moloch whose fingers are ten armies! Moloch whose breast is a cannibal dynamo! Moloch whose ear is a smoking tomb!

Moloch whose eyes are a thousand blind windows! Moloch whose skyscrapers stand in the long streets like endless Jehovahs! Moloch whose factories dream and croak in the fog! Moloch whose smokestacks and antennae crown the cities!

Moloch whose love is endless oil and stone! Moloch whose soul is electricity and banks! Moloch whose poverty is the specter of genius! Moloch whose fate is a cloud of sexless hydrogen! Moloch whose name is the Mind!

Moloch in whom I sit lonely! Moloch in whom I dream Angels! Crazy in Moloch! Cocksucker in Moloch! Lacklove and manless in Moloch!

Moloch who entered my soul early! Moloch in whom I am a consciousness without a body! Moloch who frightened me out of my natural ecstasy! Moloch whom I abandon! Wake up in Moloch! Light streaming out of the sky!

Moloch! Moloch! Robot apartments! invisible suburbs! skeleton treasuries! blind capitals! demonic industries! spectral nations! invincible madhouses! granite cocks! monstrous bombs!

They broke their backs lifting Moloch to Heaven! Pavements, trees, radios, tons! lifting the city to Heaven which exists and is everywhere about us!

Visions! omens! hallucinations! miracles! ecstasies! gone down the American river!

Dreams! adorations! illuminations! religions! the whole boatload of sensitive bullshit!

Breakthroughs! over the river! flips and crucifixions! gone down the flood! Highs! Epiphanies! Despairs! Ten years' animal screams and suicides! Minds! New loves! Mad generation! down on the rocks of Time!

Real holy laughter in the river! They saw it all! the wild eyes! the holy yells! They bade farewell! They jumped off the roof! to solitude! waving! carrying flowers! Down to the river! into the street!

3.
Carl Solomon! I'm with you in Rockland
  where you're madder than I am
I'm with you in Rockland
  where you must feel very strange
I'm with you in Rockland
  where you imitate the shade of my mother
I'm with you in Rockland
  where you've murdered your twelve secretaries
I'm with you in Rockland
  where you laugh at this invisible humor
I'm with you in Rockland
  where we are great writers on the same dreadful typewriter
I'm with you in Rockland
  where your condition has become serious and is reported on the radio
I'm with you in Rockland
  where the faculties of the skull no longer admit the worms of the
  senses
I'm with you in Rockland
  where you drink the tea of the breasts of the spinsters of Utica
I'm with you in Rockland
  where you pun on the bodies of your nurses the harpies of the Bronx
I'm with you in Rockland
  where you scream in a straightjacket that you're losing the game of
  the actual pingpong of the abyss
I'm with you in Rockland
  where you bang on the catatonic piano the soul is innocent and im-
  mortal it should never die ungodly in an armed madhouse
I'm with you in Rockland
  where fifty more shocks will never return your soul to its body again
  from its pilgrimage to a cross in the void
I'm with you in Rockland
  where you accuse your doctors of insanity and plot the Hebrew
  socialist revolution against the fascist national Golgotha
I'm with you in Rockland
  where you will split the heavens of Long Island and resurrect your
  living human Jesus from the superhuman tomb
I'm with you in Rockland
  where there are twentyfive-thousand mad comrades all together sing-
  ing the final stanzas of the Internationale

I'm with you in Rockland
   where we hug and kiss the United States under our bedsheets the
   United States that coughs all night and won't let us sleep
I'm with you in Rockland
   where we wake up electrified out of the coma by our own souls' air-
   planes roaring over the roof they've come to drop angelic bombs the
   hospital illuminates itself imaginary walls collapse   O skinny legions
   run outside   O starryspangled shock of mercy the eternal war is here
   O victory forget your underwear we're free
I'm with you in Rockland
   in my dreams you walk dripping from a sea-journey on the highway
   across America in tears to the door of my cottage in the Western
   night

FOOTNOTE TO HOWL

Holy! Holy! Holy! Holy! Holy! Holy! Holy! Holy! Holy! Holy! Holy!
   Holy! Holy! Holy! Holy!
The world is holy! The soul is holy! The skin is holy! The nose is holy!
   The tongue and cock and hand and asshole holy!
Everything is holy! everybody's holy! everywhere is holy! everyday is
   in eternity! Everyman's an angel!
The bum's as holy as the seraphim! the madman is holy as you my soul
   are holy!
The typewriter is holy the poem is holy the voice is holy the hearers are
   holy the ecstasy is holy!
Holy Peter holy Allen holy Solomon holy Lucien holy Kerouac holy
   Huncke holy Burroughs holy Cassady holy the unknown buggered
   and suffering beggars holy the hideous human angels!
Holy my mother in the insane asylum! Holy the cocks of the grand-
   fathers of Kansas!
Holy the groaning saxophone! Holy the bop apocalypse! Holy the jazz-
   bands marijuana hipsters peace & junk & drums!
Holy the solitudes of skyscrapers and pavements! Holy the cafeterias
   filled with the millions! Holy the mysterious rivers of tears under the
   streets!

Holy the lone juggernaut! Holy the vast lamb of the middleclass! Holy
    the crazy shepherds of rebellion! Who digs Los Angeles IS Los Angeles!
Holy New York Holy San Francisco Holy Peoria & Seattle Holy Paris
    Holy Tangiers Holy Moscow Holy Istanbul!
Holy time in eternity holy eternity in time holy the clocks in space holy
    the fourth dimension holy the fifth International holy the Angel in
    Moloch!
Holy the sea holy the desert holy the railroad holy the locomotive holy
    the visions holy the hallucinations holy the miracles holy the eyeball
    holy the abyss!
Holy forgiveness! mercy! charity! faith! Holy! Ours! bodies! suffering!
    magnanimity!
Holy the supernatural extra brilliant intelligent kindness of the soul!

AMERICA

America I've given you all and now I'm nothing.
America two dollars and twentyseven cents January 17, 1956.
I can't stand my own mind.
America when will we end the human war?
Go fuck yourself with your atom bomb.
I don't feel good don't bother me.
I won't write my poem till I'm in my right mind.
America when will you be angelic?
When will you take off your clothes?
When will you look at yourself through the grave?
When will you be worthy of your million Trotskyites?
America why are your libraries full of tears?
America when will you send your eggs to India?
I'm sick of your insane demands.
When can I go into the supermarket and buy what I need with my good
    looks?
America after all it is you and I who are perfect not the next world.
Your machinery is too much for me.
You made me want to be a saint.
There must be some other way to settle this argument.
Burroughs is in Tangiers I don't think he'll come back it's sinister.

Are you being sinister or is this some form of practical joke?
I'm trying to come to the point.
I refuse to give up my obsession.
America stop pushing I know what I'm doing.
America the plum blossoms are falling.
I haven't read the newspapers for months, everyday somebody goes on
  trial for murder.
America I feel sentimental about the Wobblies.
America I used to be a communist when I was a kid I'm not sorry.
I smoke marijuana every chance I get.
I sit in my house for days on end and stare at the roses in the closet.
When I go to Chinatown I get drunk and never get laid.
My mind is made up there's going to be trouble.
You should have seen me reading Marx.
My psychoanalyst thinks I'm perfectly right.
I won't say the Lord's Prayer.
I have mystical visions and cosmic vibrations.
America I still haven't told you what you did to Uncle Max after he came
  over from Russia.

I'm addressing you.
Are you going to let your emotional life be run by Time Magazine?
I'm obsessed by Time Magazine.
I read it every week.
Its cover stares at me every time I slink past the corner candystore.
I read it in the basement of the Berkeley Public Library.
It's always telling me about responsibility. Businessmen are serious.
  Movie producers are serious. Everybody's serious but me.
It occurs to me that I am America.
I am talking to myself again.

Asia is rising against me.
I haven't got a chinaman's chance.
I'd better consider my national resources.
My national resources consist of two joints of marijuana millions of
  genitals an unpublishable private literature that goes 1400 miles an
  hour and twentyfive-thousand mental institutions.
I say nothing about my prisons nor the millions of underprivileged who
  live in my flowerpots under the light of five hundred suns.

I have abolished the whorehouses of France, Tangiers is the next to go.
My ambition is to be President despite the fact that I'm a Catholic.

America how can I write a holy litany in your silly mood?
I will continue like Henry Ford my strophes are as individual as his
automobiles more so they're all different sexes.
America I will sell you strophes $2500 apiece $500 down on your old
strophe
America free Tom Mooney
America save the Spanish Loyalists
America Sacco & Vanzetti must not die
America I am the Scottsboro boys.
America when I was seven momma took me to Communist Cell meet-
ings they sold us garbanzos a handful per ticket a ticket costs a nickel
and the speeches were free everybody was angelic and sentimental
about the workers it was all so sincere you have no idea what a good
thing the party was in 1835 Scott Nearing was a grand old man a real
mensch Mother Bloor made me cry I once saw Israel Amter plain.
Everybody must have been a spy.
America you don't really want to go to war.
America it's them bad Russians.
Them Russians them Russians and them Chinamen. And them Russians.
The Russia wants to eat us alive. The Russia's power mad. She wants to
take our cars from out our garages.
Her wants to grab Chicago. Her needs a Red Readers' Digest. Her wants
our auto plants in Siberia. Him big bureaucracy running our filling-
stations.
That no good. Ugh. Him make Indians learn read. Him need big black
niggers. Hah. Her make us all work sixteen hours a day. Help.
America this is quite serious.
America this is the impression I get from looking in the television set.
America is this correct?
I'd better get right down to the job.
It's true I don't want to join the Army or turn lathes in precision parts
factories, I'm nearsighted and psychopathic anyway.
America I'm putting my queer shoulder to the wheel.

LOVE POEM ON THEME BY WHITMAN

I'll go into the bedroom silently and lie down between the bridegroom
    and the bride,
those bodies fallen from heaven stretched out waiting naked and restless,
arms resting over their eyes in the darkness,
bury my face in their shoulders and breasts, breathing their skin,
and stroke and kiss neck and mouth and make back be open and known,
legs raised up crook'd to receive, cock in the darkness driven tormented
    and attacking
roused up from hole to itching head,
bodies locked shuddering naked, hot lips and buttocks screwed into
    each other
and eyes, eyes glinting and charming, widening into looks and abandon,
and moans of movement, voices, hands in air, hands between thighs,
hands in moisture on softened lips, throbbing contraction of bellies
till the white come flow in the swirling sheets,
and the bride cry for forgiveness, and the groom be covered with tears
    of passion and compassion,
and I rise up from the bed replenished with last intimate gestures and
    kisses of farewell—
all before the mind wakes, behind shades and closed doors in a dark-
    ened house
where the inhabitants roam unsatisfied in the night,
nude ghosts seeking each other out in the silence.

PSALM III

    To God: to illuminate all men. Beginning with Skid Road.
    Let Occidental and Washington be transformed into a
higher place, the plaza of eternity.
    Illuminate the welders in shipyards with the brilliance of
their torches.
    Let the crane operator lift up his arm for joy.

Let elevators creak and speak, ascending and descending in
awe.

Let the mercy of the flower's direction beckon in the eye.

Let the straight flower bespeak its purpose in straightness—
to seek the light.

Let the crooked flower bespeak its purpose in crookedness—
to seek the light.

Let the crookedness and straightness bespeak the light.

Let Puget Sound be a blast of light.

I feed on your Name like a cockroach on a crumb—this
cockroach is holy.

WICHITA VORTEX SUTRA

1.

Turn Right Next Corner
     The Biggest Little Town in Kansas
         Macpherson
Red sun setting flat plains west streaked
        with gauzy veils, chimney mist spread
      around christmas-tree bulbed refineries—aluminum
        white tanks squat beneath
      winking signal towers' bright plane-lights,
          orange gas flares
      beneath pillows of smoke, flames in machinery—
          transparent towers at dusk

In advance of the Cold Wave
     Snow is spreading eastward to
           the Great Lakes
  News Broadcast & old clarinets
     Watertower dome Lighted on the flat plain
        car radio speeding acrost railroad tracks—

Kansas! Kansas! Shuddering at last!
     PERSON appearing in Kansas!
   angry telephone calls to the University

Police dumbfounded leaning on
    their radiocar hoods
  While Poets chant to Allah in the roadhouse Showboat!
Blue eyed children dance and hold thy Hand O aged Walt
  who came from Lawrence to Topeka to envision
    Iron interlaced upon the city plain—
  Telegraph wires strung from city to city O Melville!
    Television brightening thy *rills of Kansas lone*
I come,
   lone man from the void, riding a bus
   hypnotized by red tail lights on the straight
       space road ahead—
 & the Methodist minister with cracked eyes
      leaning over the table
    quoting Kierkegaard 'death of God'
      a million dollars
  in the bank owns all West Wichita
       come to Nothing!
    Prajnaparamita Sutra over coffee—Vortex
of telephone radio aircraft assembly frame ammunition
petroleum nightclub Newspaper streets illuminated by Bright
     EMPTINESS—

Thy sins are forgiven, Wichita!
    Thy lonesomeness annulled, O Kansas dear!
      as the western Twang prophesied
  thru banjo, when lone cowboy walked the railroad track
     past an empty station toward the sun
    sinking giant-bulbed orange down the box canyon—
  Music strung over his back
   and empty handed singing on this planet earth
      I'm a lonely Dog, O Mother!
Come, Nebraska, sing & dance with me—
   Come lovers of Lincoln and Omaha,
      hear my soft voice at last
  As Babes need the chemical touch of flesh in pink infancy
   lest they die Idiot returning to Inhuman—
        Nothing—
So, tender lipt adolescent girl, pale youth,
      give me back my soft kiss

Hold me in your innocent arms,
accept my tears as yours to harvest
equal   in nature to the Wheat
that made your bodies' muscular bones
broad shouldered, boy bicept—
from leaning on cows & drinking Milk
in Midwest Solitude—
No more fear of tenderness, much delight in weeping, ecstasy
in singing, laughter rises that confounds
staring Idiot mayors
and stony politicians eyeing
Thy breast,
O Man of America, be born!
Truth breaks through!
How big is the prick of the President?
How big is Cardinal Viet-Nam?
How little the prince of the F.B.I., unmarried all these years!
How big are all the Public Figures?
What kind of flesh hangs, hidden behind their Images?

Approaching Salina,
Prehistoric excavation, *Apache Uprising*
in the drive-in theater
Shelling Bombing Range   mapped in the distance,
Crime Prevention Show, sponsor Wrigley's Spearmint
Dinosaur Sinclair advertisement, glowing green—
South 9th Street lined with poplar & elm branch
spread over evening's tiny headlights—
Salinas Highschool's brick darkens Gothic
over a night-lit door—
What wreaths of naked bodies, thighs and faces,
small hairy bun'd vaginas,
silver cocks, armpits and breasts
moistened by tears
for 20 years, for 40 years?
Peking Radio surveyed by Luden's Coughdrops
Attacks on the Russians & Japanese,
Big Dipper leaning above the Nebraska border,
handle down to the blackened plains,
telephone-pole ghosts crossed
by roadside, dim headlights—

dark night, & giant T-bone steaks,
    and in *The Village Voice*
      New Frontier Productions present
          Camp Comedy: *Fairies I Have Met.*
Blue highway lamps strung along the horizon east at Hebron
      Homestead National Monument near Beatrice—

Language, language
    black Earth-circle in the rear window,
        no cars for miles along highway
      beacon lights on oceanic plain
    language, language
        over Big Blue River
        chanting *La Illaha El ('lill) Allah Who*
        revolving my head to my heart like my mother
        chin abreast at Allah
          Eyes closed, blackness
vaster than midnight prairies,
      Nebraskas of solitary Allah,
        Joy, I am I
          the lone One singing to myself
              God come true—
        Thrills of fear,
        nearer than the vein in my neck—?
What if I opened my soul to sing to my absolute self
    Singing as the car crash chomped thru blood & muscle
          tendon skull?
    What if I sang, and loosed the chords of fear brow?
      What exquisite noise wd
          shiver my car companions?
    I am the Universe tonite
      riding in all my Power riding
chauffeured thru my self by a long haired saint with eyeglasses
What if I sang till Students knew I was free
    of Viet-Nam, trousers, free of my own meat,
    free to die in my thoughtful shivering Throne?
      freer than Nebraska, freer than America,
        May I disappear
      in magic Joy-smoke! Pouf! reddish Vapor,
Faustus vanishes weeping & laughing
    under stars on Highway 77 between Beatrice & Lincoln—

"Better not to move but let things be" Reverend Preacher?
We've all already disappeared!

Space highway open, entering Lincoln's ear
ground to a stop Tracks Warning
Pioneer Boulevard—
William Jennings Bryan sang
Thou shalt not crucify mankind upon a cross of Gold!
O Baby Doe! Gold's
Department Store hulks o'er 10th Street now
—an unregenerate old fop who didn't want to be a monkey
now's the Highest Perfect Wisdom dust
and Lindsay's cry
survives compassionate in the Highschool Anthology—
a giant dormitory brilliant on the evening plain
drifts with his memories—
There's a nice white door over there
for me O dear!   on Zero Street.

February 15, 1966

2.
Face the Nation
Thru Hickman's rolling earth hills
icy winter
grey sky   bare trees lining the road
South to Wichita
you're in the Pepsi Generation   Signum enroute
Aiken Republican on the radio   60,000
Northvietnamese troops now infiltrated but over 250,000
South Vietnamese   armed men
our Enemy—
Not Hanoi our enemy
Not China our enemy
The Viet Cong!
MacNamara made a "bad guess"
"Bad Guess" chorused the Reporters?
Yes, no more than a Bad Guess, in 1962
"8000 American Troops handle the
Situation"

Bad Guess
in 1956, 80% of the
Vietnamese people would've voted for Ho Chi Minh
wrote Ike   years later   *Mandate for Change*
A bad guess in the Pentagon
And the Hawks were guessing all along
Bomb China's 200,000,000
cried Stennis from Mississippi
I guess it was 3 weeks ago
Holmes Alexander in Alberquerque Journal
Provincial newsman
said I guess we better begin to do that Now.
his typewriter clacking in his aged office
on a side street   under Sandia Mountain?
Half the world away from China
Johnson got some bad advice   Republican Aiken sang
to the Newsmen over the radio
The General guessed they'd stop infiltrating the South
if they bombed the North—
So I guess they bombed!
Pale Indochinese boys came thronging thru the jungle
in increased numbers
to the scene of TERROR!
While the triangle-roofed Farmer's Grain Elevator
sat quietly by the side of the road
along the railroad track
American Eagle beating its wings over Asia
million dollar helicopters
a billion dollars worth of Marines
who loved *Aunt Betty*
Drawn from the shores and farms shaking
from the high schools to the landing barge
blowing the air thru their cheeks with fear
in *Life* on Television
Put it this way on the radio
Put it this way in television language
Use the words
language, language:
"A bad guess"

Put it this way in headlines
    Omaha World Herald—   *Rusk Says Toughness*
                               Essential For Peace
Put it this way
    Lincoln Nebraska morning Star—
                   Vietnam War Brings Prosperity
Put it *this* way
        Declared MacNamara,   speaking language
        Asserted Maxwell Taylor
        General, Consultant to White House
    Vietcong losses leveling up three five zero zero
                              per month
        Front page testimony February '66
    Here in Nebraska same as Kansas same known in Saigon
        in Peking, in Moscow, same known
        by the youths of Liverpool three five zero zero
        the latest quotation in the human meat market—
            Father I cannot tell a lie!

A black horse bends its head to the stubble
    beside the silver stream winding thru the woods
    by an antique red barn on the outskirts of Beatrice—
            Quietness, quietness
      over this countryside
            except for unmistakable signals on radio
               followed by the honkytonk tinkle
                   of a city piano
to calm the nerves of taxpaying housewives of a Sunday morn.
          Has anyone looked in the eyes of the dead?
U.S. Army recruiting service sign *Careers With A Future*
    Is anyone living to look for future forgiveness?
Water hoses frozen on the street, the
    Crowd gathered to see a strange happening garage—
    Red flames on Sunday morning
          in a quiet town!
Has anyone looked in the eyes of the wounded?
    Have we seen but paper faces, Life Magazine?
    Are screaming faces made of dots,
        electric dots on Television—
            fuzzy decibels registering
               the mammal voiced howl

from the outskirts of Saigon to console model picture tubes
in Beatrice, in Hutchinson, in El Dorado
in historic Abilene
O inconsolable!

Stop, and eat more flesh.
"We will negotiate anywhere anytime"
said the giant President
Kansas City Times 2/14/66: "Word reached U.S. authorities
that Thailand's leaders feared that in Honolulu Johnson might
have tried to pursuade South Vietnam's rulers to ease their
stand against negotiating with the Viet Cong.
American officials said these fears were groundless and
Humphrey was telling the Thais so."
A.P. dispatch
The last week's paper is Amnesia.
Three five zero zero is numerals
Headline language poetry, nine decades after Democratic Vistas
and the Prophecy of the Good Grey Poet
Our nation "of the fabled damned"
or else . . .
Language, language
Ezra Pound the Chinese Written Character for truth
defined as man standing by his word
Word picture: forked creature
Man
standing by a box, birds flying out
representing mouth speech
Ham Steak please waitress, in the warm cafe.
Different from a bad guess.
The war is language,
language abused
for Advertisement,
language used
like magic for power on the planet:
Black Magic language,
formulas for reality—
Communism is a 9 letter word
used by inferior magicians with
the wrong alchemical formula for transforming earth into gold
—funky warlocks operating on guesswork,

handmedown mandrake terminology
that never worked in 1956
for grey-domed Dulles,
brooding over at State,
that never worked for Ike who knelt to take
the magic wafer in his mouth
from Dulles' hand
inside the church in Washington:
Communion of bum magicians
congress of failures from Kansas & Missouri
working with the wrong equations
Sorcerer's Apprentices who lost control
of the simplest broomstick in the world:
Language
O longhaired magician come home take care of your dumb helper
before the radiation deluge floods your livingroom,
your magic errandboy's
just made a bad guess again
that's lasted a whole decade.

N B C B S U P A P I N S L I F E
Time Mutual presents
World's Largest Camp Comedy:
Magic In Vietnam—
reality turned inside out
changing its sex in the Mass Media
for 30 days, TV den and bedroom farce
Flashing pictures Senate Foreign Relations Committee room
Generals faces flashing on and off screen
mouthing language
State Secretary speaking nothing but language
MacNamara declining to speak public language
The President talking language,
Senators reinterpreting language
General Taylor *Limited Objectives*
Owls from Pennsylvania
Clark's Face *Open Ended*
Dove's *Apocalypse*
Morse's hairy ears

Stennis orating in Mississippi
                    half billion chinamen crowding into the
                                        polling booth,
            Clean shaven Gen. Gavin's image
                                imagining *Enclaves*
                    Tactical Bombing the magic formula for
            a silver haired Symington:
Ancient Chinese apothegm:
                        Old in vain.
            Hawks swooping thru the newspapers
                    talons visible
            wings outspread in the giant updraft of hot air
                        loosing their dry screech in the skies
                                    over the Capitol
Napalm and black clouds emerging in newsprint
        Flesh soft as a Kansas girl's
                    ripped open by metal explosion—
        three five zero zero   on the other side of the planet
                    caught in barbed wire, fire ball
                    bullet shock, bayonet electricity
        bomb blast terrific in skull & belly, shrapnelled
                                    throbbing meat
While this American nation argues war:
                    conflicting language, language
                                proliferating in airwaves
        filling the farmhouse ear, filling
                    the City Manager's head in his oaken office
                    the professor's head in his bed at midnight
                    the pupil's head at the movies
                        blond haired, his heart throbbing with desire
                        for the girlish image bodied on the screen:
                                or smoking cigarettes
                                and watching Captain Kangaroo
                                that fabled damned of nations
                                prophecy come true—
Though the highway's straight,
        dipping downward through low hills,
        rising narrow on the far horizon
                black cows browse in caked fields
                    ponds in the hollows lie frozen,
                                quietness.

Is this the land that started war on China?
    This be the soil that thought Cold War for decades?
    Are these nervous naked trees & farmhouses
                    the vortex
              of oriental anxiety molecules
   that've imagined   American Foreign Policy
      and magick'd up paranoia in Peking
            and curtains of living blood
                  surrounding far Saigon?
Are these the towns where the language emerged
    from the mouths here
           that makes a Hell of riots in Dominica
    sustains the aging tyranny of Chiang in silent Taipeh city
    Paid for the lost French war in Algeria
        overthrew the Guatemalan polis in '54
    maintaining United Fruit's bannana greed
            another thirteen years
      for the secret prestige of the Dulles family lawfirm?

Here's Marysville—
    a black railroad engine in the children's park,
            at rest—
and the Track Crossing
    with Cotton Belt flatcars
          carrying autos west from Dallas
    Delaware & Hudson gondolas filled with power stuff—
    a line of boxcars far east as the eye can see
         carrying battle goods to cross the Rockies
      into the hands of rich longshoreman loading
            ships on the Pacific—
    Oakland Army Terminal lights
          blue illumined all night now—
Crash of couplings and the great American train
      moves on carrying its cushioned load of metal doom
    Union Pacific linked together with your Hoosier Line
      followed by passive Wabash
          rolling behind
      all Erie carrying cargo in the rear,
    Central Georgia's rust colored truck proclaiming
          The Right Way, concluding
   the awesome poet writ by the train

across northern Kansas,
land which gave right of way
to the massing of metal meant for explosion
in Indochina—
Passing thru Waterville,
Electronic machinery in the bus humming prophecy—
paper signs blowing in cold wind,
mid-Sunday afternoon's silence
in town
under frost-grey sky
that covers the horizon—
That the rest of earth is unseen,
an outer universe invisible,
Unknown except thru
language
airprint
magic images
or prophecy of the secret
heart the same
in Waterville as Saigon one human form:
When a woman's heart bursts in Waterville
a woman screams equal in Hanoi—
On to Wichita to prophesy! O frightful Bard!
into the heart of the Vortex
where anxiety rings
the University with millionaire pressure,
lonely crank telephone voices sighing in dread,
and students waken trembling in their beds
with dreams of a new truth warm as meat,
little girls suspecting their elders of murder
committed by remote control machinery,
boys with sexual bellies aroused
chilled in the heart by the mailman
with a letter from an aging white haired General
Director of selection for service in
Deathwar
all this black language
writ by machine!
O hopeless Fathers and Teachers
in Hué   do you know
the same woe too?

I'm an old man now, and a lonesome man in Kansas
 but not afraid
  to speak my lonesomeness in a car,
  because not only my lonesomeness
   it's Ours, all over America,
     O tender fellows—
   & spoken lonesomeness is Prophecy
   in the moon 100 years ago or in
    the middle of Kansas now.
It's not the vast plains mute our mouths
    that fill at midnite with ecstatic language
  when our trembling bodies hold each other
     breast to breast on a mattress—
Not the empty sky that hides
      the feeling from our faces
nor our skirts and trousers that conceal
   the bodylove emanating in a glow of beloved skin,
     white smooth abdomen down to the hair
        between our legs,
  It's not a God that bore us that forbid
    our Being, like a sunny rose
      all red with naked joy
    between our eyes & bellies, yes
All we do is for this frightened thing
    we call Love, want and lack—
fear that we aren't the one whose body could be
   beloved of all the brides of Kansas City,
   kissed all over by every boy of Wichita—
O but how many in their solitude weep aloud like me—
   On the bridge over Republican River
      almost in tears to know
       how to speak the right language—
on the frosty broad road
     uphill between highway embankments
   I search for the language
      that is also yours—
   almost all our language has been taxed by war.
Radio antennae high tension
   wires ranging from Junction City across the plains—

highway cloverleaf sunk in a vast meadow
              lanes curving past Abilene
                  to Denver filled with old
                        heroes of love—
        to Wichita where McClure's mind
              burst into animal beauty
              drunk, getting laid in a car
                  in a neon misted street
                      15 years ago—
   to Independence where the old man's still alive
  who loosed the bomb that's slaved all human consciousness
          and made the body universe a place of fear—
Now, speeding along the empty plain,
          no giant demon machine
            visible on the horizon
   but tiny human trees and wooden houses at the sky's edge
      I claim my birthright!
            reborn forever as long as Man
              in Kansas or other universe—Joy
        reborn after the vast sadness of War Gods!
A lone man talking to myself, no house in the brown vastness to hear,
     imagining the throng of Selves
          that make this nation one body of Prophecy
            languaged by Declaration as
              Happiness!
I call all Powers of imagination
   to my side in this auto to make Prophecy,
              all Lords
     of human kingdoms to come
Shambu Bharti Baba naked covered with ash
     Khaki Baba fat-bellied mad with the dogs
Dehorahava Baba who moans Oh how wounded, How wounded
    Citaram Onkar Das Thakur who commands
            give up your desire
Satyananda who raises two thumbs in tranquillity
    Kali Pada Guha Roy whose yoga drops before the void
     Shivananda who touches the breast and says OM
Srimata Krishnaji of Brindaban who says take for your guru
   William Blake the invisible father of English visions

Sri Ramakrishna master of ecstasy eyes
       half closed who only cries for his mother
Chaitanya arms upraised singing & dancing his own praise
    merciful Chango judging our bodies
       Durga-Ma covered with blood
           destroyer of battlefield illusions
         million-faced Tathagata gone past suffering
Preserver Harekrishna returning in the age of pain
Sacred Heart my Christ acceptable
        Allah the Compassionate One
           Jaweh Righteous One
      all Knowledge-Princes of Earth-man, all
   ancient Seraphim of heavenly Desire, Devas, yogis
        & holymen I chant to—
         Come to my lone presence
            into this Vortex named Kansas,
I lift my voice aloud,
    make Mantra of American language now,
      pronounce the words beginning my own millennium,
         I here declare the end of the War!
      Ancient days' Illusion!—
Let the States tremble,
    let the Nation weep,
      let Congress legislate its own delight
        let the President execute his own desire—
this Act done by my own voice,
        nameless Mystery—
published to my own senses,
      blissfully received by my own form
approved with pleasure by my sensations
    manifestation of my very thought
    accomplished in my own imagination
      all realms within my consciousness fulfilled
    60 miles from Wichita
        near El Dorado,
         The Golden One,
in chill earthly mist
    houseless brown farmland plains rolling heavenward
           in every direction
one midwinter afternoon Sunday called the day of the Lord—

Pure Spring Water gathered in one tower
            where Florence is
                    set on a hill,
             stop for tea & gas

Cars passing their messages along country crossroads
          to populaces cement-networked on flatness,
                    giant white mist on earth
        and a Wichita Eagle-Beacon headlines
         "Kennedy Urges Cong Get Chair in Negotiations"
The War is gone,
        Language emerging on the motel news stand,
                  the right magic
            Formula, the language known
in the back of the mind before, now in black print
                daily consciousness
Eagle News Services Saigon—
        Headline Surrounded Vietcong Charge Into Fire Fight
           the suffering not yet ended
                  for others
        The last spasms of the dragon of pain
              shoot thru the muscles
          a crackling around the eyeballs
          of a sensitive yellow boy by a muddy wall
Continued from page one   area
        after the Marines killed 256 Vietcong captured 31
        ten day operation Harvest Moon last December
              Language language
       U.S. Military Spokesmen
            Language language
                Cong death toll
     has soared to 100 in First Air Cavalry
      Division's Sector of
            Language language
        Operation White Wing near Bong Son
Some of the
      Language language
           Communist
            Language language soldiers

charged so desperately
      they were struck with six or seven bullets before they fell
    Language Language M 60 Machine Guns
           Language language in La Drang Valley
    the terrain is rougher infested with leeches and scorpions
          The war was over several hours ago!
Oh at last again the radio opens
    blue Invitations!
        Angelic Dylan singing across the nation
          "When all your children start to resent you
          Won't you come see me, Queen Jane?"
    His youthful voice making glad
          the brown endless meadows
    His tenderness penetrating aether,
      soft prayer on the airwaves,
        Language language, and sweet music too
        even unto thee,
          hairy flatness!
        even unto thee
            despairing Burns!

Future speeding on swift wheels
        straight to the heart of Wichita!
Now radio voices cry population hunger world
          of unhappy people
      waiting for Man to be born
          O man in America!
    you certainly smell good
          the radio says
passing mysterious families of winking towers
grouped round a quonset-hut on a hillock—
      feed storage or military fear factory here?
Sensitive City, Ooh! Hamburger & Skelley's Gas
         lights feed man and machine,
    Kansas Electric Substation aluminum robot
      signals thru thin antennae towers
      above the empty football field
              at Sunday dusk
to a solitary derrick that pumps oil from the unconscious
        working night & day

    & factory gas-flares edge a huge golf course
        where tired businessmen can come and play—
Cloverleaf, Merging Traffic East Wichita turnoff
          McConnel Airforce Base
              nourishing the city—
    Lights rising in the suburbs
    Supermarket Texaco brilliance starred
          over streetlamp vertebrae on Kellogg,
      green jewelled traffic lights
        confronting the windshield,
Centertown ganglion entered!
        Crowds of autos moving with their lightshine,
        signbulbs winking in the driver's eyeball—
The human nest collected, neon lit,
        and sunburst signed
      for business as usual, except on the Lord's Day—
Redeemer Lutheran's three crosses lit on the lawn
        reminder of our sins
and Titsworth offers insurance on Hydraulic
by De Voors Guard's Mortuary for outmoded bodies
        of the human vehicle
      which no Titsworth of insurance will customise
            for resale—
So home, traveller, past the newspaper language factory
    under Union Station railroad bridge on Douglas
    to the center of the Vortex, calmly returned
      to Hotel Eaton—
Carry Nation began the war on Vietnam here
        with an angry smashing axe
          attacking Wine—
    Here fifty years ago, by her violence
began a vortex of hatred that defoliated the Mekong Delta—
    Proud Wichita! vain Wichita
      cast the first stone!—
         That murdered my mother
    who died of the communist anticommunist psychosis
      in the madhouse one decade long ago
complaining about wires of masscommunication in her head
      and phantom political voices in the air
        besmirching her girlish character.

Many another has suffered death and madness
in the Vortex from Hydraulic
to the end of 17th—enough!
The war is over now—
Except for the souls
held prisoner in Niggertown
still pining for love of your tender white bodies O children of
Wichita!

WALES VISITATION

White fog lifting & falling on mountain-brow
Trees moving in rivers of wind
The clouds arise
as on a wave, gigantic eddy lifting mist
above teeming ferns exquisitely swayed
along a green crag
glimpsed thru mullioned glass in valley raine—

Bardic, O Self, Visitacione, tell naught
but what seen by one man in a vale in Albion,
of the folk, whose physical sciences end in Ecology,
the wisdom of earthly relations,
of mouths & eyes interknit ten centuries visible
orchards of mind language manifest human,
of the satanic thistle that raises its horned symmetry
flowering above sister grass-daisies' pink tiny
bloomlets angelic as lightbulbs—

Remember 160 miles from London's symmetrical thorned tower
& network of TV pictures flashing bearded your Self
the lambs on the tree-nooked hillside this day bleating
heard in Blake's old ear, & the silent thought of Wordsworth in
eld Stillness
clouds passing through skeleton arches of Tintern Abbey—
Bard Nameless as the Vast, babble to Vastness!

All the Valley quivered, one extended motion, wind
    undulating on mossy hills
  a giant wash that sank white fog delicately down red runnels
      on the mountainside
  whose leaf-branch tendrils moved asway
      in granitic undertow down—
and lifted the floating Nebulous upward, and lifted the arms of the
              trees
    and lifted the grasses an instant in balance
     and lifted the lambs to hold still
   and lifted the green of the hill, in one solemn wave

A solid mass of Heaven, mist-infused, ebbs thru the vale,
  a wavelet of Immensity, lapping gigantic through Llanthony
         Valley,
  the length of all England, valley upon valley under Heaven's ocean
      tonned with cloud-hang,
    Heaven balanced on a grassblade—
Roar of the mountain wind slow, sigh of the body,
   One Being on the mountainside stirring gently
     Exquisite scales trembling everywhere in balance,
one motion thru the cloudy sky-floor shifting on the million
      feet of daisies,
one Majesty the motion that stirred wet grass quivering
   to the farthest tendril of white fog poured down
     through shivering flowers on the mountain's
       head—

No imperfection in the budded mountain,
  Valleys breathe, heaven and earth move together,
  daisies push inches of yellow air, vegetables tremble
    green atoms shimmer in grassy mandalas,
sheep speckle the mountainside, revolving their jaws with empty
      eyes,
   horses dance in the warm rain,
  tree-lined canals network through live farmland,
    blueberries fringe stone walls
   on hill breasts nippled with hawthorn,
  pheasants croak up meadow-bellies haired with fern—

Out, out on the hillside, into the ocean sound, into delicate
                              gusts of wet air,
Fall on the ground, O great Wetness, O Mother, No harm on
                                        thy body!
Stare close, no imperfection in the grass,
                    each flower Buddha-eye, repeating the story,
                            the myriad-formed soul
Kneel before the foxglove raising green buds, mauve bells drooped
          doubled down the stem trembling antennae,
        & look in the eyes of the branded lambs that stare
            breathing stockstill under dripping hawthorn—
I lay down mixing my beard with the wet hair of the mountainside,
          smelling the brown vagina-moist ground, harmless,
              tasting the violet thistle-hair, sweetness—
One being so balanced, so vast, that its softest breath
            moves every floweret in the stillness on the valley floor,
        trembles lamb-hair hung gossamer rain-beaded in the grass,
    lifts trees on their roots, birds in the great draught
              hiding their strength in the rain, bearing same weight,

Groan thru breast and neck, a great Oh! to earth heart
                    Calling our Presence together
        The great secret is no secret
                    Senses fit the winds,
                        Visible is visible,
        rain-mist curtains wave through the bearded vale,
            grey atoms wet the wind's Kaballah
Crosslegged on a rock in dusk rain,
          rubber booted in soft grass, mind moveless,
      breath trembles in white daisies by the roadside,
                Heaven breath and my own symmetric
        Airs wavering thru antlered green fern
drawn in my navel, same breath as breathes thru Capel-Y-Ffn,
          Sounds of Aleph and Aum
                through forests of gristle,
      my skull and Lord Hereford's Knob equal,
                All Albion one.

What did I notice? Particulars! The
           vision of the great One is myriad—
     smoke curls upward from ash tray,
              house fire burned low,
The night, still wet & moody black heaven
                  starless
   upward in motion with wet wind.

                    July 29, 1967 (LSD)—August 3, 1967 (London)

G. Marshall Wilson—Ebony Magazine

LeRoi Jones

DUNCAN SPOKE OF A PROCESS

And what I have learned
of it, to repeat, repeated
as a day will repeat
its color, the tired sounds
run off its bones. In me, a balance.

Before that, what came easiest. From
wide poles, across the greenest earth,
eyes locked on, where they could live, and
whatever came from there, where the hand
could be offered, like Gideon's young troops
on their knees at the water.

                     I test myself,
with memory. A live bloody skeleton. Hung as softly
as summer. Sways like words' melody, as ugly as any
lips, or fingers stroking lakes, or flesh like a
white frightened scream.

What comes, closest, is
closest. Moving, there
is a wreck of spirit,
                     a heap of broken feeling. What

was only love
or in those cold rooms,
opinion. Still, it made

color. And filled me
as no one will. As, even
I cannot fill
myself.

       I see what I love most and will not
leave what futile lies
I have. I am where there
is nothing, save myself. And go out to
what is most beautiful. What some noncombatant Greek
or soft Italian prince
would sing, "Noble Friends."

                      Noble Selves. And which one
is truly
to rule here? And
what country is this?

PREFACE TO A TWENTY VOLUME SUICIDE NOTE

(For Kellie Jones, born 16 May 1959)

Lately, I've become accustomed to the way
The ground opens up and envelops me
Each time I go out to walk the dog.
Or the broad-edged silly music the wind
Makes when I run for a bus . . .

Things have come to that.

And now, each night I count the stars,
And each night I get the same number.
And when they will not come to be counted,
I count the holes they leave.

Nobody sings anymore.

And then last night, I tiptoed up
To my daughter's room and heard her
Talking to someone, and when I opened
The door, there was no one there . . .
Only she on her knees, peeking into

Her own clasped hands.

A POEM FOR WILLIE BEST*

1.
The face sings, alone
at the top
              of the body. All
flesh, all song, aligned. For hell
is silent, at those cracked lips
flakes of skin and mind
twist and whistle softly
as they fall.
              It was your own death
you saw. Your own face, stiff
and raw. This
without sound, or
movement. Sweet afton, the
dead beggar bleeds
yet. His blood, for a time
alive, and huddled in a door
way, struggling to sing. Rain
washes it into cracks. Pits
whose bottoms are famous. Whose sides
are innocent broadcasts
of another life.

* Willie Best was a Negro character actor whose Hollywood name was
Sleep'n'eat.

2.
At this point, neither
front nor back. A point, the
dimensionless line. The top
of a head, seen from Christ's
heaven, stripped of history
or desire.
           Fixed, perpendicular
to shadow. (even speech, vertical,
leaves no trace. Born in to death
held fast to it, where
the lover spreads his arms, the line
he makes to threaten Gods with history.
The fingers stretch to emptiness. At
each point, after flesh, even light
is speculation. But an end, his end,
failing a beginning.

                II.
A cross. The gesture, symbol, line
arms held stiff, nailed stiff, with
no sign, of what gave them strength.
The point, become a line, a cross, or
the man, and his material, driven in
the ground. If the head rolls back
and the mouth opens, screamed into
existence, there will be perhaps
only the slightest hint of movement—
a smear; no help will come. No one
will turn to that station again.

3.
At a cross roads, sits the
player. No drum, no umbrella, even
though it's raining. Again, and we
are somehow less miserable because
here is a hero, used to being wet.
One road is where you are standing now
(reading this, the other, crosses then
rushes into a wood.

5 lbs neckbones.
5 lbs hog innards.
10 bottles cheap wine.
(The contents
of a paper bag, also shoes, with holes
for the big toe, and several rusted
knives. This is a literature, of
symbols. And it is his gift, as the
bag is.
(The contents
again, holy saviours,
300 men on horseback
75 bibles
the quietness
of a field. A rich
man, though wet through
by the rain.
I said,
47 howitzers
7 polished horses jaws
a few trees being waved
softly back under
the black night
All This should be
invested.

4.
Where
ever,
he has gone. Who ever
mourns
or sits silent
to remember

There is nothing of pity
here. Nothing
of sympathy.

5.
This is the dance of the raised
leg. Of the hand on the knee
quickly.
      As a dance it punishes
speech. 'The house burned. The
old man killed.'
      As a dance it
is obscure.

6.
This is the song
of the highest C.
      The falsetto. An elegance
that punishes silence. This is the song
of the toes pointed inward, the arms swung, the
hips, moved, for fucking, slow, from side
to side. He is quoted
saying, "My father was
never a jockey,
      but
        he did teach me
        how to ride."

7.
The balance.
    (Rushed in, swarmed of dark, cloaks,
and only red lights pushed a message
to the street. Rub.
      This is the lady,
I saw you with.
This is your mother.
This is the lady I wanted
some how to sleep with.
      As a dance, or
our elegant song. Sun red and grown
from trees, fences, mud roads in dried out
river beds. This is for me, with no God

but what is given me. Give me.
                              Something more
than what is here. I must tell you
my body hurts.

The balance.
                    Can you hear? Here
I am again. Your boy, dynamite. Can
you hear? My soul is moved. The soul
you gave me. I say, my soul, and it
is moved. That soul
you gave me.
                    Yes, I'm sure
this is the lady. You
slept with her. Witness, your boy,
here, dynamite. Hear?
                              I mean
can you?

The balance.
                    He was tired of losing. (And
his walking buddies tired
of walking.
                    Bent slightly,
at the waist. Left hand low, to flick
quick showy jabs ala Sugar. The right
cocked, to complete,
                              any combination.
                                        He was
tired of losing, but he was fighting
a big dumb "farmer."
                              Such a blue bright
afternoon, and only a few hundred yards
from the beach. He said, I'm tired
of losing.
          "I *got* ta cut'cha."

8.
A renegade
behind the mask. And even
the mask, a renegade
disguise. Black skin
and hanging lip.

> Lazy
> Frightened
> Thieving
> Very potent sexually
> Scars
> Generally inferior
> > (but natural

rhythms.

His head is
at the window. The only
part
       that sings.

(The word he used
              (we are passing St. Mark's place
              and those crazy jews who fuck)
                            to provoke

in neon, still useful
in the rain,
          to provoke
some meaning, where before
there was only hell. I said
silence, at his huddled blood.

> It is an obscene invention.
> A white sticky discharge.
> "Jism," in white chalk
> on the back of Angel's garage.
> Red jackets with the head of
> Hobbes staring into space. "Jasm"
> the name the leader took, had it
> stenciled on his chest.
> > And he sits

wet at the crossroads, remembering distinctly
each weightless face that eases by. (Sun at
the back door, and that hideous mindless grin.

(Hear?

THE DEAD LADY CANONIZED

(A thread
of meaning. Meaning light. The quick
response. To breath, or the virgins
sick odor against the night.

(A trail
of objects. Dead nouns, rotted faces
propose the night's image. Erect
for that lady, a grave of her own.

(The stem
of the morning, sets itself, on
each window (of thought, where it
goes. The lady is dead, may the Gods,

(those others
beg our forgiveness. And Damballah, kind father,
sew up
her bleeding hole.

THE INVENTION OF COMICS

I am a soul in the world: in
the world of my soul the whirled
light / from the day
the sacked land
of my father.

In the world, the sad
nature of
myself. In myself
nature is sad. Small
prints of the day. Its
small dull fires. Its
sun, like a greyness
smeared on the dark.

The day of my soul, is
the nature of that
place. It is a landscape. Seen
from the top of a hill. A
grey expanse; dull fires
throbbing on its seas.

The man's soul, the complexion
of his life. The menace
of its greyness. The
fire, throbs, the sea
moves. Birds shoot
from the dark. The edge
of the waters lit
darkly for the moon.

And the moon, from the soul. Is
the world, of the man. The man
and his sea, and its moon, and
the soft fire throbbing. Kind
death. O,
my dark and sultry
love.

A POEM FOR DEMOCRATS

the city rises

       in color, our sad
ness, blanket this wood place, single drop
of rain, blue image of
someone's love.
           Net of rain. Crystal ice
glass strings, smash
(on such repertoire of memory
as:
   baskets
   the long walk up harbor
   & the insistence, rain, as they build

City, is wicked. Not
this one, where I am, where they
still move, go to, out of
(transporting your loved one
across the line is death
by drowning.

       Drowned love
hanged man, swung, cement on his feet.)
             But
the small filth of the small mind
short structures of
newark, baltimore, cincinnati, omaha. Distress,
europe has passed we are alone. Europe
frail woman dead, we are alone

A POEM FOR BLACK HEARTS

For Malcolm's eyes, when they broke
the face of some dumb white man, For
Malcolm's hands raised to bless us
all black and strong in his image
of ourselves, For Malcolm's words
fire darts, the victor's tireless
thrusts, words hung above the world
change as it may, he said it, and
for this he was killed, for saying,
and feeling, and being/ change, all
collected hot in his heart, For Malcolm's
heart, raising us above our filthy cities,
for his stride, and his beat, and his address
to the grey monsters of the world, For Malcolm's
pleas for your dignity, black men, for your life,
black man, for the filling of your minds
with righteousness, For all of him dead and
gone and vanished from us, and all of him which
clings to our speech black god of our time.
For all of him, and all of yourself, look up,
black man, quit stuttering and shuffling, look up,
black man, quit whining and stooping, for all of him,
For Great Malcolm a prince of the earth, let nothing in us rest
until we avenge ourselves for his death, stupid animals
that killed him, let us never breathe a pure breath if
we fail, and white men call us faggots till the end of
the earth.

POEM FOR HALFWHITE COLLEGE STUDENTS

Who are you, listening to me, who are you
listening to yourself? Are you white or
black, or does that have anything to do
with it? Can you pop your fingers to no

music, except those wild monkies go on
in your head, can you jerk, to no melody,
except finger poppers get it together
when you turn from starchecking to checking
yourself. How do you sound, your words, are they
yours? The ghost you see in the mirror, is it really
you, can you swear you are not an imitation greyboy,
can you look right next to you in that chair, and swear,
that the sister you have your hand on is not really
so full of Elizabeth Taylor, Richard Burton is
coming out of her ears. You may even have to be Richard
with a white shirt and face, and four million negroes
think you cute, you may have to be Elizabeth Taylor, old lady,
if you want to sit up in your crazy spot dreaming about dresses,
and the sway of certain porters' hips. Check yourself, learn who it is
speaking, when you make some ultrasophisticated point, check yourself,
when you find yourself gesturing like Steve McQueen, check it out, ask
in your black heart who it is you are, and is that image black or white,

you might be surprised right out the window, whistling dixie on the way in.

KA 'BA

A closed window looks down
on a dirty courtyard, and black people
call across or scream across or walk across
defying physics in the stream of their will

Our world is full of sound
Our world is more lovely than anyone's
tho we suffer, and kill each other
and sometimes fail to walk the air

We are beautiful people
with african imaginations
full of masks and dances and swelling chants

with african eyes, and noses, and arms,
though we sprawl in grey chains in a place
full of winters, when what we want is sun.

We have been captured,
brothers. And we labor
to make our getaway, into
the ancient image, into a new

correspondence with ourselves
and our black family. We need magic
now we need the spells, to raise up
return, destroy, and create. What will be

the sacred words?

BLACK PEOPLE: THIS IS OUR DESTINY

The road runs straight with no turning, the circle
runs complete as it is in the storm of peace, the all
embraced embracing in the circle complete turning road
straight like a burning straight with the circle complete
as in a peaceful storm, the elements, the niggers' voices
harmonized with creation on a peak in the holy black man's
eyes that we rise, whose race is only direction up, where
we go to meet the realization of makers knowing who we are
and the war in our hearts but the purity of the holy world
that we long for, knowing how to live, and what life is, and
who God is, and the many revolutions we must spin through in our
seven adventures in the endlessness of all existing feeling, all
existing forms of life, the gases, the plants, the ghost minerals
the spirits the souls the light in the stillness where the storm
the glow the nothing in God is complete except there is nothing
to be incomplete the pulse and change of rhythm, blown flight
to be anything at all . . . vibration holy nuance beating against
itself, a rhythm a playing re-understood now by one of the 1st race
the primitives the first men who evolve again to civilize the
world

BLACK ART

Poems are bullshit unless they are
teeth or trees or lemons piled
on a step. Or black ladies dying
of men leaving nickel hearts
beating them down. Fuck poems
and they are useful, wd they shoot
come at you, love what you are,
breathe like wrestlers, or shudder
strangely after pissing. We want live
words of the hip world live flesh &
coursing blood. Hearts Brains
Souls splintering fire. We want poems
like fists beating niggers out of Jocks
or dagger poems in the slimy bellies
of the owner-jews. Black poems to
smear on girdlemamma mulatto bitches
whose brains are red jelly stuck
between 'lizabeth taylor's toes. Stinking
Whores! We want "poems that kill."
Assassin poems, Poems that shoot
guns. Poems that wrestle cops into alleys
and take their weapons leaving them dead
with tongues pulled out and sent to Ireland. Knockoff
poems for dope selling wops or slick halfwhite
politicians Airplane poems, rrrrrrrrrrrrrrr
rrrrrrrrrrrrrr . . . tuhtuhtuhtuhtuhtuhtuhtuhtuh
. . . rrrrrrrrrrrrrrr . . . Setting fire and death to
whities ass. Look at the Liberal
Spokesman for the jews clutch his throat
& puke himself into eternity . . . rrrrrrrr
There's a negroleader pinned to
a bar stool in Sardi's eyeballs melting
in hot flame Another negroleader
on the steps of the white house one
kneeling between the sheriff's thighs
negotiating cooly for his people.

Agggh . . . stumbles across the room . . .
Put it on him, poem. Strip him naked
to the world! Another bad poem cracking
steel knuckles in a jewlady's mouth
Poem scream poison gas on beasts in green berets
Clean out the world for virtue and love,
Let there be no love poems written
until love can exist freely and
cleanly. Let Black People understand
that they are the lovers and the sons
of lovers and warriors and sons
of warriors Are poems & poets &
all the loveliness here in the world

We want a black poem. And a
Black World.
Let the world be a Black Poem
And Let All Black People Speak This Poem
Silently
or LOUD

© Rollie McKenna

Kenneth Koch

FRESH AIR

1.
At the Poem Society a black-haired man stands up to say
"You make me sick with all your talk about restraint and mature talent!
Haven't you ever looked out the window at a painting by Matisse,
Or did you always stay in hotels where there were too many spiders
    crawling on your visages?
Did you ever glance inside a bottle of sparkling pop,
Or see a citizen split in two by the lightning?
I am afraid you have never smiled at the hibernation
Of bear cubs except that you saw in it some deep relation
To human suffering and wishes, oh what a bunch of crackpots!"
The black-haired man sits down, and the others shoot arrows at him.
A blond man stands up and says,
"He is right! Why should we be organized to defend the kingdom
Of dullness? There are so many slimy people connected with poetry,
Too, and people who know nothing about it!
I am not recommending that poets like each other and organize to
    fight them,
But simply that lightning should strike them."
Then the assembled mediocrities shot arrows at the blond-haired man.
The chairman stood up on the platform, oh he was physically ugly!
He was small-limbed and -boned and thought he was quite seductive,
But he was bald with certain hideous black hairs,
And his voice had the sound of water leaving a vaseline bathtub,
And he said, "The subject for this evening's discussion is poetry
On the subject of love between swans." And everyone threw candy
    hearts
At the disgusting man, and they stuck to his bib and tucker,

187

And he danced up and down on the platform in terrific glee
And recited the poetry of his little friends—but the blond man stuck
  his head
Out of a cloud and recited poems about the east and thunder,
And the black-haired man moved through the stratosphere chanting
Poems of the relationships between terrific prehistoric charcoal whales,
And the slimy man with candy hearts sticking all over him
Wilted away like a cigarette paper on which the bumblebees have uri-
  nated,
And all the professors left the room to go back to their duty,
And all that were left in the room were five or six poets
And together they sang the new poem of the twentieth century
Which, though influenced by Mallarmé, Shelley, Byron, and Whitman,
Plus a million other poets, is still entirely original
And is so exciting that it cannot be here repeated.
You must go to the Poem Society and wait for it to happen.
Once you have heard this poem you will not love any other,
Once you have dreamed this dream you will be inconsolable,
Once you have loved this dream you will be as one dead,
Once you have visited the passages of this time's great art!

2.
"Oh to be seventeen years old
Once again," sang the red-haired man, "and not know that poetry
Is ruled with the sceptre of the dumb, the deaf, and the creepy!"
And the shouting persons battered his immortal body with stones
And threw his primitive comedy into the sea
From which it sang forth poems irrevocably blue.

Who are the great poets of our time, and what are their names?
Yeats of the baleful influence, Auden of the baleful influence, Eliot of
  the baleful influence
(Is Eliot a great poet? no one knows), Hardy, Stevens, Williams (is Hardy
  of our time?),
Hopkins (is Hopkins of our time?), Rilke (is Rilke of our time?), Lorca
  (is Lorca of our time?), who is still of our time?
Mallarmé, Valéry, Apollinaire, Eluard, Reverdy, French poets are still of
  our time,
Pasternak and Mayakovsky, is Jouve of our time?

Where are young poets in America, they are trembling in publishing
  houses and universities,
Above all they are trembling in universities, they are bathing the library
  steps with their spit,
They are gargling out innocuous (to whom?) poems about maple trees
  and their children,
Sometimes they brave a subject like the Villa d'Este or a lighthouse in
  Rhode Island,
Oh what worms they are! they wish to perfect their form.
Yet could not these young men, put in another profession,
Succeed admirably, say at sailing a ship? I do not doubt it, Sir, and I
  wish we could try them.
(A plane flies over the ship holding a bomb but perhaps it will not drop
  the bomb,
The young poets from the universities are staring anxiously at the skies,
Oh they are remembering their days on the campus when they looked
  up to watch birds excrete,
They are remembering the days they spent making their elegant poems.)

Is there no voice to cry out from the wind and say what it is like to be
  the wind,
To be roughed up by the trees and to bring music from the scattered
  houses
And the stones, and to be in such intimate relationship with the sea
That you cannot understand it? Is there no one who feels like a pair of
  pants?

3.
Summer in the trees! "It is time to strangle several bad poets."
The yellow hobbyhorse rocks to and fro, and from the chimney
Drops the Strangler! The white and pink roses are slightly agitated by
  the struggle,
But afterwards beside the dead "poet" they cuddle up comfortingly
  against their vase. They are safer now, no one will compare them to
  the sea.

Here on the railroad train, one more time, is the Strangler.
He is going to get that one there, who is on his way to a poetry reading.
Agh! Biff! A body falls to the moving floor.

In the football stadium I also see him,
He leaps through the frosty air at the maker of comparisons
Between football and life and silently, silently strangles him!

Here is the Strangler dressed in a cowboy suit
Leaping from his horse to annihilate the students of myth!
The Strangler's ear is alert for the names of Orpheus,
Cuchulain, Gawain, and Odysseus,
And for poems addressed to Jane Austen, F. Scott Fitzgerald,
To Ezra Pound, and to personages no longer living
Even in anyone's thoughts—O Strangler the Strangler!

He lies on his back in the waves of the Pacific Ocean.

4.
Supposing that one walks out into the air
On a fresh spring day and has the misfortune
To encounter an article on modern poetry
In *New World Writing,* or has the misfortune
To see some examples of some of the poetry
Written by the men with their eyes on the myth
And the Missus and the midterms, in the *Hudson Review,*
Or, if one is abroad, in *Botteghe Oscure,*
Or indeed in *Encounter,* what is one to do
With the rest of one's day that lies blasted to ruins
All bluely about one, what is one to do?
O surely one cannot complain to the President,
Nor even to the deans of Columbia College,
Nor to T. S. Eliot, nor to Ezra Pound,
And supposing one writes to the Princess Caetani,
"Your poets are awful!" what good would it do?
And supposing one goes to the *Hudson Review*
With a package of matches and sets fire to the building?
One ends up in prison with trial subscriptions
To the *Partisan, Sewanee,* and *Kenyon Review!*

5.
Sun out! perhaps there is a reason for the lack of poetry
In these ill-contented souls, perhaps they need air!

Blue air, fresh air, come in, I welcome you, you are an art student,
Take off your cap and gown and sit down on the chair.
Together we shall paint the poets—but no, air! perhaps you should go
    to them, quickly,
Give them a little inspiration, they need it, perhaps they are out of
    breath,
Give them a little inhuman company before they freeze the English
    language to death!
(And rust their typewriters a little, be sea air! be noxious! kill them,
    if you must, but stop their poetry!
I remember I saw you dancing on the surf on the Côte d'Azur,
And I stopped, taking my hat off, but you did not remember me,
Then afterwards you came to my room bearing a handful of orange
    flowers
And we were together all through the summer night!)

That we might go away together, it is so beautiful on the sea, there are
    a few white clouds in the sky!

But no, air! you must go . . . Ah, stay!

But she has departed and . . . Ugh! what poisonous fumes and clouds!
    what a suffocating atmosphere!
Cough! whose are these hideous faces I see, what is this rigor
Infecting the mind? where are the green Azores,
Fond memories of childhood, and the pleasant orange trolleys,
A girl's face, red-white, and her breasts and calves, blue eyes, brown
    eyes, green eyes, fahrenheit
Temperatures, dandelions, and trains, O blue?!
Wind, wind, what is happening? Wind! I can't see any bird but the gull,
    and I feel it should symbolize . . .
Oh, pardon me, there's a swan, one two three swans, a great white
    swan, hahaha how pretty they are! Smack!
Oh! stop! help! yes, I see—disrespect of my superiors—forgive me, dear
    Zeus, nice Zeus, parabolic bird, O feathered excellence! white!

There is Achilles too, and there's Ulysses, I've always wanted to see
them, hahaha!

And there is Helen of Troy, I suppose she is Zeus too, she's so terribly
pretty—hello, Zeus, my you are beautiful, Bang!

One more mistake and I get thrown out of the Modern Poetry Associa-
tion, help! Why aren't there any adjectives around?

Oh there are, there's practically nothing else—look, here's grey, *utter,
agonized, total, phenomenal, gracile, invidious, sundered,* and *fused,
Elegant, absolute, pyramidal,* and . . . Scream! but what can I describe
with these words? States!

States symbolized and divided by two, complex states, magic states,
states of consciousness governed by an aroused sincerity, cockadoodle
doo!

Another bird! is it morning? Help! where am I? am I in the barnyard?
oink oink, scratch, moo! Splash!

My first lesson. "Look around you. What do you think and feel?" *Uhhh
. . .* "Quickly!" *This Connecticut landscape would have pleased Ver-
meer.* Wham! A-Plus. "Congratulations!" I am promoted.

OOOhhhhh I wish I were dead, what a headache! My second lesson:
"Rewrite your first lesson line six hundred times. Try to make it into a
magnetic field." I can do it too. But my poor line! What a nightmare!
Here comes a tremendous horse,

Trojan, I presume. No, it's my third lesson. "Look, look! Watch him,
see what he's doing? That's what we want you to do. Of course it
won't be the same as his at first, but . . ." I demur. Is there no other
way to fertilize minds?

Bang! I give in . . . Already I see my name in two or three anthologies,
a serving girl comes into the barn bringing me the anthologies,

She is very pretty and I smile at her a little sadly, perhaps it is my last
smile! Perhaps she will hit me! But no, she smiles in return, and she
takes my hand.

My hand, my hand! what is this strange thing I feel in my hand, on
my arm, on my chest, my face—can it be . . . ? it is! AIR!

Air, air, you've come back! Did you have any success? "What do you
think?" I don't know, air. You are so strong, air.

And she breaks my chains of straw, and we walk down the road, behind
us the hideous fumes!

Soon we reach the seaside, she is a young art student who places her
head on my shoulder,

I kiss her warm red lips, and here is the Strangler, reading the *Kenyon
Review*! Good luck to you, Strangler!

Goodbye, Helen! goodbye, fumes! goodbye, abstracted dried-up boys!
goodbye, dead trees! goodbye, skunks!

Goodbye, manure! goodbye, critical manicure! goodbye, you big fat
men standing on the east coast as well as the west giving poems the
test! farewell, Valéry's stern dictum!

Until tomorrow, then, scum floating on the surface of poetry! goodbye
for a moment, refuse that happens to land in poetry's boundaries!
adieu, stale eggs teaching imbeciles poetry to bolster up your egos!
adios, boring anomalies of these same stale eggs!

Ah, but the scum is deep! Come, let me help you! and soon we pass
into the clear blue water. Oh GOODBYE, castrati of poetry! farewell,
stale pale skunky pentameters (the only honest English meter, gloop
gloop!) until tomorrow, horrors! oh, farewell!

Hello, sea! good morning, sea! hello, clarity and excitement, you great
expanse of green—

O green, beneath which all of them shall drown!

VARIATIONS ON A THEME BY WILLIAM CARLOS WILLIAMS

1.
I chopped down the house that you had been saving to live in next
summer.
I am sorry, but it was morning, and I had nothing to do
and its wooden beams were so inviting.

2.
We laughed at the hollyhocks together
and then I sprayed them with lye.
Forgive me. I simply do not know what I am doing.

3.
I gave away the money that you had been saving to live on for the next
   ten years.
The man who asked for it was shabby
and the firm March wind on the porch was so juicy and cold.

4.
Last evening we went dancing and I broke your leg.
Forgive me. I was clumsy, and
I wanted you here in the wards, where I am the doctor!

PERMANENTLY

One day the Nouns were clustered in the street.
An Adjective walked by, with her dark beauty.
The Nouns were struck, moved, changed.
The next day a Verb drove up and created the Sentence.

Each Sentence says one thing—for example, "Although it was a dark
   rainy day when the Adjective walked by, I shall remember the pure
   and sweet expression on her face until the day I perish from the
   green, effective earth."
Or, "Will you please close the window, Andrew?"
Or, for example, "Thank you, the pink pot of flowers on the window
   sill has changed color recently to a light yellow, due to the heat from
   the boiler factory which exists nearby."

In the springtime the Sentences and the Nouns lay silently on the grass.
A lonely Conjunction here and there would call, "And! But!"
But the Adjective did not emerge.

As the adjective is lost in the sentence,
So I am lost in your eyes, ears, nose, and throat—
You have enchanted me with a single kiss
Which can never be undone
Until the destruction of language.

TAKING A WALK WITH YOU

My misunderstandings: for years I thought "muso bello" meant
   "Bell Muse," I thought it was a kind of
Extra reward on the slotmachine of my shyness in the snow when
February was only a bouncing ball before the Hospital of the
   Two Sisters of the Last
Hamburger Before I go to Sleep. I thought Axel's Castle
   was a garage;
And I had beautiful dreams about it, too—sensual, mysterious
   mechanisms; horns honking, wheels turning . . .
My misunderstandings were:
1) thinking Pinocchio could really change from a puppet into a
   real boy, and back again!
2) thinking it depended on whether he was good or bad!
3) identifying him with myself!
4) and therefore every time I was bad being afraid I would turn
   into wood . . .
5) I misunderstood childhood. I usually liked the age I was.
   However, now I regard twenty-nine as an optimum age (for me).
6) I disliked Shelley between twenty and twenty-five.
All of these things I suppose are understandable, but
When you were wearing your bodice I did not understand that you
   had nothing on beneath it;
When my father turned the corner I misunderstood the light very much
On Fifty-fifth Street; and I misunderstood (like an old Chinese
   restaurant) what he was doing there.
I misunderstand generally Oklahoma and Arkansas, though I think I
   understand New Mexico;
I understand the Painted Desert, cowboy hats, and vast spaces; I do
Not understand hillbilly life—I am sure I misunderstand it.
I did not understand that you had nothing on beneath your bodice
Nor, had I understood this, would I have understood what it meant;
   even now I
(Merry Christmas! Here, Father, take your package) misunderstand it!
Merry Christmas, Uncle Leon! yes, here is your package too.

I misunderstand Renaissance life; I misunderstand:
The Renaissance;
Ancient China;
The Middle Atlantic States and what they are like;
The tubes of London and what they mean;
Titian, Michelangelo, Vermeer;
The origins of words;
What others are talking about;
Music from the beginnings to the present time;
Laughter; and tears, even more so;
Value (economic and esthetic);
Snow (and weather in the country);
The meaning of the symbols and myths of Christmas.
I misunderstand you,
I misunderstand the day we walked down the street together for ten
  hours—
Where were we going? I had thought we were going somewhere. I
  believe I misunderstand many of the places we passed and things
  you said . . .
I misunderstand "Sons of Burgundy,"
I misunderstand that you had nothing painted beneath your bodice,
I misunderstand "Notification of Arrival or Departure to Be Eradicated
  Before Affection of Deceased Tenant."
I understand that
The smoke and the clouds are both a part of the day, but

I misunderstand the words "After Departure,"
I misunderstand nothingness;
I misunderstand the attitude of people in pharmacies, on the decks of
  ships, in my bedroom, amid the pine needles, on mountains of cot-
  ton, everywhere—
When they say paralytic I hear parasite, and when they say coffee I
  think music . . .
What is wrong with me from head to toe
That I misinterpret everything I hear? I misunderstand:
French: often;
Italian: sometimes, almost always—for example, if someone says "For-
  tunate ones!" I am likely to think he is referring to the fountain with
  blue and red water (I am likely to make this mistake also in English).
I misunderstand Greek entirely;

I find ancient Greece very hard to understand: I probably misunder-
    stand it;
I misunderstand spoken German about 98% of the time, like the
    cathedral in the middle of a town;
I misunderstand "Beautiful Adventures"; I also think I probably
    misunderstand La Nausée by Jean-Paul Sartre . . .
I probably misunderstand misunderstanding itself—I misunderstand the
    Via Margutta in Rome, or Via della Vite, no matter what street, all
    of them.
I misunderstand wood in the sense of its relationship to the tree; I
    misunderstand people who take one attitude or another about it . . .
Spring I would like to say I understand, but I most probably don't—
    autumn, winter, and summer are all in the same boat
(Ruined ancient cities by the sea).

I misunderstand vacation and umbrella,
I misunderstand motion and weekly
(Though I think I understand "Daytime Pissarros"
And the octagon—I do not understand the public garden) . . .

Oh I am sure there is a use for all of them, but what is it?
My misunderstandings confuse Rome and Ireland, and can you
Bring that beautiful sex to bear upon it?
I misunderstand what I am saying, though not to you;
I misunderstand a large boat: that is a ship.
What you are feeling for me I misunderstand totally; I think I mis-
    understand the very possibilities of feeling,
Especially here in Rome, where I somehow think I am.
I see the sky, and sails.
(I misunderstand the mustard and the bottle)
Oh that we could go sailing in that sky!

What tune came with the refreshments?
I am unable to comprehend why they were playing off key.
Is it because they wanted us to jump over the cliff
Or was one of them a bad or untrained musician
Or the whole lot of them?
At any rate
San Giovanni in Laterano
Also resisted my questioning

And turned a deaf blue dome to me
Far too successfully.
I cannot understand why you walk forwards and backwards with me.
I think it is because you want to try out your shoes for their toes.
It is Causation that is my greatest problem
And after that the really attentive study of millions of details.

I love you, but it is difficult to stop writing.
As a flea could write the Divine Comedy of a water jug. Now Irish
     mists close in upon us.
Peat sails through the air, and greenness becomes bright. Are you the
     ocean or the island? Am I on Irish soil, or are your waves covering
     me?
St. Peter's bells are ringing: "Earthquake, inundation, and sleep to the
     understanding!"
(American Express! flower vendors! your beautiful straight nose!
     that delightful trattoria in Santa Maria in Trastevere!)
Let us have supper at Santa Maria in Trastevere
Where by an absolute and total misunderstanding (but not fatal) I
     once ate before I met you
I am probably misinterpreting your answer, since I hear nothing, and
     I believe I am alone.

TO YOU

I love you as a sheriff searches for a walnut
That will solve a murder case unsolved for years
Because the murderer left it in the snow beside a window
Through which he saw her head, connecting with
Her shoulders by a neck, and laid a red
Roof in her heart. For this we live a thousand years;
For this we love, and we live because we love, we are not
Inside a bottle, thank goodness! I love you as a
Kid searches for a goat; I am crazier than shirttails
In the wind, when you're near, a wind that blows from
The big blue sea, so shiny so deep and so unlike us;
I think I am bicycling across an Africa of green and white fields

Always, to be near you, even in my heart
When I'm awake, which swims, and also I believe that you
Are trustworthy as the sidewalk which leads me to
The place where I again think of you, a new
Harmony of thoughts! I love you as the sunlight leads the prow
Of a ship which sails
From Hartford to Miami, and I love you
Best at dawn, when even before I am awake the sun
Receives me in the questions which you always pose.

IN LOVE WITH YOU

1.
O what a physical effect it has on me
To dive forever into the light blue sea
Of your acquaintance! Ah, but dearest friends,
Like forms, are finished, as life has ends! Still,
It is beautiful, when October
Is over, and February is over,
To sit in the starch of my shirt, and to dream of your sweet
Ways! As if the world were a taxi, you enter it, then
Reply (to no one), "Let's go five or six blocks."
Isn't the blue stream that runs past you a translation from the Russian?
Aren't my eyes bigger than love?
Isn't this history, and aren't we a couple of ruins?
Is Carthage Pompeii? is the pillow the bed? is the sun
What glues our heads together? O midnight! O midnight!
Is love what we are,
Or has happiness come to me in a private car
That's so very small I'm amazed to see it there?

2.
We walk through the park in the sun, and you say, "There's a spider
Of shadow touching the bench, when morning's begun." I love you.
I love you fame I love you raining sun I love you cigarettes I love you
    love
I love you daggers I love smiles daggers and symbolism.

3.

Inside the symposium of your sweetest look's

Sunflower awning by the nurse-faced chrysanthemums childhood

Again represents a summer spent sticking knives into porcelain rasp-
berries, when China's

Still a country! Oh, King Edward abdicated years later, that's

Exactly when. If you were seventy thousand years old, and I were a
pill,

I know I could cure your headache, like playing baseball in drinking-
water, as baskets

Of towels sweetly touch the bathroom floor! O benches of nothing

Appear and reappear—electricity! I'd love to be how

You are, as if

The world were new, and the selves were blue

Which we don

When it's dawn,

Until evening puts on

The gray hooded selves and the light brown selves of . . .

Water! your tear-colored nail polish

Kisses me! and the lumberyard seems new

As a calm

On the sea, where, like pigeons,

I feel so mutated, sad, so breezed, so revivified, and still so unabdi-
cated—

Not like an edge of land coming over the sea!

POEM

The thing
To do
Is organize
The sea
So boats will
Automatically float
To their destinations.
Ah, the Greeks
Thought of that!
Well, what if
They
Did? We have no
Gods
Of the winds!
And therefore
Must use
Science!

© Rollie McKenna

Denise Levertov

ONE A.M.

The kitchen patio in snowy
moonlight.   That
snowsilence, that
abandon to stillness.
The sawhorse, the concrete
washtub, snowblue. The washline
bowed under its snowfur!
Moon has silenced
the crickets, the summer frogs
hold their breath.
Summer night, summer night, standing
one-legged, a crane
in the snowmarsh, staring
at snowmoon!

PLEASURES

I like to find
what's not found
at once, but lies

within something of another nature,
in repose, distinct.
Gull feathers of glass, hidden

in white pulp: the bones of squid
which I pull out and lay
blade by blade on the draining board—

tapered as if for swiftness, to pierce
the heart, but fragile, substance
belying design.   Or a fruit, *mamey,*

cased in rough brown peel, the flesh
rose-amber, and the seed:
the seed a stone of wood, carved and

polished, walnut-colored, formed
like a brazilnut, but large,
large enough to fill
the hungry palm of a hand.

I like the juicy stem of grass that grows
within the coarser leaf folded round,
and the butteryellow glow
in the narrow flute from which the morning-glory
opens blue and cool on a hot morning.

ART

(After Gautier)

The best work is made
from hard, strong materials,
        obstinately precise—
the line of the poem, onyx, steel.

It's not a question of
false constraints—but
        to move well and get somewhere
wear shoes that fit.

To hell with easy rhythms—
sloppy mules that anyone can
    kick off or
step into.

Sculptor, don't bother with modeling
pliant clay; don't let
    a touch of your thumb
set your vision while it's still vague.

Pit yourself against granite,
hew basalt, carve hard ebony—
    intractable
guardians of contour.

Renew the power men had in Azerbaijan
to cast ethereal intensity in bronze
    and give it
force to endure any number of thousand years.

Painter, let be the 'nervous scratches' the
trick spontaneity; learn to see again,
    construct, break through
to 'the thrill of continuance with the appearance of all its changes,'[1]

towards that point where 'art becomes
a realization with which the urge to live
    collaborates as a mason.'[2] Use
'the mind's tongue, that works and tastes into the very rock heart.'[3]

Our lives flower and pass. Only robust
works of the imagination live in eternity,
    Tlaloc, Apollo,
dug out alive from dead cities.

[1] Cézanne
[2] Jean Hélion
[3] Ruskin

And the austere coin
a tractor turns up in a
    building site
reveals an emperor.

The gods die every day
but sovereign poems go on breathing
    in a counter-rhythm that mocks
the frenzy of weapons, their impudent power.

Incise, invent, file to poignance;
make your elusive dream
    seal itself
in the resistant mass of crude substance.

THE PEACHTREE

from **During the Eichmann Trial**

The Danube orchards
are full of fruit
but in the city one tree
haunts a boy's dreams

a tree in a villa garden
the Devil's garden
a peach tree

and of its fruit one peach
calls to him

he sees it yellow and ripe
the vivid blood
bright in its round cheek

Next day he knows
he cannot withstand desire
it is no common fruit

it holds some secret
it speaks to the yellow star within him

he scales the wall
enters the garden of death
takes the peach
and death pounces

mister death who rushes out
from his villa
mister death who loves yellow

who wanted that yellow peach
for himself
mister death who signs papers
then eats

telegraphs simply: *Shoot them*
then eats
mister death who orders
more transports
then eats

he would have enjoyed
the sweetest of all the peaches on his tree
with sour-cream
with brandy

Son of David
's blood, vivid red
and trampled juice
yellow and sweet
flow together beneath the tree

there is more blood than
sweet juice
always more blood—mister
death goes indoors
exhausted

Note: This poem is based on the earliest men-
tion, during the trial, of this incident. In a later

statement it was said that the fruit was cherries, that the boy was already in the garden, doing forced labor, when he was accused of taking the fruit, and that Eichmann killed him in a tool shed, not beneath the tree. The poem therefore is not to be taken as a report of what happened but of what I envisioned.

HYPOCRITE WOMEN

Hypocrite women, how seldom we speak
of our own doubts, while dubiously
we mother man in his doubt!

And if at Mill Valley perched in the trees
the sweet rain drifting through western air
a white sweating bull of a poet told us

our cunts are ugly—why didn't we
admit we have thought so too? (And
what shame? They are not for the eye!)

No, they are dark and wrinkled and hairy,
caves of the Moon . . .   And when a
dark humming fills us, a

coldness towards life,
we are too much women to
own to such unwomanliness.

Whorishly with the psychopomp
we play and plead—and say
nothing of this later.   And our dreams,

with what frivolity we have pared them
like toenails, clipped them like ends of
split hair.

A PSALM PRAISING THE HAIR
OF MAN'S BODY

My great brother
      Lord of the Song
wears the ruff of
      forest bear.

Husband, thy fleece of silk is black,
      a black adornment;
lies so close to the turns of the flesh,
burns my palm-stroke.

My great brother
      Lord of the Song
wears the ruff of
      forest bear.

Strong legs of our son are dusted
      dark with hair.
Told of long roads,
we know his stride.

My great brother
      Lord of the Song
wears the ruff of
      forest bear.

Hair of man, man-hair, hair of
breast and groin, marking contour as
      silverpoint marks in cross-
      hatching, as river-
      grass on the woven current
      indicates ripple,
praise.

THE WINGS

Something hangs in back of me,
I can't see it, can't move it.

I know it's black,
a hump on my back.

It's heavy. You
can't see it.

What's in it? Don't tell me
you don't know. It's

what you told me about—
black

inimical power, cold
whirling out of it and

around me and
sweeping you flat.

But what if,
like a camel, it's

pure energy I store,
and carry humped and heavy?

Not black, not
that terror, stupidity

of cold rage; or black
only for being pent there?

What if released in air
it became a white

source of light, a fountain
of light? Could all that weight

be the power of flight?
Look inward: see me

with embryo wings, one
feathered in soot, the other

blazing ciliations of ember, pale
flare-pinions. Well—

could I go
on one wing,

the white one?

STEPPING WESTWARD

What is green in me
darkens, muscadine.

If woman is inconstant,
good, I am faithful to

ebb and flow, I fall
in season and now

is a time of ripening.
If her part

is to be true,
a north star,

good, I hold steady
in the black sky

and vanish by day,
yet burn there

in blue or above
quilts of cloud.

There is no savor
more sweet, more salt

than to be glad to be
what, woman,

and who, myself,
I am, a shadow

that grows longer as the sun
moves, drawn out

on a thread of wonder.
If I bear burdens

they begin to be remembered
as gifts, goods, a basket

of bread that hurts
my shoulders but closes me

in fragrance. I can
eat as I go.

THE ALTARS IN THE STREET

*On June 17th, 1966, The New York
Times reported that, as part of the
Buddhist campaign of passive non-
resistance, Viet-Namese children were
building altars in the streets of
Saigon and Hue, effectively jamming
traffic.*

Children begin at green dawn nimbly to build
topheavy altars, overweighted with prayers,
thronged each instant more densely

with almost-visible ancestors.
Where tanks have cracked the roadway
the frail altars shake; here a boy

with red stumps for hands steadies a corner,
here one adjusts with his crutch the holy base.
The vast silence of Buddha overtakes

and overrules the oncoming roar
of tragic life that fills alleys and avenues;
it blocks the way of pedicabs, police, convoys.

The hale and maimed together
hurry to construct for the Buddha
a dwelling at each intersection. Each altar

made from whatever stones, sticks, dreams, are at hand,
is a facet of one altar; by noon
the whole city in all its corruption,

all its shed blood the monsoon cannot wash away,
has become a temple,
fragile, insolent, absolute.

A NOTE TO OLGA (1966)

1.
Of lead and emerald
the reliquary
that knocks my breastbone,

slung round my neck
on a rough invisible rope
that rubs the knob of my spine.

Though I forget you
a red coal from your fire
burns in that box.

2.
On the Times Square sidewalk
we shuffle along, cardboard signs
—Stop the War—
slung round our necks.

The cops
hurry about,
shoulder to shoulder,
comic.

Your high soprano
sings out from just
in back of me—

We shall—I turn,
you're, I very well know,
not there,

and your voice, they say,
grew hoarse
from shouting at crowds . . .

yet *overcome*
sounds then hoarsely
from somewhere in front,

the paddywagon
gapes.   —It seems
you that is lifted

limp and ardent
off the dark snow
and shoved in, and driven away.

John Logan

THREE MOVES

Three moves in six months and I remain
the same.
Two homes made two friends.
The third leaves me with myself again.
(We hardly speak.)
Here I am with tame ducks
and my neighbors' boats,
only this electric heat
against the April damp
I have a friend named Frank—
The only one who ever dares to call
and ask me, "How's your soul?"
I hadn't thought about it for a while,
and was ashamed to say I didn't know.
I have no priest for now.
Who
will forgive me then. Will you?
Tame birds and my neighbors' boats.
The ducks honk about the floats . . .
They walk dead drunk onto the land and grounds,
iridescent blue and black and green and brown.
They live on swill
our aged houseboats spill.
But still they are beautiful.
Look! The duck with its unlikely beak
has stopped to pick
and pull
at the potted daffodil.

Then again they sway home
to dream
bright gardens of fish in the early night.
Oh these ducks are all right.
They will survive.
But I am sorry I do not often see them climb.
Poor sons-a-bitching ducks.
You're all fucked up.
What do you do that for?
Why don't you hover near the sun anymore?
Afraid you'll melt?
These foolish ducks lack a sense of guilt,
and so all their multi-thousand-mile range
is too short for the hope of change.

Seattle, April 1965

ON A PRIZE CRUCIFIX
BY A STUDENT SCULPTOR

To Catherine Brunot

The cross of boy with man within is an
Anguished one. The boy who made this curve
Of Christ, the man who made this anxious cross
Of Christ, stripped, inside a classroom case,
Has hung, stripped, inside the college gym.
He knows. He sees the bodies of the boy
Men, beautiful with beauty caught
In him also, with agony, with grace.

His Christ has his turned shape of muscle,
Lean with this leanness of the young
Becoming men; lithe within the brass
Along the hand and limb; bright as skin
In light of campus sun upon the rolled-up
Arm. This Christ's chest heaves with the
Runner's breath, the legs torqued, the tight,
Powered thighs not at rest, as though

They jump in contest. The belly caves beneath
The holy human building of his ribs;
His thin belly feels the touch of hands,
Of lance. His navel buds above his loins
Where lies his genital, secret as a
Boy's, breeched, denied, terrible with weight
Of seed and with the supple strength of God.
The student Christ tries for middle thirty:

Ah God, if Christ has not a body as
The student (and the older) artist does,
And all of that, what good is He to us?
The student Christ has lived through being born
And through the awful time of being young,
And not so young, I think. He sees the lasting
Crucifixion in the growing man
Who every passing day lets die a little more

The body of the boy grieved for.

LINES TO HIS SON ON REACHING ADOLESCENCE

I've always thought Polonius a dry
And senile fop, fool to those he didn't love
Though he had given life to them as father—
To his beautiful young boy and beautiful
Young daughter; and loathed Augustine's
Lecherous old man who noticed that his son
Naked at his bath, was growing up
And told his wife a dirty joke. But
I have given my own life to you my son
Remembering my fear, my joy and unbelief
(And my disgust) when I saw you monkey
Blue and blooded, shrouded with the light down
Of the new born, the cord of flesh
That held you to my wife cut free from her
And from my own remote body,

And I could fill you up with epithets
Like Ophelia's father, full of warnings,
For I have learned what we must avoid
And what must choose and how to be of use.
My father never taught me anything
I needed for myself. It's no excuse,
For what he might have said I think
I would refuse, and besides (is it despair
I reach?) I feel we learn too late to teach.
And like Augustine's dad I have watched you bathe
Have seen as my own hair begins to fall
The fair gold beard upon your genital
That soon will flow with seed
And swell with love and pain (I almost add
Again). I cannot say to you whether
In a voice steady or unsteady, ah Christ
Please wait your father isn't ready.
You cannot wait, as he could not.
But for both our sakes I ask you, wrestle
Manfully against the ancient curse of snakes,
The bitter mystery of love, and learn to bear
The burden of the tenderness
That is hid in us. Oh you cannot
Spare yourself the sadness of Hippolytus
Whom the thought of Phaedra
Turned from his beloved horse and bow,
My son, the arrow of my quiver,
The apple of my eye, but you can save your father
The awful agony of Laocoön
Who could not stop the ruin of his son.
And as I can I will help you with my love.
Last I warn you, as Polonius,
Yet not as him, from now on I will not plead
As I have always done, for sons
Against their fathers who have wronged them.
I plead instead for us
Against the sons we hoped we would not hurt.

TO A YOUNG POET WHO FLED

Your cries make us afraid, but we love
your delicious music!
            Kierkegaard

So you said you'd go home to work on your father's farm.
We've talked of how it is the poet alone can touch
with words, but I would touch you with my hand, my lost son,
to say good-bye again. You left some work, and have gone.
You don't know what you mean. Oh, not to me as a son,
for I have others. Perhaps too many. I cannot
answer all the letters. If I seem to brag, I add
I know how to shatter an image of the father
(twice have tried to end the yearning of an orphan son,
but opened up in him, and in me, another wound).
No—I say this: you don't know the reason of your gift.
It's not the suffering. Others have that. The gift of tears
is the hope of saints, Monica again and Austin.
I mean the gift of the structure of a poet's jaw,
which makes the mask that's cut out of the flesh of his face
a megaphone—as with the goat clad Greeks—to ampli-
fy the light gestures of his soul toward the high stone seats.
The magic of the mouth that can melt to tears the rock
of hearts. I mean the wand of tongues that charms the exile
of listeners into a bond of brothers, breaking
down the lines of lead that separate a man from a
man, and the husbands from their wives, in these old, burned glass
panels of our lives. The poet's jaw has its tongue ripped
as Philomel, its lips split (and kissed beside the grave),
the jawbone patched and cracked with fists and then with the salve
of his fellows. If they make him bellow, like a slave
cooked inside the ancient, brass bull, still that small machine
inside its throat makes music for an emperor's guest
out of his cries. Thus his curse: the poet cannot weep
but with a public and musical grief, and he laughs
with the joys of others. Yet, when the lean blessings come,
they are sweet, and great. My son, I could not make your choice.

Let me take your hand. I am too old or young to say,
"I'd rather be a swineherd in the hut, understood
by swine, than be a poet misunderstood by men."

LINES ON HIS BIRTHDAY

I was born on a street named Joy
of which I remember nothing,
but since I was a boy
I've looked for its lost turning.
Still I seem to hear my mother's cry
echo in the street of joy.
She was sick as Ruth for home
when I was born. My birth
took away my father's wife
and left me half
my life. Christ will my remorse
be less when my father's dead?
Or more. As Lincoln's minister of war
kept the body of his infant boy
in a silver coffin on his desk,
so I keep
in a small heirloom box of teak
the picture of my living father.
Or perhaps it is an image of myself
dead in this box she held?
I know her milk like ivory blood
still runs in my thick veins
and leaves in me an almost
lickerish taste for ghosts:
my mother's wan face,
full brown hair, the mammoth breast
death cuts off at the bone—
to which she draws her bow
again, brazen Amazon,

and aiming deadly as a saint
shoots her barb
of guilt into my game heart.

January 23, 1961

SPRING OF THE THIEF

But if I look the ice is gone from the lake
and the altered air
no longer fills with the small
terrible bodies of the snow.
Only once these late winter weeks
the dying flakes
fell instead as manna or as wedding rice
blooming in the light
about the bronze Christ
and the thieves. There these three
still hang, more than man-
sized and heavier than life
on a hill over the lake
where I walk
this Third Sunday of Lent.
I come from Mass
melancholy at its ancient story
of the unclean ghost
a man thought he'd lost.
It came back into his well-swept house
and at the final state that man
was worse than he began.
Yet again today
there is the faintest edge of green
to trees about St. Joseph's Lake.
Ah God if our confessions show contempt
because we let them free us of our guilt
to sin again
forgive us still . . . before the leaves . . .

before the leaves have formed
you can glimpse the Christ and Thieves
on top of the hill. One of them was saved.
That day the snow had seemed to drop like grace
upon the four of us,
or like the peace of intercourse,
suddenly I wanted to confess—
or simply talk.
I paid a visit to the mammoth Sacred Heart
Church, and found it shut.
Who locked him out or in?
Is the name of God changing in our time?
What is his winter name?
Where was his winter home.
Oh I've kept my love to myself before.
Even those ducks weave down the shore
together, drunk with hope
for the April water. One spring festival
near here I stripped and strolled
through a rain filled field.
Spread eagled on the soaking earth
I let the rain
move its audible little hands
gently on my skin . . . let the dark rain
raise up my love.
But why? I was alone
and no one saw how ardent I grew.
And when I rolled naked in the snow one night
as St. Francis with his Brother Ass
or a hard bodied Finn
I was alone. Underneath
the howling January moon
I knelt and dug my fist
full of the cold winter sand
and rubbed and
hid my manhood under it.
Washed up at some ancient or half-heroic shore
I was ashamed that I was naked there.
Before Nausicaä and the saints. Before myself.
But who took off my coat? Who put it on?

Who drove me home?
Blessed be sin if it teaches men shame.
Yet because of it we cannot talk
and I am separated from myself.
So what is all this reveling in snow and rain?
Or in the summer sun when the heavy gold
body weeps with joy or grief or love?
When we speak of God, is it God we speak of?
Perhaps his winter home
is in that field where I rolled or ran . . .
this hill where once the snow
fell serene as rain.
Oh I have walked around the lake
when I was not alone—
sometimes with my wife have seen these swans
dip down their necks
graceful as a girl, showering white and wet!
I've seen their heads delicately turn.
Have gone sailing with my quiet, older son.
And once on a morning walk
a student who had just come back
in fall found a perfect hickory shell
among the bronze and red
leaves and purple flowers of the time
and puts its white bread into my hand.
Ekelöf said there is a freshness
nothing can destroy in us—
not even we ourselves.
Perhaps that
Freshness is the changed name of God.
Where all the monsters also hide
I bear him in the ocean of my blood
and in the pulp of my enormous head.
He lives beneath the unkempt potter's grass
of my belly and chest.
I feel his terrible, aged heart
moving under mine . . . can see the shadows
of the gorgeous light
that plays at the edges of his giant eye . . .
or tell the faint press and hum

of his eternal pool of sperm.
Like sandalwood! *Like sandalwood*
the righteous man
perfumes the axe that falls on him.
The cords of elm, of cedar oak and pine
will pile again in fall.
The ribs and pockets of the barns will swell.
Winds and fires in the field rage
and again burn out each
of the ancient roots.
Again at last the late November snow
will fill those fields, change this hill,
throw these figures in relief
and raining on them
will transform
the bronze Christ's brow and cheek,
the white face and thigh of the thief.

March–April, 1962

LINES FOR MICHAEL IN THE PICTURE

There is a sense in which darkness
has more of God than light has.
He dwells in the thick dark.
                    F. W. Robertson

1.
You are my shadow in the picture.
Once I thought you were my brother,
but to be honest, he and I were never friends.
(Even our boyhood secrets never brought us closer.)
Odd the way you stand behind and to the side,
like a shade. Still it is your own
darknesses you stay in.
You generate shadow like a light
or like an odor
falling from your arrogant shoulder,
eddying into your eyes.

The great eyes almost seem to glaze.
Look! They seem to tip!
Your eyes are alive with the gestures of death.
You've got something of mine shut in there, Michael.
I must enlarge the picture
and let it out
of your ancient, melancholy face.
My shadow yearns for peace.

2.
You came to my house
just separated from your life,
your clothes still burning in the chimney
(fires tended by furious women),
books piled or bent ("She has made
me stupid," you said)
or lost. Dishes in boxes, smashed.
Pieces of your life gaped from paper sacks.
Shelves were stripped like flesh,
letters from your friends destroyed—
family scowling, all utterly annoyed.
Who was to blame?
Your marriage already gone
at twenty-one,
you said, "I have abandoned myself," and wept.

3.
Something binds every kind of orphan.
I could find my own loneliness in your face,
hear it in your voice.
But there is something else,
some lost part of myself I seem to track
(did you know I used to be called Jack?),
so I follow like a blind animal
with hope (and with fear)
your brilliant, shadow spoor.

4.
I followed in the sun
until we reached the silent pine
the day we climbed the mountain.

We were with your friends, Marie, Jim.
I was jealous of them
for they had known you longer.
It was then I began to wish
you were my brother. We cut
some sticks and walked behind.
Suddenly the pied fields, farms
and iridescent waters of The Sound
blue or black
simply fell away from where we watched
like the holdings of a haughty god,
and from the mountain top
I found an island in a lake
on the other island where we stood.
That is the way you seem,
there is your home.
Your eyes are like the inwardmost island
of that inwardmost lake,
and your tears are the springs of that.
Ah well, we all weep, Michael.
One of our eyes cannot even know the other
(except, perhaps, with a picture).

5.
Down the mountain again
we stopped to swim
in a cove of The Sound—the water
actual ebony beside the brilliant sky.
You walked away from the rest
for you had seen
another hill you hoped to scale
rising down into the sea.
Marie sat on the steps behind
as we undressed.
(She wouldn't swim with us.)
Tall, classical, you poised at your own place
on the stones black from the wet
of waves, and dove suddenly
into the heartcold sea.

And for a silent while
you were gone with no sign,
the time of a cold change.
Coming back you brought up
a part of the dark
of the seas in your eyes
and some of the blue, obscure snow of the hill
drifted on your thighs and arms
in the shattering sun.
Jim and I dunked briefly,
chattering and quickly pimpled.
We carefully kept our backs
to Marie as we dressed. You
simply stood, naked and plumed,
half hard
on the bridge of the rock
and (almost as an afterthought) turned
toward the steps.
Marie looked easily at your body
and smiled. You grinned
and climbed toward your clothes.
Suddenly I felt that she
had watched the dark
rich-haired shadow of me.

6.
You and I, Marie and Jim
that night on the island shore
piled up log
on log on log (we couldn't stop)
and built a driftwood fire so big
I think it scared the four of us
into dancing barefoot on the sand.
The greatest fire we'd ever seen!
We didn't join our hands,
but the eyes of flames
grew huge
and struck us blue,
then red. Blue. Then yellow.
Blue. And as we danced and danced higher

the freshly made fire
threw our shadows each on each
and blurred us into a family
sometimes three, sometimes four
close as lovers on the beach!

7.
It was the last ember
of that transforming island fire
that seems to fade in your eyes in the picture.
It makes you brother, friend, son, father.
If it isn't death, it is change,
and in that fine shadow flame
what was locked is yours, Michael, as much as mine.

Seattle, May 1965

LETTER TO A YOUNG FATHER IN EXILE

When I last wrote
I was so hung up with old guilt
or fright
       I could not think
what *you* might need—you who are
caught by this fucking war
in another land,
gone from parent, from calming scene, friend,
who had to leave school just as that
began to help
          shape
the keen blessing of your insight,
which is bright and quick
with presence as a fresh, dawn-white
drop of milk.
        And now you have a son
  whom you are also exiled from
  double-walled away
            by
both an outer and the terrible inner fight

(more bloody than any human battle yet,
Rimbaud said).
Sweat, tears and sperm
press together from the muscles of a man
such as you are in our time—
an age which is only made
(it seems) for the old
who dare to send
                  their gifted young
off to the predicted geld-
ing of a war, or jail, or to some other land
from which as you they never can
come back.
So you've become a lumberjack—
and undertake
the most dangerous of lumber jobs
choking, hooking, lassoing logs,
risking your young arms and legs
because you are not afraid.
Better to take the lives of bears and trees
than any of those
you feel inside yourself or in the eyes
of brothers, or in your own
yet unseen son's
                  burgeoning flesh.
He learns to nurse—
a sharp and tender boy
we have the hope to say—
and grows out guts, limbs:
desires to return what his mother gives.

Next, as do all kids, I guess,
he will try to learn to piss
with all the strength of giants, Gulliver
and Pantagruel, heroes who could stop a war
alone, or Leopold Bloom, higher
than two hundred fellow scholars
against the white wall
of his elementary school.
(Or the young man in Freud's dream
whose powerful river could rinse clean,

as in a famous, ancient marvel,
the filthy Augean stable.)
And one day your son will learn to swim and ski
with your own passing grace and beauty.
And perhaps in a heavy, red
woolen sweater and a massive, black beard
he will hunt swift and kill (as you) the lithe
heavy bear, and pose squatting alongside
its great, steaming, brownfelled thigh.
Michael, your son's rifle will resound
and resound
though you may only see his young kind
and not himself,
since you are banned, and since you do not have
his mother for your wife.
And you have lost one daughter or son
already, under
the murdering stress
of our own human hopelessness.
After the tender pulsing in
of your full tide of semen,
with the clouded image of a son
(which always brightens when we come)
once there
was the fusing of the sea and shore—
meeting of another half
                              life
to carry yours.
But then war
on the womb, solid hits—
and death for the quick new part
of you and her.
And now again the grotesque hidden scars
that form and grow in all our hidden wars.
With this slow grief and your present loss of roots,
with all your unwritten books
and your rock hard, exiled life
(its vicious, black, summer logging flies):
Jesus, how in hell do you survive!

And finally this, my own thoughtless role:
you write me a note
                    about your first son,
a bastard like the rare and brilliant one
of St. Augustine,
and in my brief reply I do not even
mention
           him. Well, I see (sadly) I am cruel.
And I too know how to kill!
For when I last wrote
and said I wanted to forget
                    (abort
your image out of my mind)
simply because you are not around
for my solace and my life, now
I see I raised what came
                 into my hand
against you. Thus
I am loving and as treacherous
as parent or as child—in the black
ancient figure you and he may fight to break.
Oh my lost, abandoned brother,
you know you had a father.
Now let your son
say so with the jets of milk
his drawn from yours
and from the breasts of a mother,
whose fecund spurts
of white
as in the Tintoretto work
where young Hercules is nursed
by a god—have formed the brilliant wash
and brush
           of stars across the dark, inner wall
of our still radiant, woman world.

Buffalo, December 1968

LOVE POEM

Last night you would not come,
and you have been gone so long.
I yearn to find you in my aging, earthen arms
again (your alchemy can change my clay to skin).
I long to turn and watch again
from my half-hidden place
the lost, beautiful slopes and fallings of your face,
the black, rich leaf of each eyelash,
fresh, beach-brightened stones of your teeth.
I want to listen as you breathe yourself to sleep
(for by our human art we mime
the sleeper til we dream).
I want to smell the dark
herb gardens of your hair—touch the thin shock
that drifts over your high brow when
you rinse it clean,
for it is so fine.
I want to hear the light,
long wind of your sigh.
But again tonight I know you will not come.
I will never feel again
your gentle, sleeping calm
from which I took
so much strength, so much of my human heart.
Because the last time
I reached to you
as you sat upon the bed
and talked, you caught both my hands
in yours and crossed them gently on my breast.
I died mimicking the dead.

WHITE PASS SKI PATROL

His high-boned, young face is so brown
from the winter's sun,
the few brief lines in each green eye's
edge as of a leaf
that is not yet gone from the limb—
as of a nut which is gold or brown.

For he has become very strong
living on the slopes.
His belly and thighs are newly
lean from the thin skis.
Tough torso of the man, blue wooled.
Thin waist. White, tasseled cap of the child.

Beneath the fury of those great,
dark panes of glass, that
seem to take a man out of grace,
his gentle eyes wait.
(We feel their melancholy gaze
which is neither innocent nor wise.)

Like those knights of the winter snows—
with a healing pack
(sign of the cross on breast and back)—
serene, snow-lonely,
he patrols the beautiful peaks
and the pale wastes that slide like a beast.

Sometimes still blind from his patrol,
you'll see him pull down
from the dangerous Cascades his
heavy sledge of pain,
its odd, black-booted, canvas-laced
shape alive or dead, without a face.

Colors blooming in the sun, he
caroms down his own
path, speeds (bending knees), dances side

to side, balancing.
Under-skis glow golden in the
snow spume around his Christiana.

And as he lifts away from us,
skis dangle like the
outstretched limbs of a frog in spring.
He swings gently in
the air, vulnerable, so much
the "poor, bare, forked" human animal.

And now he slowly rises up
over trees and snow.
He begins to grow more thin, and then
vanishes in air!
as, high in the lithe boughs of pines,
the silver leaves flake silently down.

There are the shadow tracks he left
down the long, white hill
beside the lift. Wait! Look up! Cloud
trails in the bright sky!
Breathing a wake of snow ribbons,
something has just flown over the mountain!

Washington, February 19, 1966

Robert Lowell

COLLOQUY IN BLACK ROCK

Here the jack-hammer jabs into the ocean;
My heart, you race and stagger and demand
More blood-gangs for your nigger-brass percussions,
Till I, the stunned machine of your devotion,
Clanging upon this cymbal of a hand,
Am rattled screw and footloose. All discussions

End in the mud-flat detritus of death.
My heart, beat faster, faster. In Black Mud
Hungarian workmen give their blood
For the martyre Stephen, who was stoned to death.

Black Mud, a name to conjure with: O mud
For watermelons gutted to the crust,
Mud for the mole-tide harbor, mud for mouse,
Mud for the armored Diesel fishing tubs that thud
A year and a day to wind and tide; the dust
Is on this skipping heart that shakes my house,

House of our Savior who was hanged till death.
My heart, beat faster, faster. In Black Mud
Stephen the martyre was broken down to blood:
Our ransom is the rubble of his death.

Christ walks on the black water. In Black Mud
Darts the kingfisher. On Corpus Christi, heart,
Over the drum-beat of St. Stephen's choir
I hear him, *Stupor Mundi,* and the mud
Flies from his hunching wings and beak—my heart,
The blue kingfisher dives on you in fire.

CHRISTMAS EVE UNDER HOOKER'S STATUE

Tonight a blackout. Twenty years ago
I hung my stocking on the tree, and hell's
Serpent entwined the apple in the toe
To sting the child with knowledge. Hooker's heels
Kicking at nothing in the shifting snow,
A cannon and a cairn of cannon balls
Rusting before the blackened Statehouse, know
How the long horn of plenty broke like glass
In Hooker's gauntlets. Once I came from Mass;

Now storm-clouds shelter Christmas, once again
Mars meets his fruitless star with open arms,
His heavy saber flashes with the rime,
The war-god's bronzed and empty forehead forms
Anonymous machinery from raw men;
The cannon on the Common cannot stun
The blundering butcher as he rides on Time—
The barrel clinks with holly. I am cold:
I ask for bread, my father gives me mould;

His stocking is full of stones. Santa in red
Is crowned with wizened berries. Man of war,
Where is the summer's garden? In its bed
The ancient speckled serpent will appear,
And black-eyed susan with her frizzled head.
When Chancellorsville mowed down the volunteer,
"All wars are boyish," Herman Melville said;
But we are old, our fields are running wild:
Till Christ again turn wanderer and child.

MR. EDWARDS AND THE SPIDER

I saw the spiders marching through the air,
Swimming from tree to tree that mildewed day
  In latter August when the hay
  Came creaking to the barn. But where
    The wind is westerly,
Where gnarled November makes the spiders fly
Into the apparitions of the sky,
They purpose nothing but their ease and die
Urgently beating east to sunrise and the sea;

What are we in the hands of the great God?
It was in vain you set up thorn and briar
  In battle array against the fire
  And treason crackling in your blood;
    For the wild thorns grow tame
And will do nothing to oppose the flame;
Your lacerations tell the losing game
You play against a sickness past your cure.
How will the hands be strong? How will the heart endure?

A very little thing, a little worm,
Or hourglass-blazoned spider, it is said,
  Can kill a tiger. Will the dead
  Hold up his mirror and affirm
    To the four winds the smell
And flash of his authority? It's well
If God who holds you to the pit of hell,
Much as one holds a spider, will destroy,
Baffle and dissipate your soul. As a small boy

On Windsor Marsh, I saw the spider die
When thrown into the bowels of fierce fire:
  There's no long struggle, no desire
  To get up on its feet and fly—
    It stretches out its feet
And dies. This is the sinner's last retreat;
Yes, and no strength exerted on the heat
Then sinews the abolished will, when sick
And full of burning, it will whistle on a brick.

But who can plumb the sinking of that soul?
Josiah Hawley, picture yourself cast
    Into a brick-kiln where the blast
    Fans your quick vitals to a coal—
        If measured by a glass.
How long would it seem burning! Let there pass
A minute, ten, ten trillion; but the blaze
Is infinite, eternal: this is death,
To die and know it. This is the Black Widow, death.

MEMORIES OF WEST STREET AND LEPKE

Only teaching on Tuesdays, book-worming
in pajamas fresh from the washer each morning,
I hog a whole house on Boston's
"hardly passionate Marlborough Street,"
where even the man
scavenging filth in the back alley trash cans,
has two children, a beach wagon, a helpmate,
and is a "young Republican."
I have a nine months' daughter,
young enough to be my granddaughter.
Like the sun she rises in her flame-flamingo infants' wear.

These are the tranquillized *Fifties,*
and I am forty. Ought I to regret my seedtime?
I was a fire-breathing Catholic C. O.,
and made my manic statement,
telling off the state and president, and then
sat waiting sentence in the bull pen
beside a Negro boy with curlicues
of marijuana in his hair.

Given a year,
I walked on the roof of the West Street Jail, a short
enclosure like my school soccer court,
and saw the Hudson River once a day
through sooty clothesline entanglements
and bleaching khaki tenements.

Strolling, I yammered metaphysics with Abramowitz,
a jaundice-yellow ("it's really tan")
and fly-weight pacifist,
so vegetarian,
he wore rope shoes and preferred fallen fruit.
He tried to convert Bioff and Brown,
the Hollywood pimps, to his diet.
Hairy, muscular, suburban,
wearing chocolate double-breasted suits,
they blew their tops and beat him black and blue.

I was so out of things, I'd never heard
of the Jehovah's Witnesses.
"Are you a C. O.?" I asked a fellow jailbird.
"No," he answered, "I'm a J. W."
He taught me the "hospital tuck,"
and pointed out the T shirted back
of *Murder Incorporated's* Czar Lepke,
there piling towels on a rack,
or dawdling off to his little segregated cell full
of things forbidden the common man:
a portable radio, a dresser, two toy American
flags tied together with a ribbon of Easter palm.
Flabby, bald, lobotomized,
he drifted in a sheepish calm,
where no agonizing reappraisal
jarred his concentration on the electric chair—
hanging like an oasis in his air
of lost connections. . . .

"TO SPEAK OF WOE THAT IS IN MARRIAGE"

*"It is the future generation that presses
into being by means of these exu-
berant feelings and supersensible soap
bubbles of ours."*
                              Schopenhauer

"The hot night makes us keep our bedroom windows open.
Our magnolia blossoms. Life begins to happen.
My hopped up husband drops his home disputes,
and hits the streets to cruise for prostitutes,
free-lancing out along the razor's edge.
This screwball might kill his wife, then take the pledge.
Oh the monotonous meanness of his lust. . . .
It's the injustice . . . he is so unjust—
whiskey-blind, swaggering home at five.
My only thought is how to keep alive.
What makes him tick? Each night now I tie
ten dollars and his car key to my thigh. . . .
Gored by the climacteric of his want,
he stalls above me like an elephant."

SKUNK HOUR

(*For Elizabeth Bishop*)

Nautilus Island's hermit
heiress still lives through winter in her Spartan cottage;
her sheep still graze above the sea.
Her son's a bishop. Her farmer
is first selectman in our village;
she's in her dotage.

Thirsting for
the hierarchic privacy
of Queen Victoria's century,

she buys up all
the eyesores facing her shore,
and lets them fall.

The season's ill—
we've lost our summer millionaire,
who seemed to leap from an L. L. Bean
catalogue. His nine-knot yawl
was auctioned off to lobstermen.
A red fox stain covers Blue Hill.

And now our fairy
decorator brightens his shop for fall;
his fishnet's filled with orange cork,
orange, his cobbler's bench and awl;
there is no money in his work,
he'd rather marry.

One dark night,
my Tudor Ford climbed the hill's skull;
I watched for love-cars. Lights turned down,
they lay together, hull to hull,
where the graveyard shelves on the town. . . .
My mind's not right.

A car radio bleats,
"Love, O careless Love. . . ." I hear
my ill-spirit sob in each blood cell,
as if my hand were at its throat. . . .
I myself am hell;
nobody's here—

only skunks, that search
in the moonlight for a bite to eat.
They march on their soles up Main Street:
white stripes, moonstruck eyes' red fire
under the chalk-dry and spar spire
of the Trinitarian Church.

I stand on top
of our back steps and breathe the rich air—
a mother skunk with her column of kittens swills the garbage pail.
She jabs her wedge-head in a cup
of sour cream, drops her ostrich tail,
and will not scare.

EYE AND TOOTH

My whole eye was sunset red,
the old cut cornea throbbed,
I saw things darkly,
as through an unwashed goldfish globe.

I lay all day on my bed.
I chain-smoked through the night,
learning to flinch
at the flash of the matchlight.

Outside, the summer rain,
a simmer of rot and renewal,
fell in pinpricks.
Even new life is fuel.

My eyes throb.
Nothing can dislodge
the house with my first tooth
noosed in a knot to the doorknob.

Nothing can dislodge
the triangular blotch
of rot on the red roof,
a cedar hedge, or the shade of a hedge.

No ease from the eye
of the sharp-shinned hawk in the birdbook there,
with reddish brown buffalo hair
on its shanks, one ascetic talon

clasping the abstract imperial sky.
It says:
an eye for an eye,
a tooth for a tooth.

No ease for the boy at the keyhole,
his telescope,
when the women's white bodies flashed
in the bathroom. Young, my eyes began to fail.

Nothing! No oil
for the eye, nothing to pour
on those waters or flames.
I am tired. Everyone's tired of my turmoil.

FOURTH OF JULY IN MAINE

(For Harriet Winslow)

Another summer! Our Independence
Day Parade, all innocence
of children's costumes, helps resist
the communist and socialist.
Five nations: Dutch, French, Englishmen,
Indians, and we, who held Castine,
rise from their graves in combat gear—
world-losers elsewhere, conquerors here!

Civil Rights clergy face again
the scions of the good old strain,
the poor who always must remain
poor and Republicans in Maine,
upholders of the American Dream,
who will not sink and cannot swim—
Emersonian self-reliance,
lethargy of Russian peasants!

High noon. Each child has won his blue,
red, yellow ribbon, and our statue,
a dandyish Union Soldier, sees
his fields reclaimed by views and spruce—
he seems a convert to old age,
small, callous, elbowed off the stage,
while the canned martial music fades
from scene and green—no more parades!

Blue twinges of mortality
remind us the theocracy
drove in its stakes here to command
the infinite, and gave this land
a ministry that would have made
short work of Christ, the Son of God,
and then exchanged His crucifix,
hardly our sign, for politics.

This white Colonial frame house,
willed downward, Dear, from you to us,
still matters—the Americas'
best artifact produced en masse.
The founders' faith was in decay,
and yet their building seems to say:
"Every time I take a breath,
my God you are the air I breathe."

New England, everywhere I look,
old letters crumble from the Book,
China trade rubble, one more line
unravelling from the dark design
spun by God and Cotton Mather—
our *bel età dell' oro*, another
bright thing thinner than a cobweb,
caught in Calvinism's ebb.

Dear Cousin, life is much the same,
though only fossils know your name
here since you left this solitude,
gone, as the Christians say, for good.

Your house, still outwardly in form
lasts, though no emissary come
to watch the garden running down,
or photograph the propped-up barn.

If memory is genius, you
had Homer's, enough gossip to
repeople Trollope's Barchester,
nurses, Negro, diplomat, down-easter,
cousins kept up with, nipped, corrected,
kindly, majorfully directed,
though family furniture, decor,
and rooms redone meant almost more.

How often when the telephone
brought you to us from Washington,
we had to look around the room
to find the objects you would name—
lying there, ten years paralyzed,
half blind, no voice unrecognized,
not trusting in the afterlife,
teasing us for a carving knife.

High New England summer, warm
and fortified against the storm
by nightly nips you once adored,
though never going overboard,
Harriet, when you used to play
your chosen Nadia Boulanger
Monteverdi, Purcell, and Bach's
precursors on the Magnavox.

Blue-ribboned, blue-jeaned, named for you,
our daughter cartwheels on the blue—
may your proportion strengthen her
to live through the millennial year
Two Thousand, and like you possess
friends, independence, and a house,
herself God's plenty, mistress of
your tireless sedentary love.

Her two angora guinea pigs
are nibbling seed, the news, and twigs—
untroubled, petrified, atremble,
a mother and her daughter, so humble,
giving, idle and sensitive,
few animals will let them live,
and only a vegetarian God
could look on them and call them good.

Man's poorest cousins, harmonies
of lust and appetite and ease,
little pacific things, who graze
the grass about their box, they praise
whatever stupor gave them breath
to multiply before their death—
Evolution's snails, by birth,
outrunning man who runs the earth.

And now the frosted summer night-dew
brightens, the north wind rushes through
your ailing cedars, finds the gaps;
thumbtacks rattle from the white maps,
food's lost sight of, dinner waits,
in the cold oven, icy plates—
repeating and repeating, one
Joan Baez on the gramophone.

And here in your converted barn,
we burn our hands a moment, borne
by energies that never tire
of piling fuel on the fire;
monologue that will not hear,
logic turning its deaf ear,
wild spirits and old sores in league
with inexhaustible fatigue.

Far off that time of gentleness,
when man, still licensed to increase,
unfallen and unmated, heard
only the uncreated Word—

when God the Logos still had wit
to hide his bloody hands, and sit
in silence, while his peace was sung.
Then the universe was young.

We watch the logs fall. Fire once gone,
we're done for: we escape the sun,
rising and setting, a red coal,
until it cinders like the soul.
Great ash and sun of freedom, give
us this day the warmth to live,
and face the household fire. We turn
our backs, and feel the whiskey burn.

from HARRIET

An unaccustomed ripeness in the wood;
move but an inch and moldy splinters fall
in sawdust from the aluminum-paint wall,
once loud and fresh, now aged to weathered wood.
Squalls of the seagulls' exaggerated outcry,
dimmed out by fog . . . Peace, peace. All day the words
hid rusty fish-hooks. Now, heart's-ease and wormwood,
we rest from all discussion, drinking, smoking,
pills for high blood, three pairs of glasses—soaking
in the sweat of our hard-earned supremacy,
offering a child our leathery love. We're fifty,
and free! Young, tottering on the dizzying brink
of discretion once, we wanted nothing,
but to be old, do nothing, type and think.

from LONG SUMMER

Everyone now is crowding everyone
to put off leaving till the Indian Summer;
and why? Because the others will be gone—
we too, dull drops in the decamping mass,
one in a million buying solitude. . . .
We asked to linger on past fall in Eden;
there must be good in man. Life fears us. Death
keeps our respect by keeping at a distance—
death we've never outdistanced as the Apostle boasted . . .
stream of heady, terrified poured stone,
suburban highway, rural superhighway,
foot of skunkweed, masts of scrub . . . the rich poor. . . .
We are loved by being distant; love-longing
mists the windshield, soothes the eye with milk.

W. S. Merwin

THE DRUNK IN THE FURNACE

For a good decade
The furnace stood in the naked gully, fireless
And vacant as any hat. Then when it was
No more to them than a hulking black fossil
To erode unnoticed with the rest of the junk-hill
By the poisonous creek, and rapidly to be added
To their ignorance.

They were afterwards astonished
To confirm, one morning, a twist of smoke like a pale
Resurrection, staggering out of its chewed hole,
And to remark then other tokens that someone,
Cosily bolted behind the eye-holed iron
Door of the drafty burner, had there established
His bad castle.

Where he gets his spirits
It's a mystery. But the stuff keeps him musical:
Hammer-and-anvilling with poker and bottle
To his jugged bellowings, till the last groaning clang
As he collapses onto the rioting
Springs of a litter of car-seats ranged on the grates,
To sleep like an iron pig.

In their tar-paper church
On a text about stoke-holes that are sated never
Their Reverend lingers. They nod and hate trespassers.
When the furnace wakes, though, all afternoon

Their witless offspring flock like piped rats to its siren
Crescendo, and agape on the crumbling ridge
Stand in a row and learn.

LEMUEL'S BLESSING

Let Lemuel bless with the wolf, which is
a dog without a master, but the Lord hears
his cries and feeds him in the desert.

Christopher Smart: Jubilate Agno

You that know the way,
Spirit,
I bless your ears which are like cypruses on a mountain
With their roots in wisdom. Let me approach.
I bless your paws and their twenty nails which tell their own prayer
And are like dice in command of their own combinations.
Let me not be lost.
I bless your eyes for which I know no comparison.
Run with me like the horizon, for without you
I am nothing but a dog lost and hungry,
Ill-natured, untrustworthy, useless.

My bones together bless you like an orchestra of flutes.
Divert the weapons of the settlements and lead their dogs a dance.
Where a dog is shameless and wears servility
In his tail like a banner,
Let me wear the opprobrium of possessed and possessors
As a thick tail properly used
To warm my worst and my best parts. My tail and my laugh bless you.
Lead me past the error at the fork of hesitation.
Deliver me

From the ruth of the lair, which clings to me in the morning,
Painful when I move, like a trap;
Even debris has its favorite positions but they are not yours;

From the ruth of kindness, with its licked hands;
I have sniffed baited fingers and followed
Toward necessities which were not my own: it would make me
An habitué of back steps, faithful custodian of fat sheep;

From the ruth of prepared comforts, with its
Habitual dishes sporting my name and its collars and leashes of vanity;

From the ruth of approval, with its nets, kennels, and taxidermists;
It would use my guts for its own rackets and instruments, to play its own
   games and music;
Teach me to recognize its platforms, which are constructed like
   scaffolds;

From the ruth of known paths, which would use my feet, tail, and ears
   as curios,
My head as a nest for tame ants,
My fate as a warning.

I have hidden at wrong times for wrong reasons.
I have been brought to bay. More than once.
Another time, if I need it,
Create a little wind like a cold finger between my shoulders, then
Let my nails pour out a torrent of aces like grain from a threshing
   machine;
Let fatigue, weather, habitation, the old bones, finally,
Be nothing to me,
Let all lights but yours be nothing to me.
Let the memory of tongues not unnerve me so that I stumble or quake.
But lead me at times beside the still waters;
There when I crouch to drink let me catch a glimpse of your image
Before it is obscured with my own.

Preserve my eyes, which are irreplaceable.
Preserve my heart, veins, bones,
Against the slow death building in them like hornets until the place is
   entirely theirs.
Preserve my tongue and I will bless you again and again.

Let my ignorance and my failings
Remain far behind me like tracks made in a wet season,
At the end of which I have vanished,
So that those who track me for their own twisted ends
May be rewarded only with ignorance and failings.
But let me leave my cry stretched out behind me like a road
On which I have followed you.
And sustain me for my time in the desert
On what is essential to me.

AIR

Naturally it is night.
Under the overturned lute with its
One string I am going my way
Which has a strange sound.

This way the dust, that way the dust.
I listen to both sides
But I keep right on.
I remember the leaves sitting in judgment
And then winter.

I remember the rain with its bundle of roads.
The rain taking all its roads.
Nowhere.

Young as I am, old as I am,

I forget tomorrow, the blind man.
I forget the life among the buried windows.
The eyes in the curtains.
The wall
Growing through the immortelles.
I forget silence
The owner of the smile.

This must be what I wanted to be doing,
Walking at night between the two deserts,
Singing.

DEAD HAND

Temptations still nest in it like basilisks.
Hang it up till the rings fall.

I LIVE UP HERE

I live up here
And a little bit to the left
And I go down only

For the accidents and then
Never a moment too soon

Just the same it's a life it's plenty

The stairs the petals she loves me
Every time
Nothing has changed

Oh down there down there
Every time
The glass knights lie by their gloves of blood

In the pans of the scales the helmets
Brim over with water
It's perfectly fair

The pavements are dealt out the dice
Every moment arrive somewhere

You can hear the hearses getting lost in lungs
Their bells stalling
And then silence comes with the plate and I
Give what I can

Feeling *It's worth it*

For I see
What my votes the mice are accomplishing
And I know I'm free

This is how I live
Up here and simply

Others do otherwise
Maybe

SOME LAST QUESTIONS

What is the head
        A. Ash
What are the eyes
        A. The wells have fallen in and have
           Inhabitants
What are the feet
        A. Thumbs left after the auction
No what are the feet
        A. Under them the impossible road is moving
           Down which the broken necked mice push
           Balls of blood with their noses
What is the tongue
        A. The black coat that fell off the wall
           With sleeves trying to say something
What are the hands
        A. Paid

No what are the hands
      A. Climbing back down the museum wall
         To their ancestors the extinct shrews that will
         Have left a message
What is the silence
      A. As though it had a right to more
Who are the compatriots
      A. They make the stars of bone

FOR THE ANNIVERSARY OF MY DEATH

Every year without knowing it I have passed the day
When the last fires will wave to me
And the silence will set out
Tireless traveller
Like the beam of a lightless star

Then I will no longer
Find myself in life as in a strange garment
Surprised at the earth
And the love of one woman
And then shamelessness of men
As today writing after three days of rain
Hearing the wren sing and the falling cease
And bowing not knowing to what

THE ASIANS DYING

When the forests have been destroyed their darkness remains
The ash the great walker follows the possessors
Forever
Nothing they will come to is real
Nor for long
Over the watercourses

Like ducks in the time of the ducks
The ghosts of the villages trail in the sky
Making a new twilight

Rain falls into the open eyes of the dead
Again again with its pointless sound
When the moon finds them they are the color of everything

The nights disappear like bruises but nothing is healed
The dead go away like bruises
The blood vanishes into the poisoned farmlands
Pain the horizon
Remains
Overhead the seasons rock
They are paper bells
Calling to nothing living

The possessors move everywhere under Death their star
Like columns of smoke they advance into the shadows
Like thin flames with no light
They with no past
And fire their only future

WE CONTINUE

For Galway Kinnell

The rust, a little pile of western color, lies
At the end of its travels,
Our instrument no longer.

Those who believe
In death have their worship cut out for them.
As for myself, we
Continue,

An old
Scar of light our trumpet,

Pilgrims with thorns
To the eye of the cold
Under flags made by the blind,
In one fist

This letter that vanishes
If the hand opens:

Charity, come home,
Begin.

DECEMBER NIGHT

The cold slope is standing in darkness
But the south of the trees is dry to the touch

The heavy limbs climb into the moonlight bearing feathers
I came to watch these
White plants older at night
The oldest
Come first to the ruins

And I hear magpies kept awake by the moon
The water flows through its
Own fingers without end

Tonight once more
I find a single prayer and it is not for men

Kenward Elmslie

Frank O'Hara

PERSONAL POEM

Now when I walk around at lunchtime
I have only two charms in my pocket
an old Roman coin Mike Kanemitsu gave me
and a bolt-head that broke off a packing case
when I was in Madrid the others never
brought me too much luck though they did
help keep me in New York against coercion
but now I'm happy for a time and interested

I walk through the luminous humidity
passing the House of Seagram with its wet
and its loungers and the construction to
the left that closed the sidewalk if
I ever get to be a construction worker
I'd like to have a silver hat please
and get to Moriarty's where I wait for
LeRoi and hear who wants to be a mover and
shaker the last five years my batting average
is .016 that's that, and LeRoi comes in
and tells me Miles Davis was clubbed 12
times last night outside BIRDLAND by a cop
a lady asks us for a nickel for a terrible
disease but we don't give her one we
don't like terrible diseases, then
we go eat some fish and some ale it's
cool but crowded we don't like Lionel Trilling
we decide, we like Don Allen we don't like
Henry James so much we like Herman Melville

we don't want to be in the poets' walk in
San Francisco even we just want to be rich
and walk on girders in our silver hats
I wonder if one person out of the 8,000,000 is
thinking of me as I shake hands with LeRoi
and buy a strap for my wristwatch and go
back to work happy at the thought possibly so

THE DAY LADY DIED

It is 12:20 in New York a Friday
three days after Bastille day, yes
it is 1959 and I go get a shoeshine
because I will get off the 4:19 in Easthampton
at 7:15 and then go straight to dinner
and I don't know the people who will feed me

I walk up the muggy street beginning to sun
and have a hamburger and a malted and buy
an ugly NEW WORLD WRITING to see what the poets
in Ghana are doing these days
                                        I go on to the bank
and Miss Stillwagon (first name Linda I once heard)
doesn't even look up my balance for once in her life
and in the GOLDEN GRIFFIN I get a little Verlaine
for Patsy with drawings by Bonnard although I do
think of Hesiod, trans. Richmond Lattimore or
Brendan Behan's new play or *Le Balcon* or *Les Nègres*
of Genet, but I don't, I stick with Verlaine
after practically going to sleep with quandariness

and for Mike I just stroll into the PARK LANE
Liquor Store and ask for a bottle of Strega and
then I go back where I came from to 6th Avenue
and the tobacconist in the Ziegfeld Theatre and
casually ask for a carton of Gauloises and a carton
of Picayunes, and a NEW YORK POST with her face on it

and I am sweating a lot by now and thinking of
leaning on the john door in the 5 SPOT
while she whispered a song along the keyboard
to Mal Waldron and everyone and I stopped breathing

ON RACHMANINOFF'S BIRTHDAY

Quick! a last poem before I go
off my rocker. Oh Rachmaninoff!
Onset, Massachusets. Is it the fig-newton
playing the horn? Thundering windows
of hell, will your tubes ever break
into powder? Oh my palace of oranges,
junk shop, staples, umber, basalt;
I'm a child again when I was really
miserable, a grope pizzicato. My pocket
of rhinestone, yoyo, carpenter's pencil,
amethyst, hypo, campaign button,
is the room full of smoke? Shit
on the soup, let it burn. So it's back.
You'll never be mentally sober.

LES ETIQUETTES JAUNES

I picked up a leaf
today from the sidewalk.
This seems childish.

Leaf! you are so big!
How can you change your
color, then just fall!

As if there were no
such thing as integrity!

You are too relaxed
to answer me. I am too
frightened to insist.

Leaf! don't be neurotic
like the small chameleon.

MEDITATIONS IN AN EMERGENCY

Am I to become profligate as if I were a blonde? Or religious as if I were French?

Each time my heart is broken it makes me feel more adventurous (and how the same names keep recurring on that interminable list!), but one of these days there'll be nothing left with which to venture forth.

Why should I share you? Why don't you get rid of someone else for a change?

I am the least difficult of men. All I want is boundless love.

Even trees understand me! Good heavens, I lie under them, too, don't I? I'm just like a pile of leaves.

However, I have never clogged myself with the praises of pastoral life, nor with nostalgia for an innocent past of perverted acts in pastures. No. One need never leave the confines of New York to get all the greenery one wishes—I can't even enjoy a blade of grass unless I know there's a subway handy, or a record store or some other sign that people do not totally *regret* life. It is more important to affirm the least sincere; the clouds get enough attention as it is and even they continue to pass. Do they know what they're missing? Uh huh.

My eyes are vague blue, like the sky, and change all the time; they are indiscriminate but fleeting, entirely specific and disloyal, so that no one trusts me. I am always looking away. Or again at something after it has given me up. It makes me restless and that makes me unhappy, but I cannot keep them still. If only I had grey, green, black, brown, yellow eyes; I would stay at home and do something. It's not that I'm curious. On the contrary, I am bored but it's my duty to be attentive, I am needed by things as the sky must be above the earth. And lately, so great has *their* anxiety become, I can spare myself little sleep.

Now there is only one man I love to kiss when he is unshaven. Hetero-sexuality! you are inexorably approaching. (How discourage her?)

St. Serapion, I wrap myself in the robes of your whiteness which is like midnight in Dostoevsky. How am I to become a legend, my dear? I've tried love, but that hides you in the bosom of another and I am always springing forth from it like the lotus—the ecstasy of always bursting forth! (but one must not be distracted by it!) or like a hyacinth, "to keep the filth of life away," yes, there, even in the heart, where the filth is pumped in and slanders and pollutes and determines. I will my will, though I may become famous for a mysterious vacancy in that department, that greenhouse.

Destroy yourself, if you don't know!

It is easy to be beautiful; it is difficult to appear so. I admire you, beloved, for the trap you've set. It's like a final chapter no one reads because the plot is over.

"Fanny Brown is run away—scampered off with a Cornet of Horse; I do love that little Minx, & hope She may be happy, tho' She has vexed me by this Exploit a little too. --Poor silly Cecchina! or F: B: as we used to call her. —I wish She had a good Whipping and 10,000 pounds." —Mrs. Thrale.

I've got to get out of here. I choose a piece of shawl and my dirtiest suntans. I'll be back, I'll re-emerge, defeated, from the valley; you don't want me to go where you go, so I go where you don't want me to. It's only afternoon, there's a lot ahead. There won't be any mail downstairs. Turning, I spit in the lock and the knob turns.

STEPS

How funny you are today New York
like Ginger Rogers in *Swingtime*
and St. Bridget's steeple leaning a little to the left

here I have just jumped out of a bed full of V-days
(I got tired of D-days) and blue you there still
accepts me foolish and free
all I want is a room up there
and you in it
and even the traffic halt so thick is a way
for people to rub up against each other
and when their surgical appliances lock
they stay together
for the rest of the day (what a day)
I go by to check a slide and I say
that painting's not so blue

where's Lana Turner
she's out eating
and Garbo's backstage at the Met
everyone's taking their coat off
so they can show a rib-cage to the rib-watchers
and the park's full of dancers with their tights and shoes
in little bags
who are often mistaken for worker-outers at the West Side Y
why not
the Pittsburgh Pirates shout because they won
and in a sense we're all winning
we're alive

the apartment was vacated by a gay couple
who moved to the country for fun
they moved a day too soon
even the stabbings are helping the population explosion
though in the wrong country

and all those liars have left the U N
the Seagram Building's no longer rivalled in interest
not that we need liquor (we just like it)

and the little box is out on the sidewalk
next to the delicatessen
so the old man can sit on it and drink beer
and get knocked off it by his wife later in the day
while the sun is still shining

oh god it's wonderful
to get out of bed
and drink too much coffee
and smoke too many cigarettes
and love you so much

TO THE FILM INDUSTRY IN CRISIS

Not you, lean quarterlies and swarthy periodicals
with your studious incursions toward the pomposity of ants,
nor you, experimental theatre in which Emotive Fruition
is wedding Poetic Insight perpetually, nor you,
promenading Grand Opera, obvious as an ear (though you
are close to my heart), but you, Motion Picture Industry,
it's you I love!

In times of crisis, we must all decide again and again whom we love.
And give credit where it's due: not to my starched nurse, who taught me
how to be bad and not bad rather than good (and has lately availed
herself of this information), not to the Catholic Church
which is at best an over-solemn introduction to cosmic entertainment,
not to the American Legion, which hates everybody, but to you,
glorious Silver Screen, tragic Technicolor, amorous Cinemascope,
stretching Vistavision and startling Stereophonic Sound, with all
your heavenly dimensions and reverberations and iconoclasms! To
Richard Barthelmess as the "tol'able" boy barefoot and in pants,

Jeanette MacDonald of the flaming hair and lips and long, long neck,
Sue Carroll as she sits for eternity on the damaged fender of a car
and smiles, Ginger Rogers with her pageboy bob like a sausage
on her shuffling shoulders, peach-melba-voiced Fred Astaire of the feet,
Eric Von Stroheim, the seducer of mountain-climbers' gasping spouses,
the Tarzans, each and every one of you (I cannot bring myself to prefer
Johnny Weissmuller to Lex Barker, I cannot!), Mae West in a furry sled,
her bordello radiance and bland remarks, Rudolph Valentino of the
    moon,
its crushing passions, and moon-like, too, the gentle Norma Shearer,
Miriam Hopkins dropping her champagne glass off Joel McCrea's yacht
and crying into the dappled sea, Clark Gable rescuing Gene Tierney
from Russia and Allan Jones rescuing Kitty Carlisle from Harpo Marx,
Cornel Wilde coughing blood on the piano keys while Merle Oberon
    berates,
Marilyn Monroe in her little spike heels reeling through Niagara Falls,
Joseph Cotten puzzling and Orson Welles puzzled and Dolores del Rio
eating orchids for lunch and breaking mirrors, Gloria Swanson reclining,
and Jean Harlow reclining and wiggling, and Alice Faye reclining
and wiggling and singing, Myrna Loy being calm and wise, William
    Powell
in his stunning urbanity, Elizabeth Taylor blossoming, yes, to you

and to all you others, the great, the neargreat, the featured, the extras
who pass quickly and return in dreams saying your one or two lines,
my love!
Long may you illumine space with your marvellous appearances, delays
and enunciations, and may the money of the world glitteringly cover
    you
as you rest after a long day under the kleig lights with your faces
in packs for our edification, the way the clouds come often at night
but the heavens operate on the star system. It is a divine precedent
you perpetuate! Roll on, reels of celluloid, as the great earth rolls on!

POEM

Lana Turner has collapsed!
I was trotting along and suddenly
it started raining and snowing
and you said it was hailing
but hailing hits you on the head
hard so it was really snowing and
raining and I was in such a hurry
to meet you but the traffic
was acting exactly like the sky
and suddenly I see a headline
LANA TURNER HAS COLLAPSED!
there is no snow in Hollywood
there is no rain in California
I have been to lots of parties
and acted perfectly disgraceful
but I never actually collapsed
oh Lana Turner we love you get up

Sylvia Plath

THE COLOSSUS

I shall never get you put together entirely,
Pieced, glued, and properly jointed.
Mule-bray, pig-grunt and bawdy cackles
Proceed from your great lips.
It's worse than a barnyard.

Perhaps you consider yourself an oracle,
Mouthpiece of the dead, or of some god or other.
Thirty years now I have labored
To dredge the silt from your throat.
I am none the wiser.

Scaling little ladders with gluepots and pails of lysol
I crawl like an ant in mourning
Over the weedy acres of your brow
To mend the immense skull plates and clear
The bald, white tumuli of your eyes.

A blue sky out of the Oresteia
Arches above us. O father, all by yourself
You are pithy and historical as the Roman Forum.
I open my lunch on a hill of black cypress.
Your fluted bones and acanthine hair are littered

In their old anarchy to the horizon-line.
It would take more than a lightning-stroke
To create such a ruin.
Nights, I squat in the cornucopia
Of your left ear, out of the wind,

Counting the red stars and those of plum-color.
The sun rises under the pillar of your tongue.
My hours are married to shadow.
No longer do I listen for the scrape of a keel
On the blank stones of the landing.

ALL THE DEAD DEARS

*In the Archæological Museum in Cam-
bridge is a stone coffin of the fourth
century A.D. containing the skeletons
of a woman, a mouse and a shrew.
The ankle-bone of the woman has
been slightly gnawn.*

Rigged poker-stiff on her back
With a granite grin
This antique museum-cased lady
Lies, companioned by the gimcrack
Relics of a mouse and a shrew
That battened for a day on her ankle-bone.

These three, unmasked now, bear
Dry witness
To the gross eating game
We'd wink at if we didn't hear
Stars grinding, crumb by crumb,
Our own grist down to its bony face.

How they grip us through thin and thick,
These barnacle dead!
This lady here's no kin
Of mine, yet kin she is: she'll suck
Blood and whistle my marrow clean
To prove it. As I think now of her head,

From the mercury-backed glass
Mother, grandmother, greatgrandmother
Reach hag hands to haul me in,

And an image looms under the fishpond surface
Where the daft father went down
With orange duck-feet winnowing his hair—

All the long gone darlings: they
Get back, though, soon,
Soon: be it by wakes, weddings,
Childbirths or a family barbecue:
Any touch, taste, tang's
Fit for those outlaws to ride home on,

And to sanctuary: usurping the armchair
Between tick
And tack of the clock, until we go,
Each skulled-and-crossboned Gulliver
Riddled with ghosts, to lie
Deadlocked with them, taking root as cradles rock.

THE STONES

This is the city where men are mended.
I lie on a great anvil.
The flat blue sky-circle

Flew off like the hat of a doll
When I fell out of the light. I entered
The stomach of indifference, the wordless cupboard.

The mother of pestles diminished me.
I became a still pebble.
The stones of the belly were peacable,

The head-stone quiet, jostled by nothing.
Only the mouth-hole piped out,
Importunate cricket

In a quarry of silences.
The people of the city heard it.
They hunted the stones, taciturn and separate,

The mouth-hole crying their locations.
Drunk as a fetus
I suck at the paps of darkness.

The food tubes embrace me. Sponges kiss my lichens away.
The jewelmaster drives his chisel to pry
Open one stone eye.

This is the after-hell: I see the light.
A wind unstoppers the chamber
Of the ear, old worrier.

Water mollifies the flint lip,
And daylight lays its sameness on the wall.
The grafters are cheerful,

Heating the pincers, hoisting the delicate hammers.
A current agitates the wires
Volt upon volt. Catgut stitches my fissures.

A workman walks by carrying a pink torso.
The storerooms are full of hearts.
This is the city of spare parts.

My swaddled legs and arms smell sweet as rubber.
Here they can doctor heads, or any limb.
On Fridays the little children come

To trade their hooks for hands.
Dead men leave eyes for others.
Love is the uniform of my bald nurse.

Love is the bone and sinew of my curse.
The vase, reconstructed, houses
The elusive rose.

Ten fingers shape a bowl of shadows.
My mendings itch. There is nothing to do.
I shall be good as new.

AN APPEARANCE

The smile of iceboxes annihilates me.
Such blue currents in the veins of my loved one!
I hear her great heart purr.

From her lips ampersands and percent signs
Exit like kisses.
It is Monday in her mind: morals

Launder and present themselves.
What am I to make of these contradictions?
I wear white cuffs, I bow.

Is this love then, this red material
Issuing from the steel needle that flies so blindingly?
It will make little dresses and coats,

It will cover a dynasty.
How her body opens and shuts—
A Swiss watch, jeweled in the hinges!

O heart, such disorganization!
The stars are flashing like terrible numerals.
ABC, her eyelids say.

MARY'S SONG

The Sunday lamb cracks in its fat.
The fat
Sacrifices its opacity. . . .

A window, holy gold.
The fire makes it precious,
The same fire

Melting the tallow heretics,
Ousting the Jews.
Their thick palls float

Over the cicatrix of Poland, burnt-out
Germany.
They do not die.

Grey birds obsess my heart,
Mouth-ash, ash of eye.
They settle. On the high

Precipice
That emptied one man into space
The ovens glowed like heavens, incandescent.

It is a heart,
This holocaust I walk in,
O golden child the world will kill and eat.

NICK AND THE CANDLESTICK

I am a miner. The light burns blue.
Waxy stalactites
Drip and thicken, tears

The earthen womb
Exudes from its dead boredom.
Black bat airs

Wrap me, raggy shawls,
Cold homicides.
They weld to me like plums.

Old caves of calcium
Icicles, old echoer.
Even the newts are white,

Those holy Joes.
And the fish, the fish—
Christ! They are panes of ice,

A vice of knives,
A piranha
Religion, drinking

Its first communion out of my live toes.
The candle
Gulps and recovers its small altitude,

Its yellows hearten.
O love, how did you get here?
O embryo

Remembering, even in sleep,
Your crossed position.
The blood blooms clean

In you, ruby.
The pain
You wake to is not yours.

Love, love,
I have hung our cave with roses.
With soft rugs—

The last of Victoriana.
Let the stars
Plummet to their dark address,

Let the mercuric
Atoms that cripple drip
Into the terrible well,

You are the one
Solid the spaces lean on, envious.
You are the baby in the barn.

MEDUSA

Off that landspit of stony mouth-plugs,
Eyes rolled by white sticks,
Ears cupping the sea's incoherences,
You house your unnerving head—God-ball,
Lens of mercies,

Your stooges
Plying their wild cells in my keel's shadow,
Pushing by like hearts,
Red stigmata at the very centre,
Riding the rip tide to the nearest point of departure,

Dragging their Jesus hair.
Did I escape, I wonder?
My mind winds to you
Old barnacled umbilicus, Atlantic cable,
Keeping itself, it seems, in a state of miraculous repair.

In any case, you are always there,
Tremulous breath at the end of my line,
Curve of water upleaping
To my water rod, dazzling and grateful,
Touching and sucking.

I didn't call you.
I didn't call you at all.
Nevertheless, nevertheless
You steamed to me over the sea,
Fat and red, a placenta

Paralyzing the kicking lovers.
Cobra light
Squeezing the breath from the blood bells
Of the fuchsia. I could draw no breath,
Dead and moneyless,

Overexposed, like an X-ray.
Who do you think you are?
A Communion wafer? Blubbery Mary?
I shall take no bite of your body,
Bottle in which I live,

Ghastly Vatican.
I am sick to death of hot salt.
Green as eunuchs, your wishes
Hiss at my sins.
Off, off, eely tentacle!

There is nothing between us.

CUT

For Susan O'Neill Roe

What a thrill—
My thumb instead of an onion.
The top quite gone
Except for a sort of a hinge

Of skin,
A flap like a hat,
Dead white.
Then that red plush.

Little pilgrim,
The Indian's axed your scalp.
Your turkey wattle
Carpet rolls

Straight from the heart.
I step on it,
Clutching my bottle
Of pink fizz.

A celebration, this is.
Out of a gap
A million soldiers run,
Redcoats, every one.

Whose side are they on?
O my
Homunculus, I am ill.
I have taken a pill to kill

The thin
Papery feeling.
Saboteur,
Kamikaze man—

The stain on your
Gauze Ku Klux Klan
Babushka
Darkens and tarnishes and when

The balled
Pulp of your heart
Confronts its small
Mill of silence

How you jump—
Trepanned veteran,
Dirty girl,
Thumb stump.

LADY LAZARUS

I have done it again.
One year in every ten
I manage it—

A sort of walking miracle, my skin
Bright as a Nazi lampshade,
My right foot

A paperweight,
My face a featureless, fine
Jew linen.

Peel off the napkin
O my enemy.
Do I terrify?—

The nose, the eye pits, the full set of teeth?
The sour breath
Will vanish in a day.

Soon, soon the flesh
The grave cave ate will be
At home on me

And I a smiling woman.
I am only thirty.
And like the cat I have nine times to die.

This is Number Three.
What a trash
To annihilate each decade.

What a million filaments.
The peanut-crunching crowd
Shoves in to see

Them unwrap me hand and foot—
The big strip tease.
Gentleman, ladies,

These are my hands,
My knees.
I may be skin and bone,

Nevertheless, I am the same, identical woman.
The first time it happened I was ten.
It was an accident.

The second time I meant
To last it out and not come back at all.
I rocked shut

As a seashell.
They had to call and call
And pick the worms off me like sticky pearls.

Dying
Is an art, like everything else.
I do it exceptionally well.

I do it so it feels like hell.
I do it so it feels real.
I guess you could say I've a call.

It's easy enough to do it in a cell.
It's easy enough to do it and stay put.
It's the theatrical

Comeback in broad day
To the same place, the same face, the same brute
Amused shout:

"A miracle!"
That knocks me out.
There is a charge

For the eyeing of my scars, there is a charge
For the hearing of my heart—
It really goes.

And there is a charge, a very large charge,
For a word or a touch
Or a bit of blood

Or a piece of my hair or my clothes.
So, so, Herr Doktor.
So, Herr Enemy.

I am your opus,
I am your valuable,
The pure gold baby

That melts to a shriek.
I turn and burn.
Do not think I underestimate your great concern.

Ash, ash—
You poke and stir.
Flesh, bone, there is nothing there—

A cake of soap,
A wedding ring,
A gold filling.

Herr God, Herr Lucifer,
Beware
Beware.

Out of the ash
I rise with my red hair
And I eat men like air.

DADDY

You do not do, you do not do
Any more, black shoe
In which I have lived like a foot
For thirty years, poor and white,
Barely daring to breathe or Achoo.

Daddy, I have had to kill you.
You died before I had time—
Marble-heavy, a bag full of God,
Ghastly statue with one grey toe
Big as a Frisco seal

And a head in the freakish Atlantic
Where it pours bean green over blue
In the waters off beautiful Nauset.
I used to pray to recover you.
Ach, du.

In the German tongue, in the Polish town
Scraped flat by the roller
Of wars, wars, wars.
But the name of the town is common.
My Polack friend

Says there are a dozen or two.
So I never could tell where you
Put your foot, your root,
I never could talk to you.
The tongue stuck in my jaw.

It stuck in a barb wire snare.
Ich, ich, ich, ich,
I could hardly speak.
I thought every German was you.
And the language obscene

An engine, an engine
Chuffing me off like a Jew.
A Jew to Dachau, Auschwitz, Belsen.
I began to talk like a Jew.
I think I may well be a Jew.

The snows of the Tyrol, the clear beer of Vienna
Are not very pure or true.
With my gypsy ancestress and my weird luck
And my Taroc pack and my Taroc pack
I may be a bit of a Jew.

I have always been scared of *you*,
With your Luftwaffe, your gobbledygoo.
And your neat moustache
And your Aryan eye, bright blue.
Panzer-man, panzer-man, O You—

Not God but a swastika
So black no sky could squeak through.
Every woman adores a Fascist,
The boot in the face, the brute
Brute heart of a brute like you.

You stand at the blackboard, daddy,
In the picture I have of you,
A cleft in your chin instead of your foot
But no less a devil for that, no not
Any less the black man who

Bit my pretty red heart in two.
I was ten when they buried you.
At twenty I tried to die
And get back, back, back to you.
I thought even the bones would do.

But they pulled me out of the sack,
And they stuck me together with glue.
And then I knew what to do.
I made a model of you,
A man in black with a Meinkampf look

And a love of the rack and the screw.
And I said I do, I do.
So daddy, I'm finally through.
The black telephone's off at the root,
The voices just can't worm through.

If I've killed one man, I've killed two—
The vampire who said he was you
And drank my blood for a year,
Seven years, if you want to know.
Daddy, you can lie back now.

There's a stake in your fat black heart
And the villagers never liked you.
They are dancing and stamping on you.
They always *knew* it was you.
Daddy, daddy, you bastard, I'm through.

Anne Sexton

RINGING THE BELLS

And this is the way they ring
the bells in Bedlam
and this is the bell-lady
who comes each Tuesday morning
to give us a music lesson
and because the attendants make you go
and because we mind by instinct,
like bees caught in the wrong hive,
we are the circle of the crazy ladies
who sit in the lounge of the mental house
and smile at the smiling woman
who passes us each a bell,
who points at my hand
that holds my bell, E flat,
and this is the gray dress next to me
who grumbles as if it were special
to be old, to be old,
and this is the small hunched squirrel girl
on the other side of me
who picks at the hairs over her lip,
who picks at the hairs over her lip all day,
and this is how the bells really sound,
as untroubled and clean
as a workable kitchen,
and this is always my bell responding
to my hand that responds to the lady
who points at me, E flat;
and although we are no better for it,
they tell you to go. And you do.

WITH MERCY FOR THE GREEDY

For my friend, Ruth, who urges me
to make an appointment for the
Sacrament of Confession

Concerning your letter in which you ask
me to call a priest and in which you ask
me to wear The Cross that you enclose;
your own cross,
your dog-bitten cross
no larger than a thumb,
small and wooden, no thorns, this rose—

I pray to its shadow,
that gray place
where it lies on your letter . . . deep, deep.
I detest my sins and I try to believe
in The Cross. I touch its tender hips, its dark jawed face,
its solid neck, its brown sleep.

True. There is
a beautiful Jesus.
He is frozen to his bones like a chunk of beef.
How desperately he wanted to pull his arms in!
How desperately I touch his vertical and horizontal axes!
But I can't. Need is not quite belief.

All morning long
I have worn
your cross, hung with package string around my throat.
It tapped me lightly as a child's heart might,
tapping secondhand, softly waiting to be born.
Ruth, I cherish the letter you wrote.

My friend, my friend, I was born
doing reference work in sin, and born
confessing it. This is what poems are:

with mercy
for the greedy,
they are the tongue's wrangle,
the world's pottage, the rat's star.

FOR GOD WHILE SLEEPING

Sleeping in fever, I am unfit
to know just who you are:
hung up like a pig on exhibit,
the delicate wrists,
the beard drooling blood and vinegar;
hooked to your own weight,
jolting toward death under your nameplate.

Everyone in this crowd needs a bath.
I am dressed in rags.
The mother wears blue. You grind your teeth
and with each new breath
your jaws gape and your diaper sags.
I am not to blame
for all this. I do not know your name.

Skinny man, you are somebody's fault.
You ride on dark poles—
a wooden bird that a trader built
for some fool who felt
that he could make the flight. Now you roll
in your sleep, seasick
on your own breathing, poor old convict.

THE ABORTION

Somebody who should have been born
is gone.

Just as the earth puckered its mouth,
each bud puffing out from its knot,
I changed my shoes, and then drove south.

Up past the Blue Mountains, where
Pennsylvania humps on endlessly,
wearing, like a crayoned cat, its green hair,

its roads sunken in like a gray washboard;
where, in truth, the ground cracks evilly,
a dark socket from which the coal has poured,

Somebody who should have been born
is gone.

the grass as bristly and stout as chives,
and me wondering when the ground would break,
and me wondering how anything fragile survives;

up in Pennsylvania, I met a little man,
not Rumpelstiltskin, at all, at all . . .
he took the fullness that love began.

Returning north, even the sky grew thin
like a high window looking nowhere.
The road was as flat as a sheet of tin.

Somebody who should have been born
is gone.

Yes, woman, such logic will lead
to loss without death. Or say what you meant,
you coward . . . this baby that I bleed.

MENSTRUATION AT FORTY

I was thinking of a son.
The womb is not a clock
nor a bell tolling,
but in the eleventh month of its life
I feel the November
of the body as well as of the calendar.
In two days it will be my birthday
and as always the earth is done with its harvest.
This time I hunt for death,
the night I lean toward,
the night I want.
Well then—
speak of it!
It was in the womb all along.

I was thinking of a son . . .
You! The never acquired,
the never seeded or unfastened,
you of the genitals I feared,
the stalk and the puppy's breath.
Will I give you my eyes or his?
Will you be the David or the Susan?
(Those two names I picked and listened for.)
Can you be the man your fathers are—
the leg muscles from Michelangelo,
hands from Yugoslavia,
somewhere the peasant, Slavic and determined,
somewhere the survivor, bulging with life—
and could it still be possible,
all this with Susan's eyes?
All this without you—
two days gone in blood.

I myself will die without baptism,
a third daughter they didn't bother.
My death will come on my name day.

What's wrong with the name day?
It's only an angel of the sun.
Woman,
weaving a web over your own,
a thin and tangled poison.
Scorpio,
bad spider—
die!

My death from the wrists,
two name tags,
blood worn like a corsage
to bloom
one on the left and one on the right—
It's a warm room,
the place of the blood.
Leave the door open on its hinges!

Two days for your death
and two days until mine.

Love! That red disease—
year after year, David, you would make me wild!
David! Susan! David! David!
full and disheveled, hissing into the night,
never growing old,
waiting always for you on the porch . . .
year after year,
my carrot, my cabbage,
I would have possessed you before all women,
calling your name,
calling you mine.

IN CELEBRATION OF MY UTERUS

Everyone in me is a bird.
I am beating all my wings.
They wanted to cut you out
but they will not.
They said you were immeasurably empty
but you are not.
They said you were sick unto dying
but they were wrong.
You are singing like a school girl.
You are not torn.

Sweet weight,
in celebration of the woman I am
and of the soul of the woman I am
and of the central creature and its delight
I sing for you. I dare to live.
Hello, spirit. Hello, cup.
Fasten, cover. Cover that does contain.
Hello to the soil of the fields.
Welcome, roots.

Each cell has a life.
There is enough here to please a nation.
It is enough that the populace own these goods.
Any person, any commonwealth would say of it,
"It is good this year that we may plant again
and think forward to a harvest.
A blight had been forecast and has been cast out."
Many women are singing together of this:
one is in a shoe factory cursing the machine,
one is at the aquarium tending a seal,
one is dull at the wheel of her Ford,
one is at the toll gate collecting,
one is tying the cord of a calf in Arizona,
one is straddling a cello in Russia,
one is shifting pots on the stove in Egypt,
one is painting her bedroom walls moon color,

one is dying but remembering a breakfast,
one is stretching on her mat in Thailand,
one is wiping the ass of her child,
one is staring out the window of a train
in the middle of Wyoming and one is
anywhere and some are everywhere and all
seem to be singing, although some can not
sing a note.

Sweet weight,
in celebration of the woman I am
let me carry a ten-foot scarf,
let me drum for the nineteen-year-olds,
let me carry bowls for the offering
(if that is my part).
Let me study the cardiovascular tissue,
let me examine the angular distance of meteors,
let me suck on the stems of flowers
(if that is my part).
Let me make certain tribal figures
(if that is my part).
For this thing the body needs
let me sing
for the supper,
for the kissing,
for the correct
yes.

MAN AND WIFE

To speke of wo
   that is in mariage. . .

We are not lovers.
We do not even know each other.
We look alike
but we have nothing to say.
We are like pigeons . . .

that pair who came to the suburbs
by mistake,
forsaking Boston where they bumped
their small heads against a blind wall,
having worn out the fruit stalls in the North End,
the amethyst windows of Louisburg Square,
the seats on the Common
And the traffic that kept stamping
and stamping.

Now there is green rain for everyone
as common as eyewash.
Now they are together
like strangers in a two-seater outhouse,
eating and squatting together.
They have teeth and knees
but they do not speak.
A soldier is forced to stay with a soldier
because they share the same dirt
and the same blows.

They are exiles
soiled by the same sweat and the drunkard's dream.
As it is they can only hang on,
their red claws wound like bracelets
around the same limb.
Even their song is not a sure thing.
It is not a language;
it is a kind of breathing.
They are two asthmatics
whose breath sobs in and out
through a small fuzzy pipe.

Like them
we neither talk nor clear our throats.
Oh darling,
we gasp in unison beside our window pane,
drunk on the drunkard's dream.
Like them
we can only hang on.

But they would pierce our heart
if they could only fly the distance.

US

I was wrapped in black
fur and white fur and
you undid me and then
you placed me in gold light
and then you crowned me,
while snow fell outside
the door in diagonal darts.
While a ten-inch snow
came down like stars
in small calcium fragments,
we were in our own bodies
(that room that will bury us)
and you were in my body
(that room that will outlive us)
and at first I rubbed your
feet dry with a towel
because I was your slave
and then you called me princess.
Princess!

Oh then
I stood up in my gold skin
and I beat down the psalms
and I beat down the clothes
and you undid the bridle
and you undid the reins
and I undid the buttons,
the bones, the confusions,
the New England postcards,
the January ten o'clock night,
and we rose up like wheat,
acre after acre of gold,
and we harvested,
we harvested.

DECEMBER 18TH

from **Eighteen Days Without You**

Swift boomerang, come get!
I am delicate. You've been gone.
The losing has hurt me some, yet
I must bend for you. See me arch. I'm turned on.
My eyes are lawn-colored, my hair brunette.

Kiss the package, Mr. Bind!
Yes? Would you consider hurling yourself
upon me, rigorous but somehow kind?
I am laid out like paper on your cabin kitchen shelf.
So draw me a breast. I like to be underlined.

Look, lout! Say yes!
Draw me like a child. I shall need
merely two round eyes and a small kiss.
A small o. Two earrings would be nice. Then proceed
to the shoulder. You may pause at this.

Catch me. I'm your disease.
Please go slow all along the torso
drawing beads and mouths and trees
and o's, a little *graffiti* and a small *hello*
for I grab, I nibble, I lift, I please.

Draw me good, draw me warm.
Bring me your raw-boned wrist and your
strange, Mr. Bind, strange stubborn horn.
Darling, bring with this an hour of undulations, for
this is the music for which I was born.

Lock in! Be alert, my acrobat
and I will be soft wood and you the nail
and we will make fiery ovens for Jack Sprat
and you will hurl yourself into my tiny jail
and we will take a supper together and that
will be that.

John C. Burlage

W. D. Snodgrass

HEART'S NEEDLE

1.
Child of my winter, born
When the new fallen soldiers froze
In Asia's steep ravines and fouled the snows,
When I was torn

By love I could not still,
By fear that silenced my cramped mind
To that cold war where, lost, I could not find
My peace in my will,

All those days we could keep
Your mind a landscape of new snow
Where the chilled tenant-farmer finds, below,
His fields asleep

In their smooth covering, white
As quilts to warm the resting bed
Of birth or pain, spotless as paper spread
For me to write,

And thinks: Here lies my land
Unmarked by agony, the lean foot
Of the weasel tracking, the thick trapper's boot;
And I have planned

My chances to restrain
The torments of demented summer or
Increase the deepening harvest here before
It snows again.

2.

Late April and you are three; today
  We dug your garden in the yard.
To curb the damage of your play,
Strange dogs at night and the moles tunneling,
  Four slender sticks of lath stand guard
    Uplifting their thin string.

So you were the first to tramp it down.
  And after the earth was sifted close
You brought your watering can to drown
All earth *and* us. But these mixed seeds are pressed
  With light loam in their steadfast rows.
    Child, we've done our best.

Someone will have to weed and spread
  The young sprouts. Sprinkle them in the hour
When shadow falls across their bed.
You should try to look at them every day
  Because when they come to full flower
    I will be away.

3.

The child between them on the street
Comes to a puddle, lifts his feet
  And hangs on their hands. They start
At the live weight and lurch together,
Recoil to swing him through the weather,
  Stiffen and pull apart.

We read of cold war soldiers that
Never gained ground, gave none, but sat
  Tight in their chill trenches.
Pain seeps up from some cavity
Through the ranked teeth in sympathy;
  The whole jaw grinds and clenches

Till something somewhere has to give.
It's better the poor soldiers live
  In someone else's hands

Than drop where helpless powers fall
On crops and barns, on towns where all
    Will burn. And no man stands.

For good, they sever and divide
Their won and lost land. On each side
    Prisoners are returned
Excepting a few unknown names.
The peasant plods back and reclaims
    His fields that strangers burned

And nobody seems very pleased.
It's best. Still, what must not be seized
    Clenches the empty fist.
I tugged your hand, once, when I hated
Things less: a mere game dislocated
    The radius of your wrist.

Love's wishbone, child, although I've gone
As men must and let you be drawn
    Off to appease another,
It may help that a Chinese play
Or Solomon himself might say
    I am your real mother.

4.
    No one can tell you why
  the season will not wait;
    the night I told you I
must leave, you wept a fearful rate
    to stay up late.

    Now that it's turning Fall,
  we go to take our walk
    among municipal
flowers, to steal one off its stalk,
    to try and talk.

    We huff like windy giants
  scattering with our breath
    gray-headed dandelions;
Spring is the cold wind's aftermath.
    The poet saith.

But the asters, too, are gray,
ghost-gray. Last night's cold
is sending on their way
petunias and dwarf marigold,
hunched sick and old.

Like nerves caught in a graph,
the morning-glory vines
frost has erased by half
still scrawl across their rigid twines.
Like broken lines

of verses I can't make.
In its unraveling loom
we find a flower to take,
with some late buds that might still bloom,
back to your room.

Night comes and the stiff dew.
I'm told a friend's child cried
because a cricket, who
had minstreled every night outside
her window, died.

5.
Winter again and it is snowing;
Although you are still three,
You are already growing
Strange to me.

You chatter about new playmates, sing
Strange songs; you do not know
Hey ding-a-ding-a-ding
Or where I go

Or when I sang for bedtime, *Fox*
Went out on a chilly night,
Before I went for walks
And did not write;

You never mind the squalls and storms
That are renewed long since;
Outside, the thick snow swarms
Into my prints

And swirls out by warehouses, sealed,
Dark cowbarns, huddled, still,
Beyond to the blank field,
The fox's hill

Where he backtracks and sees the paw,
Gnawed off, he cannot feel;
Conceded to the jaw
Of toothed, blue steel.

6.
      Easter has come around
   again; the river is rising
      over the thawed ground
and the banksides. When you come you bring
      an egg dyed lavender.
  We shout along our bank to hear
our voices returning from the hills to meet us.
  We need the landscape to repeat us.

      You lived on this bank first.
  While nine months filled your term, we knew
      how your lungs, immersed
in the womb, miraculously grew
      their useless folds till
  the fierce, cold air rushed in to fill
them out like bushes thick with leaves. You took your hour,
  caught breath, and cried with your full lung power.

      Over the stagnant bight
  we see the hungry bank swallow
      flaunting his free flight
still; we sink in mud to follow
      the killdeer from the grass
  that hides her nest. That March there was
rain; the rivers rose; you could hear killdeers flying
  all night over the mudflats crying.

You bring back how the red-
winged blackbird shrieked, slapping frail wings,
      diving at my head—
I saw where her tough nest, cradled, swings
      in tall reeds that must sway
with the winds blowing every way.
If you recall much, you recall this place. You still
      live nereby—on the opposite hill.

      After the sharp windstorm
of July Fourth, all that summer
      through the gentle, warm
afternoons, we heard great chain saws chirr
      like iron locusts. Crews
of roughneck boys swarmed to cut loose
branches wrenched in the shattering wind, to hack free
      all the torn limbs that could sap the tree.

      In the debris lay
starlings, dead. Near the park's birdrun
      we surprised one day
a proud, tan-spatted, buff-brown pigeon.
      In my hands she flapped so
fearfully that I let her go.
Her keeper came. And we helped snarl her in a net.
      You bring things I'd as soon forget.

      You raise into my head
a Fall night that I came once more
      to sit on your bed;
sweat beads stood out on your arms and fore-
      head and you wheezed for breath,
for help, like some child caught beneath
its comfortable woolly blankets, drowning there.
      Your lungs caught and would not take the air.

      Of all things, only we
have power to choose that we should die;
      nothing else is free
in this world to refuse it. Yet I

who say this, could not raise
    myself from bed how many days
to the thieving world. Child, I have another wife,
    another child. We try to choose our life.

7.
Here in the scuffled dust
    is our ground of play.
I lift you on your swing and must
    shove you away,
see you return again,
    drive you off again, then

stand quiet till you come.
    You, though you climb
higher, farther from me, longer,
    will fall back to me stronger.
Bad penny, pendulum,
    you keep my constant time

to bob in blue July
    where fat goldfinches fly
over the glittering, fecund
    reach of our growing lands.
Once more now, this second,
    I hold you in my hands.

8.
I thumped on you the best I could
        which was no use;
you would not tolerate your food
until the sweet, fresh milk was soured
        with lemon juice.

That puffed you up like a fine yeast.
    The first June in your yard
like some squat Nero at a feast
you sat and chewed on white, sweet clover.
        That is over.

When you were old enough to walk
     we went to feed
the rabbits in the park milkweed;
saw the paired monkeys, under lock,
     consume each other's salt.

Going home we watched the slow
stars follow us down Heaven's vault.
You said, let's catch one that comes low,
     pull off its skin
     and cook it for our dinner.

     As absentee bread-winner,
I seldom got you such cuisine;
we ate in local restaurants
or bought what lunches we could pack
     in a brown sack

with stale, dry bread to toss for ducks
     on the green-scummed lagoons,
crackers for porcupine and fox,
life-savers for the footpad coons
     to scour and rinse,

snatch after in their muddy pail
     and stare into their paws.
When I moved next door to the jail
     I learned to fry
omelettes and griddlecakes so I

could set you supper at my table.
As I built back from helplessness,
     when I grew able,
the only possible answer was
     you had to come here less.

This Hallowe'en you come one week.
     You masquerade
     as a vermilion, sleek,
fat, crosseyed fox in the parade
or, where grim jackolanterns leer,

go with your bag from door to door
foraging for treats. How queer:
    when you take off your mask
my neighbors must forget and ask
      whose child you are.

Of course you lose your appetite,
    whine and won't touch your plate;
      as local law
I set your place on an orange crate
in your own room for days. At night

you lie asleep there on the bed
      and grate your jaw.
Assuredly your father's crimes
      are visited
on you. You visit me sometimes.

The time's up. Now our pumpkin sees
    me bringing your suitcase.
      He holds his grin;
the forehead shrivels, sinking in.
You break this year's first crust of snow

off the runningboard to eat.
    We manage, though for days
I crave sweets when you leave and know
they rot my teeth. Indeed our sweet
      foods leave us cavities.

9.
      I get numb and go in
though the dry ground will not hold
    the few dry swirls of snow
and it must not be very cold.
A friend asks how you've been
      and I don't know

or see much right to ask.
Or what use it could be to know.
    In three months since you came

the leaves have fallen and the snow;
your pictures pinned above my desk
        seem much the same.

    Somehow I come to find
myself upstairs in the third floor
      museum's halls,
walking to kill my time once more
among the enduring and resigned
        stuffed animals,

    where, through a century's
caprice, displacement and
      known treachery between
its wars, they hear some old command
and in their peaceable kingdoms freeze
        to this still scene,

    Nature Morte. Here
by the door, its guardian,
      the patchwork dodo stands
where you and your stepsister ran
laughing and pointing. Here, last year,
        you pulled my hands

    and had your first, worst quarrel,
so toys were put up on your shelves.
      Here in the first glass cage
the little bobcats arch themselves,
still practicing their snarl
        of constant rage.

    The bison, here, immense,
shoves at his calf, brow to brow,
      and looks it in the eye
to see what it is thinking now.
I forced you to obedience;
        I don't know why.

Still the lean lioness
beyond them, on her jutting ledge
    of shale and desert shrub,
stands watching always at the edge,
stands hard and tanned and envious
      above her cub;

    with horns locked in tall heather,
two great Olympian Elk stand bound,
    fixed in their lasting hate
till hunger brings them both to ground.
Whom equal weakness binds together
      none shall separate.

    Yet separate in the ocean
of broken ice, the white bear reels
    beyond the leathery groups
of scattered, drab Arctic seals
arrested here in violent motion
      like Napoleon's troops.

    Our states have stood so long
At war, shaken with hate and dread,
    they are paralyzed at bay;
once we were out of reach, we said,
we would grow reasonable and strong.
      Some other day.

    Like the cold men of Rome,
we have won costly fields to sow
    in salt, our only seed.
Nothing but injury will grow.
I write you only the bitter poems
      that you can't read.

    Onan who would not breed
a child to take his brother's bread
    and be his brother's birth,
rose up and left his lawful bed,
went out and spilled his seed
      in the cold earth.

I stand by the unborn,
by putty-colored children curled
  in jars of alcohol,
that waken to no other world,
unchanging where no eye shall mourn
   I see the caul

  that wrapped a kitten, dead.
I see the branching, doubled throat
  of a two-headed foal;
I see the hydrocephalic goat;
here is the curled and swollen head,
   there, the burst skull;

  skin of a limbless calf;
a horse's foetus, mummified;
  mounted and joined forever,
the Siamese twin dogs that ride
belly to belly, half and half,
   that none shall sever.

  I walk among the growths,
by gangrenous tissue, goitre, cysts,
  by fistulas and cancers,
where the malignancy man loathes
is held suspended and persists.
  And I don't know the answers.

  The window's turning white.
The world moves like a diseased heart
  packed with ice and snow.
Three months now we have been apart
less than a mile. I cannot fight
   or let you go.

10.
The vicious winter finally yields
  the green winter wheat;
the farmer, tired in the tired fields
  he dare not leave will eat.

Once more the runs come fresh; prevailing
    piglets, stout as jugs,
harry their old sow to the railing
    to ease her swollen dugs

and game colts trail the herded mares
    that circle the pasture courses;
our seasons bring us back once more
    like merry-go-round horses.

With crocus mouths, perennial hungers,
    into the park Spring comes;
we roast hot dogs on old coat hangers
    and feed the swan bread crumbs,

pay our respects to the peacocks, rabbits,
    and leathery Canada goose
who took, last Fall, our tame white habits
    and now will not turn loose.

In full regalia, the pheasant cocks
    march past their dubious hens;
the porcupine and the lean, red fox
    trot around bachelor pens

and the miniature painted train
    wails on its oval track:
you said, I'm going to Pennsylvania!
    and waved. And you've come back.

If I loved you, they said, I'd leave
    and find my own affairs.
Well, once again this April, we've
    come around to the bears;

punished and cared for, behind bars,
    the coons on bread and water
stretch thin black fingers after ours.
    And you are still my daughter.

APRIL INVENTORY

The green catalpa tree has turned
All white; the cherry blooms once more.
In one whole year I haven't learned
A blessed thing they pay you for.
The blossoms snow down in my hair;
The trees and I will soon be bare.

The trees have more than I to spare.
The sleek, expensive girls I teach,
Younger and pinker every year,
Bloom gradually out of reach.
The pear tree lets its petals drop
Like dandruff on a tabletop.

The girls have grown so young by now
I have to nudge myself to stare.
This year they smile and mind me how
My teeth are falling with my hair.
In thirty years I may not get
Younger, shrewder, or out of debt.

The tenth time, just a year ago,
I made myself a little list
Of all the things I'd ought to know,
Then told my parents, analyst,
And everyone who's trusted me
I'd be substantial, presently.

I haven't read one book about
A book or memorized one plot.
Or found a mind I did not doubt.
I learned one date. And then forgot.
And one by one the solid scholars
Get the degrees, the jobs, the dollars.

And smile above their starchy collars.
I taught my classes Whitehead's notions;
One lovely girl, a song of Mahler's.
Lacking a source-book or promotions,
I showed one child the colors of
A luna moth and how to love.

I taught myself to name my name,
To bark back, loosen love and crying;
To ease my woman so she came,
To ease an old man who was dying.
I have not learned how often I
Can win, can love, but choose to die.

I have not learned there is a lie
Love shall be blonder, slimmer, younger;
That my equivocating eye
Loves only by my body's hunger;
That I have forces, true to feel,
Or that the lovely world is real.

While scholars speak authority
And wear their ulcers on their sleeves,
My eyes in spectacles shall see
These trees procure and spend their leaves.
There is a value underneath
The gold and silver in my teeth.

Though trees turn bare and girls turn wives,
We shall afford our costly seasons;
There is a gentleness survives
That will outspeak and has its reasons.
There is a loveliness exists,
Preserves us, not for specialists.

THE EXAMINATION

Under the thick beams of that swirly smoking light,
    The black robes are clustering, huddled in together.
Hunching their shoulders, they spread short, broad sleeves like night-
    Black grackles' wings; then they reach bone-yellow leather-

y fingers, each to each. And are prepared. Each turns
    His single eye—or since one can't discern their eyes,
That reflective, single, moon-pale disc which burns
    Over each brow—to watch this uncouth shape that lies

Strapped to their table. One probes with his ragged nails
    The slate-sharp calf, explores the thigh and the lean thews
Of the groin. Others raise, red as piratic sails,
    His wing, stretching, trying the pectoral sinews.

One runs his finger down the whet of that cruel
    Golden beak, lifts back the horny lids from the eyes,
Peers down in one bright eye malign as a jewel,
    And steps back suddenly. "He is anaesthetized?"

"He is. He is. Yes. Yes." The tallest of them, bent
    Down by the head, rises: "This drug possesses powers
Sufficient to still all gods in this firmament.
    This is Garuda who was fierce. He's yours for hours.

"We shall continue, please." Now, once again, he bends
    To the skull, and its clamped tissues. Into the cran-
ial cavity, he plunges both of his hands
    Like obstetric forceps and lifts out the great brain,

Holds it aloft, then gives it to the next who stands
    Beside him. Each, in turn, accepts it, although loath,
Turns it this way, that way, feels it between his hands
    Like a wasp's nest or some sickening outsized growth.

They must decide what thoughts each part of it must think;
    They tap at, then listen beside, each suspect lobe;
Next, with a crow's quill dipped into India ink,
    Mark on its surface, as if on a map or globe,

Those dangerous areas which need to be excised.
    They rinse it, then apply antiseptics to it;
Now silver saws appear which, inch by inch, slice
    Through its ancient folds and ridges, like thick suet.

It's rinsed, dried, and daubed with thick salves. The smoky saws
    Are scrubbed, resterilized, and polished till they gleam.
The brain is repacked in its case. Pinched in their claws,
    Glimmering needles stitch it up, that leave no seam.

Meantime, one of them has set blinders to the eyes
    Inserted light packing beneath each of the ears
And calked the nostrils in. One, with thin twine, ties
    The genitals off. With long wooden-handled shears,

Another chops pinions out of the scarlet wings.
    It's hoped that with disuse he will forget the sky
Or, at least, in time, learn, among others things,
    To fly no higher than his superiors fly.

Well; that's a beginning. The next time, they can split
    His tongue and teach him to talk correctly, can give
Him opinions on fine books and choose clothing fit
    For the integrated area where he'll live.

Their candidate may live to give them thanks one day.
    He will recover and may hope for such success
He might return to join their ranks. Bowing away,
    They nod, whispering, "One of ours; one of ours. Yes. Yes."

A FLAT ONE

Old Fritz, on this rotating bed
For seven wasted months you lay
Unfit to move, shrunken, gray,
No good to yourself or anyone
But to be babied—changed and bathed and fed.
      At long last, that's all done.

Before each meal, twice every night
We set pads on your bedsores, shut
Your catheter tube off, then brought
The second canvas-and-black-iron
Bedframe and clamped you in between them, tight,
      Scared, so we could turn

You over. We washed you, covered you,
Cut up each bite of meat you ate;
We watched your lean jaws masticate
As ravenously your useless food
As thieves at hard labor in their chains chew
      Or insects in the wood.

Such pious sacrifice to give
You all you could demand of pain:
Receive this haddock's body, slain
For you, old tyrant; take this blood
Of a tomato, shed that you might live.
      You had that costly food.

You seem to be all finished, so
We'll plug your old recalcitrant anus
And tie up your discouraged penis
In a great, snow-white bow of gauze.
We wrap you, pin you, and cart you down below,
      Below, below, because

Your credit has finally run out.
On our steel table, trussed and carved,
You'll find this world's hardworking, starved
Teeth working in your precious skin.
The earth turns, in the end, by turn about
        And opens to take you in.

    Seven months gone down the drain; thank God
That's through. Throw out the four-by-fours,
Swabsticks, the thick salve for bedsores,
    Throw out the diaper pads and drug
Containers, pile the bedclothes in a wad,
        And rinse the cider jug

    Half-filled with the last urine. Then
Empty out the cotton cans,
Autoclave the bowls and spit pans,
    Unhook the pumps and all the red
Tubes—catheter, suction, oxygen;
        Next, wash the empty bed.

    —All this Dark Age machinery
On which we had tormented you
To life. Last, we collect the few
    Belongings: snapshots, some odd bills,
Your mail, and half a pack of Luckies we
        Won't light you after meals.

    Old man, these seven months you've lain
Determined—not that you would live—
Just not to die. No one would give
    You one chance you could ever wake
From that first night, much less go well again,
        Much less go home and make

    Your living; how could you hope to find
A place for yourself in all creation?—
Pain was your only occupation.
    And pain that should content and will
A man to give it up, nerved you to grind
        Your clenched teeth, breathing, till

Your skin broke down, your calves went flat
And your legs lost all sensation. Still,
You took enough morphine to kill
A strong man. Finally, nitrogen
Mustard: you could last two months after that;
     It would kill you then.

Even then you wouldn't quit.
Old soldier, yet you must have known
Inside the animal had grown
Sick of the world, made up its mind
To stop. Your mind ground on its separate
     Way, merciless and blind,

Into these last weeks when the breath
Would only come in fits and starts
That puffed out your sections like the parts
Of some enormous, damaged bug.
You waited, not for life, not for your death,
     Just for the deadening drug

That made your life seem bearable.
You still whispered you would not die.
Yet in the nights I heard you cry
Like a whipped child; in fierce old age
You whimpered, tears stood on your gun-metal
     Blue cheeks shaking with rage

And terror. So much pain would fill
Your room that when I left I'd pray
That if I came back the next day
I'd find you gone. You stayed for me—
Nailed to your own rapacious, stiff self-will.
     You've shook loose, finally.

They'd say this was a worthwhile job
Unless they tried it. It is mad
To throw our good lives after bad;
     Waste time, drugs, and our minds, while strong
Men starve. How many young men did we rob
     To keep you hanging on?

I can't think we did *you* much good.
Well, when you died, none of us wept.
You killed for us, and so we kept
You, because we need to earn our pay.
No. We'd still have to help you try. We would
        Have killed for you today.

"AFTER EXPERIENCE TAUGHT ME . . ."

After experience taught me that all the ordinary
surroundings of social life are futile and vain;

        I'm going to show you something very
        Ugly: someday, it might save your life.

Seeing that none of the things I feared contain
In themselves anything either good or bad

        What if you get caught without a knife;
        Nothing—even a loop of piano wire;

Excepting only in the effect they had
Upon my mind, I resolved to inquire

        Take the first two fingers of this hand;
        Fork them out—kind of a "V for Victory"—

Whether there might be something whose discovery
Would grant me supreme, unending happiness.

        And jam them into the eyes of your enemy.
        You have to do this hard. Very hard. Then press

No virtue can be thought to have priority
Over this endeavor to preserve one's being.

        Both fingers down around the cheekbone
        And setting your foot high into the chest

No man can desire to act rightly, to be blessed,
To live rightly, without simultaneously

You must call up every strength you own
And you can rip off the whole facial mask.

Wishing to be, to act, to live. He must ask
First, in other words, to actually exist.

And you, whiner, who wastes your time
Dawdling over the remorseless earth,
What evil, what unspeakable crime
Have you made your life worth?

Nathan Sivins

Gary Snyder

PIUTE CREEK

One granite ridge
A tree, would be enough
Or even a rock, a small creek,
A bark shred in a pool.
Hill beyond hill, folded and twisted
Tough trees crammed
In thin stone fractures
A huge moon on it all, is too much.
The mind wanders. A million
Summers, night air still and the rocks
Warm.   Sky over endless mountains.
All the junk that goes with being human
Drops away, hard rock wavers
Even the heavy present seems to fail
This bubble of a heart.
Words and books
Like a small creek off a high ledge
Gone in the dry air.

A clear, attentive mind
Has no meaning but that
Which sees is truly seen.
No one loves rock, yet we are here.
Night chills. A flick
In the moonlight
Slips into Juniper shadow:
Back there unseen
Cold proud eyes
Of Cougar or Coyote
Watch me rise and go.

MILTON BY FIRELIGHT

Piute Creek, August, 1955

"Oh hell, what do mine eyes
      with grief behold?"
Working with an old
Singlejack miner, who can sense
The vein and cleavage
In the very guts of rock, can
Blast granite, build
Switchbacks that last for years
Under the beat of snow, thaw, mule-hooves.
What use, Milton, a silly story
Of our lost general parents,
      eaters of fruit?

The Indian, the chainsaw boy,
And a string of six mules
Came riding down to camp
Hungry for tomatoes and green apples.
Sleeping in saddle-blankets
Under a bright night-sky
Han River slantwise by morning.
Jays squall
Coffee boils

In ten thousand years the Sierras
Will be dry and dead, home of the scorpion.
Ice-scratched slabs and bent trees.
No paradise, no fall,
Only the weathering land
The wheeling sky,
Man, with his Satan
Scouring the chaos of the mind.
Oh Hell!

Fire down
Too dark to read, miles from a road
The bell-mare clangs in the meadow
That packed dirt for a fill-in
Scrambling through loose rocks
On an old trail
All of a summer's day.

THINGS TO DO AROUND A LOOKOUT

Wrap up in a blanket in cold weather and just read.
Practise writing Chinese characters with a brush
Paint pictures of the mountains
Put out salt for deer
Bake coffee cake and biscuit in the iron oven,
Hours off hunting twisty firewood, packing it all back up and chopping.
Rice out for the ptarmigan and the conies
Mark well sunrise and sunset—drink lapsang soochong.
Rolling smokes
The Flower book and the Bird book and the Star book
Old Readers Digests left behind
Bullshitting on the radio with a distant pinnacle, like you, hid in clouds;
Drawing little sexy sketches of bare girls.
Reading maps, checking on the weather, airing out musty Forest Service
     sleeping bags and blankets
Oil the saws, sharpen axes,
Learn the names of all the peaks you see
               and which is highest
Learn by heart the drainages between.
Go find a shallow pool of snowmelt on a good day, bathe in the luke-
     warm water.
Take off in foggy weather and go climbing all alone
The Rock book,—strata, dip, and strike
Get ready for the snow, get ready
To go down.

THINGS TO DO AROUND A SHIP AT SEA

Go out with a small flashlight and a star chart, on a good night, and
    check out the full size of Eridanus.
Sunbathe on a cot on the boatdeck
Go forward and talk to the lookout, away from the engines, the silence
    and shudder
Watch running lights pass in the night.
Dolphins and sharks.
Phosphorescing creatures alongside the shipside, burning spots in the
    wake.
Stag, Argosy, Playboy, and Time.
Do pushups.
Make coffee in the galley, telling jokes.
Type letters to his girl friend in Naples for the twelve-to-four Oiler
Sew up jeans.
Practise tying knots and whipping
With the Chief Cook singing blues
Tell big story lies
Grow a beard
Learn to weld and run a lathe
Study for the Firemans Oilers and Watertenders exam
Tropic- and sea-bird watching
Types of ships
Listening to hours of words and lifetimes—fuck & shit—
Figuring out the revolution.
Hammer pipes and flanges
Paint a picture on a bulkhead with leftover paints
Jack off in the shower
Dreams of girls, about yr girl friend, writing letters, wanting children,
Making plans.

BURNING THE SMALL DEAD

Burning the small dead
          branches
broke from beneath
   thick spreading
               whitebark pine.

               a hundred summers
snowmelt   rock   and air

hiss in a twisted bough.

   sierra granite;
          mt. Ritter—
               black rock twice as old.

Deneb, Altair

windy fire

FROM MYTHS AND TEXTS

Logging

5.

Again the ancient, meaningless
Abstractions of the educated mind.
               wet feet and the campfire out.
Drop a mouthful of useless words.
—The book's in the crapper
They're up to the part on Ethics now

               skidding logs in pine-flat heat
               long summer sun
               the flax bag sweet
Summer professors
          elsewhere meet

Indiana? Seattle? Ann Arbor?
        bug clack in sage
Sudden rumble of wheels on cattle-guard rails.
        hitching & hiking
        looking for work.

"We rule you" all crownéd or be-Homburged heads
"We fool you" those guys with P.H.D.s
"We eat for you" you
"We work for you" who?
        a big picture of K. Marx with an axe,
"Where I cut off one it will never grow again."
        O Karl would it were true
        I'd put my saw to work for you
& the wicked social tree would fall right down.
(The only logging we'll do here is trees
And do it quick, with big trucks and machines)
        "That Cat wobbles like a sick whore"
So we lay on our backs tinkering
                all afternoon
The trees and the logs stood still
It was so quiet we could hear the birds.

Hunting

8.

this poem is for deer

"I dance on all the mountains
On five mountains, I have a dancing place
When they shoot at me I run
To my five mountains"

Missed a last shot
At the Buck, in twilight
So we came back sliding
On dry needles through cold pines.
Scared out a cottontail
Whipped up the winchester
Shot off its head.

The white body rolls and twitches
In the dark ravine
As we run down the hill to the car.

                              deer foot down scree
Picasso's fawn, Issa's fawn,
Deer on the autumn mountain
Howling like a wise man
Stiff springy jumps down the snowfields
Head held back, forefeet out,
Balls tight in a tough hair sack
Keeping the human soul from care
                       on the autumn mountain
Standing in late sun, ear-flick
Tail-flick, gold mist of flies
Whirling from nostril to eyes.

               *   *   *

Home by night
               drunken eye
Still picks out Taurus
Low, and growing high:
               four-point buck
Dancing in the headlights
               on the lonely road
A mile past the mill-pond,
With the car stopped, shot
That wild silly blinded creature down.

Pull out the hot guts
               with hard bare hands
While night-frost chills the tongue
               and eye
The cold horn-bones.
The hunter's belt
               just below the sky
Warm blood in the car trunk.
Deer-smell,
               the limp tongue.

               *   *   *

Deer don't want to die for me.
        I'll drink sea-water
Sleep on beach pebbles in the rain
Until the deer come down to die
            in pity for my pain.

16.

How rare to be born a human being!
Wash him off with cedar-bark and milkweed
            send the damned doctors home.
Baby, baby, noble baby
Noble-hearted baby

One hand up, one hand down
"I alone am the honored one"
Birth of the Buddha.
And the whole world-system trembled.
"If that baby really said that,
I'd cut him up and throw him to the dogs!"
said Chao-chou the Zen Master. But
Chipmunks, gray squirrels, and
Golden-mantled ground squirrels
            brought him each a nut.
Truth being the sweetest of flavors.

Girls would have in their arms
A wild gazelle or wild wolf-cubs
And give them their white milk,
            those who had new-born infants home
Breasts still full.
Wearing a spotted fawnskin
            sleeping under trees
            bacchantes, drunk
On wine or truth, what you will,
Meaning: compassion.
Agents: man and beast, beasts
Got the buddha-nature
All but
Coyote.

VAPOR TRAILS

Twin streaks twice higher than cumulus,
Precise plane icetracks in the vertical blue
Cloud-flaked light-shot shadow-arcing
Field of all future war, edging off to space.

Young expert U. S. pilots waiting
The day of criss-cross rockets
And white blossoming smoke of bomb,
The air world torn and staggered for these
Specks of brushy land and ant-hill towns—

   I stumble on the cobble rockpath,
Passing through temples,
Watching for two-leaf pine
   —spotting that design.

in Daitoku-ji

THIS TOKYO

Peace, war, religion,
Revolution, will not help.
This horror seeds in the agile
Thumb and greedy little brain
That learned to catch bananas
With a stick.
      The millions of us worthless
To each other or the world
Or selves, the sufferers of the real
Or of the mind—this world
Is but a dream?   Or human life
A nightmare grafted on solidity
Of planet—mental, mental,
Shudder of the sun—praise

Evil submind freedom with de Sade
Or highest Dantean radiance of the God
Or endless Light or Life or Love
Or simple tinsel angel in the
Candy heaven of the poor—
Mental divinity or beauty, all,
Plato, Aquinas, Buddha,
Dionysius of the Cross, all
Pains or pleasures hells or
What in sense of flesh
Logic, eye, music, or
Concoction of all faculties
& thought tend—tend—to this:
      This gaudy apartment of the rich.
The comfort of the U.S. for its own.
The shivering pair of girls
Who dyked each other for a show
A thousand yen before us men
—In an icy room—to buy their relatives
A meal. This scramble spawn of
Wire dirt rails tin boards blocks
Babies, students, crookt old men.
   We live
On the meeting of sun and earth.
We live—we live—and all our lives
Have led to this, this city,
Which is soon the world, this
Hopelessness where love of man
Or hate of man could matter
None, love if you will or
Contemplate or write or teach
But know in your human marrow you
Who read, that all you tread
Is earthquake rot and matter mental
Trembling, freedom is a void,
Peace war religion revolution
Will not help.

© Rollie McKenna

Richard Wilbur

PRAISE IN SUMMER

Obscurely yet most surely called to praise,
As sometimes summer calls us all, I said
The hills are heavens full of branching ways
Where star-nosed moles fly overhead the dead;
I said the trees are mines in air, I said
See how the sparrow burrows in the sky!
And then I wondered why this mad *instead*
Perverts our praise to uncreation, why
Such savor's in this wrenching things awry.
Does sense so stale that it must needs derange
The world to know it? To a praiseful eye
Should it not be enough of fresh and strange
That trees grow green, and moles can course in clay,
And sparrows sweep the ceiling of our day?

LOVE CALLS US TO THE THINGS OF THIS WORLD

The eyes open to a cry of pulleys,
And spirited from sleep, the astounded soul
Hangs for a moment bodiless and simple
As false dawn.
                    Outside the open window
The morning air is all awash with angels.

Some are in bed-sheets, some are in blouses,
Some are in smocks: but truly there they are.
Now they are rising together in calm swells
Of halcyon feeling, filling whatever they wear
With the deep joy of their impersonal breathing;

Now they are flying in place, conveying
The terrible speed of their omnipresence, moving
And staying like white water; and now of a sudden
They swoon down into so rapt a quiet
That nobody seems to be there.
       The soul shrinks

From all that it is about to remember,
From the punctual rape of every blessèd day,
And cries,
    "Oh, let there be nothing on earth but laundry,
Nothing but rosy hands in the rising steam
And clear dances done in the sight of heaven."

Yet, as the sun acknowledges
With a warm look the world's hunks and colors,
The soul descends once more in bitter love
To accept the waking body, saying now
In a changed voice as the man yawns and rises,

"Bring them down from their ruddy gallows;
Let there be clean linen for the backs of thieves;
Let lovers go fresh and sweet to be undone,
And the heaviest nuns walk in a pure floating
Of dark habits,
    keeping their difficult balance."

POTATO

for André du Bouchet

An underground grower, blind and a common brown;
Got a misshapen look, it's nudged where it could;
Simple as soil yet crowded as earth with all.

Cut open raw, it looses a cool clean stench,
Mineral acid seeping from pores of prest meal;
It is like breaching a strangely refreshing tomb:

Therein the taste of first stones, the hands of dead slaves,
Waters men drank in the earliest frightful woods,
Flint chips, and peat, and the cinders of buried camps.

Scrubbed under faucet water the planet skin
Polishes yellow, but tears to the plain insides;
Parching, the white's blue-hearted like hungry hands.

All of the cold dark kitchens, and war-frozen gray
Evening at window; I remember so many
Peeling potatoes quietly into chipt pails.

"It was potatoes saved us, they kept us alive."
Then they had something to say akin to praise
For the mean earth-apples, too common to cherish or steal.

Times being hard, the Sikh and the Senegalese,
Hobo and Okie, the body of Jesus the Jew,
Vestigial virtues, are eaten; we shall survive.

What has not lost its savor shall hold us up,
And we are praising what saves us, what fills the need.
(Soon there'll be packets again, with Algerian fruits.)

Oh, it will not bear polish, the ancient potato,
Needn't be nourished by Caesars, will blow anywhere,
Hidden by nature, counted-on, stubborn and blind.

You may have noticed the bush that it pushes to air,
Comical-delicate, sometimes with second-rate flowers
Awkward and milky and beautiful only to hunger.

A BAROQUE WALL-FOUNTAIN
IN THE VILLA SCIARRA

for Dore and Adja

Under the bronze crown
Too big for the head of the stone cherub whose feet
A serpent has begun to eat,
Sweet water brims a cockle and braids down

Past spattered mosses, breaks
On the tipped edge of a second shell, and fills
The massive third below. It spills
In threads then from the scalloped rim, and makes

A scrim or summery tent
For a faun-ménage and their familiar goose.
Happy in all that ragged, loose
Collapse of water, its effortless descent

And flatteries of spray,
The stocky god upholds the shell with ease,
Watching, about his shaggy knees,
The goatish innocence of his babes at play;

His fauness all the while
Leans forward, slightly, into a clambering mesh
Of water-lights, her sparkling flesh
In a saecular ecstasy, her blinded smile

Bent on the sand floor
Of the trefoil pool, where ripple-shadows come
And go in swift reticulum,
More addling to the eye than wine, and more

Interminable to thought
Than pleasure's calculus. Yet since this all
  Is pleasure, flash, and waterfall,
Must it not be too simple? Are we not

  More intricately expressed
In the plain fountains that Maderna set
  Before St. Peter's—the main jet
Struggling aloft until it seems at rest

  In the act of rising, until
The very wish of water is reversed,
  That heaviness borne up to burst
In a clear, high, cavorting head, to fill

  With blaze, and then in gauze
Delays, in a gnatlike shimmering, in a fine
  Illumined version of itself, decline,
And patter on the stones its own applause?

  If that is what men are
Or should be, if those water-saints display
  The pattern of our areté,
What of these showered fauns in their bizarre,

  Spangled, and plunging house?
They are at rest in fulness of desire
  For what is given, they do not tire
Of the smart of the sun, the pleasant water-douse

  And riddled pool below,
Reproving our disgust and our ennui
  With humble insatiety.
Francis, perhaps, who lay in sister snow

  Before the wealthy gate
Freezing and praising, might have seen in this
  No trifle, but a shade of bliss—
That land of tolerable flowers, that state

As near and as far as grass
Where eyes become the sunlight, and the hand
  Is worthy of water: the dreamt land
Toward which all hungers leap, all pleasures pass.

YEAR'S END

Now winter downs the dying of the year,
And night is all a settlement of snow;
From the soft street the rooms of houses show
A gathered light, a shapen atmosphere,
Like frozen-over lakes whose ice is thin
And still allows some stirring down within.

I've known the wind by water banks to shake
The late leaves down, which frozen where they fell
And held in ice as dancers in a spell
Fluttered all winter long into a lake;
Graved on the dark in gestures of descent,
They seemed their own most perfect monument.

There was perfection in the death of ferns
Which laid their fragile cheeks against the stone
A million years. Great mammoths overthrown
Composedly have made their long sojourns,
Like palaces of patience, in the gray
And changeless lands of ice. And at Pompeii

The little dog lay curled and did not rise
But slept the deeper as the ashes rose
And found the people incomplete, and froze
The random hands, the loose unready eyes
Of men expecting yet another sun
To do the shapely thing they had not done.

These sudden ends of time must give us pause.
We fray into the future, rarely wrought
Save in the tapestries of afterthought.

More time, more time. Barrages of applause
Come muffled from a buried radio.
The New-year bells are wrangling with the snow.

A DUBIOUS NIGHT

A bell diphthonging in an atmosphere
Of shying night air summons some to prayer
Down in the town, two deep lone miles from here,

Yet wallows faint or sudden everywhere,
In every ear, as if the twist wind wrung
Some ten years' tangled echoes from the air.

What kyries it says are mauled among
The queer elisions of the mist and murk,
Of lights and shapes; the senses were unstrung,

Except that one star's synecdochic smirk
Burns steadily to me, that nothing's odd
And firm as ever is the masterwork.

I weary of the confidence of God.

ADVICE TO A PROPHET

When you come, as you soon must, to the streets of our city,
Mad-eyed from stating the obvious,
Not proclaiming our fall but begging us
In God's name to have self-pity,

Spare us all word of the weapons, their force and range,
The long numbers that rocket the mind;
Our slow, unreckoning hearts will be left behind,
Unable to fear what is too strange.

Nor shall you scare us with talk of the death of the race.
How should we dream of this place without us?—
The sun mere fire, the leaves untroubled about us,
A stone look on the stone's face?

Speak of the world's own change. Though we cannot conceive
Of an undreamt thing, we know to our cost
How the dreamt cloud crumbles, the vines are blackened
    by frost,
How the view alters. We could believe,

If you told us so, that the white-tailed deer will slip
Into perfect shade, grown perfectly shy,
The lark avoid the reaches of our eye,
The jack-pine lose its knuckled grip

On the cold ledge, and every torrent burn
As Xanthus once, its gliding trout
Stunned in a twinkling. What should we be without
The dolphin's arc, the dove's return,

These things in which we have seen ourselves and spoken?
Ask us, prophet, how we shall call
Our natures forth when that live tongue is all
Dispelled, that glass obscured or broken

In which we have said the rose of our love and the clean
Horse of our courage, in which beheld
The singing locust of the soul unshelled,
And all we mean or wish to mean.

Ask us, ask us whether with the worldless rose
Our hearts shall fail us; come demanding
Whether there shall be lofty or long standing
When the bronze annals of the oak-tree close.

THE UNDEAD

Even as children they were late sleepers,
Preferring their dreams, even when quick with monsters,
To the world with all its breakable toys,
Its compacts with the dying;

From the stretched arms of withered trees
They turned, fearing contagion of the mortal,
And even under the plums of summer
Drifted like winter moons.

Secret, unfriendly, pale, possessed
Of the one wish, the thirst for mere survival,
They came, as all extremists do
In time, to a sort of grandeur:

Now, to their Balkan battlements
Above the vulgar town of their first lives,
They rise at the moon's rising. Strange
That their utter self-concern

Should, in the end, have left them selfless:
Mirrors fail to perceive them as they float
Through the great hall and up the staircase;
Nor are the cobwebs broken.

Into the pallid night emerging,
Wrapped in their flapping capes, routinely maddened
By a wolf's cry, they stand for a moment
Stoking the mind's eye.

With lewd thoughts of the pressed flowers
And bric-a-brac of rooms with something to lose,—
Of love-dismembered dolls, and children
Buried in quilted sleep.

Then they are off in a negative frenzy,
Their black shapes cropped into sudden bats
That swarm, burst, and are gone. Thinking
Of a thrush cold in the leaves

Who has sung his few summers truly,
Or an old scholar resting his eyes at last,
We cannot be much impressed with vampires,
Colorful though they are;

Nevertheless, their pain is real,
And requires our pity. Think how sad it must be
To thirst always for a scorned elixir,
The salt quotidian blood

Which, if mistrusted, has no savor;
To prey on life forever and not possess it,
As rock-hollows, tide after tide,
Glassily strand the sea.

A MILTONIC SONNET FOR MR. JOHNSON ON HIS REFUSAL OF PETER HURD'S OFFICIAL PORTRAIT

Heir to the office of a man not dead
Who drew our Declaration up, who planned
Range and Rotunda with his drawing-hand
And harbored Palestrina in his head,
Who would have wept to see small nations dread
The imposition of our cattle-brand,
With public truth at home mistold or banned,
And in whose term no army's blood was shed,

Rightly you say the picture is too large
Which Peter Hurd by your appointment drew,
And justly call that Capitol too bright
Which signifies our people in your charge;
Wait, Sir, and see how time will render you,
Who talk of vision but are weak of sight.

6 January 1967

ON THE MARGINAL WAY

for J. C. P.

Another cove of shale,
But the beach here is rubbled with strange rock
    That is sleek, fluent, and taffy-pale.
I stare, reminded with a little shock
How, by a shore in Spain, George Borrow saw
A hundred women basking in the raw.

They must have looked like this,
That catch of bodies on the sand, that strew
    Of rondure, crease, and orifice,
Lap, flank, and knee—a too abundant view
Which, though he'd had the lenses of a fly,
Could not have waked desire in Borrow's eye.

Has the light altered now?
The rocks flush rose and have the melting shape
    Of bodies fallen anyhow.
It is a Géricault of blood and rape,
Some desert town despoiled, some caravan
Pillaged, its people murdered to a man,

And those who murdered them
Galloping off, a rumpling line of dust
    Like the wave's white, withdrawing hem.
But now the vision of a colder lust
Clears, as the wind goes chill and all is greyed
By a swift cloud that drags a carrion shade.

If these are bodies still,
Theirs is a death too dead to look asleep
    Like that of Auschwitz' final kill,
Poor slaty flesh abandoned in a heap
And then, like sea-rocks buried by a wave,
Bulldozed at last into a common grave.

It is not tricks of sense
But the time's fright within me which distracts
Least fancies into violence
And makes my thought take cover in the facts,
As now it does, remembering how the bed
Of layered rock two miles above my head

Hove ages up and broke
Soundless asunder, when the shrinking skin
Of Earth, blacked out by steam and smoke,
Gave passage to the muddled fire within,
Its crannies flooding with a sweat of quartz,
And lathered magmas out of deep retorts

Welled up, as here, to fill
With tumbled rockmeal, stone-fume, lithic spray,
The dike's brief chasm and the sill.
Weathered until the sixth and human day
By sanding winds and water, scuffed and brayed
By the slow glacier's heel, these forms were made

That now recline and burn
Comely as Eve and Adam, near a sea
Transfigured by the sun's return.
And now three girls lie golden in the lee
Of a great arm or thigh, and are as young
As the bright boulders that they lie among.

Though, high above the shore
On someone's porch, spread wings of newsprint flap
The tidings of some dirty war,
It is a perfect day: the waters clap
Their hands and kindle, and the gull in flight
Loses himself at moments, white in white,

And like a breaking thought
Joy for a moment floods into the mind,
Blurting that all things shall be brought
To the full state and stature of their kind,
By what has found the manhood of this stone.
May that vast motive wash and wash our own.

James Wright

IN SHAME AND HUMILIATION

He will launch a curse upon the world,
and as only man can curse (it is his
privilege, the primary distinction be-
tween him and other animals), maybe
by his curse alone he will attain his
object—that is, convince himself that
he is a man and not a piano-key!
      Dostoyevsky, Notes from Underground

What can a man do that a beast cannot,
A bird, a reptile, any fiercer thing?
      He can amaze the ground
With anger never hissed in a snake's throat
      Or past a bitch's fang,
Though, suffocate, he cannot make a sound.

He can out-rage the forked tongue with a word,
The iron forged of his pain, over and over,
      Till the cold blade can fall
And beak an enemy's heart quick as a bird,
      And then retire to cover,
To vines of hair, declivities of skull.

Outright the snake, faster than man, can kill.
A mongrel's teeth can snarl as man's cannot.
      And a bird, unbodied soul
Soaring and dazzling, in the cloud at will
      Outbeautifies the flight
Of halt man's clavicles that flop and wheel.

Their cries last longer. Sinew of wing and coil,
Or sprung thighs of hounds impinge their iron
    Easy and quick, to leap
Over the brooks, the miles and days, like oil
    Flung on a surge of green
A man limps into nothing more than sleep.

But under the dream he always dreams too late,
That stark abounding dream of wretchedness
    Where stones and very trees
Ignore his name, and crows humiliate,
    And fiends below the face,
Serpents, women, and dogs dance to deny his face—

He will not deny, he will not deny his own.
Thrashing in lakes or pools of broken glass,
    He hunches over to look
And feel his mouth, his nostrils, feel of the bone,
    A man's ultimate face:
The individual bone, that burns like ice.

That fire, that searing cold is what I claim:
What makes me man, that dogs can never share,
    Woman or brilliant bird,
The beaks that mock but cannot speak the names
    Of the blind rocks, of the stars.
Sprawling in dark, I burn my sudden pride.

Let my veins wither now, my words revolt
Serpent or bird or pure untroubled mind.
    I will avow my face
Unto my face and, through the spirit's vault,
    Deliberate underground,
Devour the locusts of my bitterness.

That angel, wheeled upon my heart, survives,
Nourished by food the righteous cannot eat
    And loathe to move among.
They die, fastidious, while the spirit thrives
    Out of its own defeat.
The pure, the pure! will never live so long.

AS I STEP OVER A PUDDLE AT THE END OF WINTER, I THINK OF AN ANCIENT CHINESE GOVERNOR

And how can I, born in evil days
And fresh from failure, ask a kindness
of Fate?
Written A.D. 819

Po Chu-i, balding old politician,
What's the use?
I think of you,
Uneasily entering the gorges of the Yang-Tze,
When you were being towed up the rapids
Toward some political job or other
In the city of Chungshou.
You made it, I guess,
By dark.

But it is 1960, it is almost spring again,
And the tall rocks of Minneapolis
Build me my own black twilight
Of bamboo ropes and waters.
Where is Yuan Chen, the friend you loved?
Where is the sea, that once solved the whole loneliness
Of the Midwest? Where is Minneapolis? I can see nothing
But the great terrible oak tree darkening with winter.
Did you find the city of isolated men beyond mountains?
Or have you been holding the end of a frayed rope
For a thousand years?

AUTUMN BEGINS IN MARTINS FERRY, OHIO

In the Shreve High football stadium,
I think of Polacks nursing long beers in Tiltonsville,
And gray faces of Negroes in the blast furnace at Benwood,
And the ruptured night watchman of Wheeling Steel,
Dreaming of heroes.

All the proud fathers are ashamed to go home.
Their women cluck like starved pullets,
Dying for love.

Therefore,
Their sons grow suicidally beautiful
At the beginning of October,
And gallop terribly against each other's bodies.

LYING IN A HAMMOCK AT WILLIAM DUFFY'S FARM IN PINE ISLAND, MINNESOTA

Over my head, I see the bronze butterfly,
Asleep on the black trunk,
Blowing like a leaf in green shadow.
Down the ravine behind the empty house,
The cowbells follow one another
Into the distances of the afternoon.
To my right,
In a field of sunlight between two pines,
The droppings of last year's horses
Blaze up into golden stones.
I lean back, as the evening darkens and comes on.
A chicken hawk floats over, looking for home.
I have wasted my life.

THE JEWEL

There is this cave
In the air behind my body
That nobody is going to touch:
A cloister, a silence
Closing around a blossom of fire.
When I stand upright in the wind,
My bones turn to dark emeralds.

EISENHOWER'S VISIT TO FRANCO, 1959

". . . we die of cold, and not of
darkness."
                              Unamuno

The American hero must triumph over
The forces of darkness.
He has flown through the very light of heaven
And come down in the slow dusk
Of Spain.

Franco stands in a shining circle of police.
His arms open in welcome.
He promises all dark things
Will be hunted down.

State police yawn in the prisons.
Antonio Machado follows the moon
Down a road of white dust,
To a cave of silent children
Under the Pyrenees.
Wine darkens in stone jars in villages.
Wine sleeps in the mouths of old men, it is a dark red
    color.
Smiles glitter in Madrid.
Eisenhower has touched hands with Franco, embracing
In a glare of photographers.
Clean new bombers from America muffle their engines
And glide down now.

Their wings shine in the searchlights
Of bare fields,
In Spain.

LATE NOVEMBER IN A FIELD

Today I am walking alone in a bare place,
And winter is here.
Two squirrels near a fence post
Are helping each other drag a branch
Toward a hiding place; it must be somewhere
Behind those ash trees.
They are still alive, they ought to save acorns
Against the cold.
Frail paws rifle the troughs between cornstalks
    when the moon
Is looking away.
The earth is hard now,
The soles of my shoes need repairs.
I have nothing to ask a blessing for,
Except these words.
I wish they were
Grass.

THE LIGHTS IN THE HALLWAY

The lights in the hallway
Have been out a long time.
I clasp her,
Terrified by the roundness of the earth
And its apples and the voluptuous rings
Of poplar trees, the secret Africas,
The children they give us.
She is slim enough.
Her knee feels like the face
Of a surprised lioness
Nursing the lost children
Of a gazelle by pure accident.
In that body I long for,
The Gabon poets gaze for hours

Between boughs toward heaven, their noble faces
Too secret to weep.
How do I know what color her hair is? I float among
Lonely animals, longing
For the red spider who is God.

IN RESPONSE TO A RUMOR THAT THE OLDEST WHOREHOUSE IN WHEELING, WEST VIRGINIA, HAS BEEN CONDEMNED

I will grieve alone,
As I strolled alone, years ago, down along
The Ohio shore.
I hid in the hobo jungle weeds
Upstream from the sewer main,
Pondering, gazing.

I saw, down river,
At Twenty-third and Water Streets
By the vinegar works,
The doors open in early evening.
Swinging their purses, the women
Poured down the long street to the river
And into the river.

I do not know how it was
They could drown every evening.
What time near dawn did they climb up the other shore,
Drying their wings?

For the river at Wheeling, West Virginia
Has only two shores:
The one in hell, the other
In Bridgeport, Ohio.

And nobody would commit suicide, only
To find beyond death
Bridgeport, Ohio.

CONFESSION TO J. EDGAR HOOVER

Hiding in the church of an abandoned stone,
A Negro soldier
Is flipping the pages of the Articles of War,
That he can't read.

Our father,
Last evening I devoured the wing
Of a cloud.
And, in the city, I sneaked down
To pray with a sick tree.

I labor to die, father,
I ride the great stones,
I hide under stars and maples,
And yet I cannot find my own face.
In the mountains of blast furnaces,
The trees turn their backs on me.
Father, the dark moths
Crouch at the sills of the earth, waiting.

And I am afraid of my own prayers.
Father, forgive me.
I did not know what I was doing.

Notes on the Poets

JOHN ASHBERY (1927)

Poetry

Some Trees, New Haven: Yale University Press, 1956.
The Tennis Court Oath, Middletown: Wesleyan University Press, 1962.
Rivers and Mountains, New York: Holt, Rinehart and Winston, Inc., 1966.
The Double Dream of Spring, New York: E. P. Dutton & Co., Inc., 1970.

A graduate of Harvard and Columbia, John Ashbery has been art critic for the New York *Herald Tribune, Art International* and editor of *Art and Literature.* Currently an editor of *Art News,* he has written several plays and, with James Schuyler, a novel, *A Nest of Ninnies* (1969).

Although Ashbery's early work was conventional enough, his later poems are enigmatic and exasperating. Known tools of explication, even the most unorthodox, fail to pry a sustained meaning out of most of them. Lost and baffled after the first, second or third line, the reader suddenly feels like Charlie Brown in Alice's Wonderland: montages of words and images leap, screaming sense and threatening the listener to attention, but they inevitably explode into seemingly meaningless fragments. Still, after these verbal hallucinations, the atmosphere remains charged with elusive emotional impact.

In Ashbery's work critics have recognized the presence of Dadaists, Wallace Stevens and action painters, the theories of Ezra Pound, the technique of James Joyce, and also a kind of McLuhanesque non-linear verbal all-at-onceness. But this sophisticated technical anarchy is also moved by the consequences of the innocent eye confronting experience: the lingering pain of loss.

JOHN BERRYMAN (1914)

Poetry

Homage to Mistress Bradstreet, New York: Farrar, Straus & Giroux, 1956.
77 Dream Songs, New York: Farrar, Straus & Giroux, 1964.
Berryman's Sonnets, New York: Farrar, Straus & Giroux, 1967.

Short Poems, New York: Farrar, Straus & Giroux, 1967.
His Toy, His Dream, His Rest, New York: Farrar, Straus & Giroux, 1968.
The Dream Songs, New York: Farrar, Straus & Giroux, 1970.

Critical Study

Martz, William J. *John Berryman,* Minneapolis: University of Minnesota
    Press, 1969.

John Berryman is a graduate of Columbia and Clare College (Cambridge). He has taught at Brown, Harvard and Princeton, and is currently Professor of the Humanities at the University of Minnesota. A recipient of Rockefeller and Guggenheim fellowships and a special award from the National Arts Council, he has also won both the Pulitzer Prize (1965) and the National Book Award (1969).

In the course of his career Berryman has written not only the distinguished long poem in homage to Anne Bradstreet and the equally notable sonnet sequence, but also short stories, criticism and a critical biography of Stephen Crane (1950). To date, however, his major work is his sequence of 385 dream songs, for which he may well be recognized as one of the truly great poets of the century. The stupendous scope, depth and craftsmanship of these poems have caused critics to compare Berryman with Homer, Dante and Whitman.

The dream songs constitute a loose narrative about a multi-dimensional figure most often called Henry (Pussycat). Berryman has written that Henry is "an imaginary character (not the poet . . .), a white American in early middle age sometimes in blackface, who has suffered an irreversible loss and talks to himself sometimes in the first person, sometimes in the third, sometimes even in the second; he has a friend, never named, who addresses himself as Mr Bones and variants thereof." There are moments when Henry, Mr Bones and the poet are barely indistinguishable from one another. Thus Berryman achieves a linear-multi-dimensional vision—maneuvered by a dazzling shift of pronouns—similar to that which Picasso achieved on canvas.

Like Odysseus, Henry Pussycat undergoes a fantastic range of experience. He even dies and comes back to life. His emotions shift from incredible panic, horror and self-pity to sheer joy and self-deprecating slapstick. If Henry gets out of hand, meanwhile, his friend and conscience, his side-kick and minstrel chorus is always there to cut him down to size or support him through despair. At the end of his journey, which takes him across spiritual as well as geographical contemporary boundaries, Henry, the schizophrenic Odysseus of the atomic age, returns to his wife and child, scarred but having learned that most ancient and essential lesson: to be a man is to suffer.

ROBERT BLY (1926)

Poetry

The Lion's Tail and Eyes, Poems Written Out of Laziness and Silence (with James Wright and William Duffy), Madison, Minnesota: The Sixties Press, 1962.

Silence in the Snowy Fields, Middletown: Wesleyan University Press, 1962.

The Light Around the Body, New York: Harper & Row, Publishers, 1967.

The Morning Glory, San Francisco: Kayak Books, Inc., 1969.

Translations

Twenty Poems of Georg Trakl (with James Wright), Madison, Minnesota: The Sixties Press, 1961.

Twenty Poems of Cesar Vallejo (with James Wright and John Knoepfle), Madison, Minnesota: The Sixties Press, 1962.

I Do Best Alone At Night, Selected Poems of Gunnar Ekelof, Washington, D.C.: Charioteer Press, 1968.

Twenty Poems of Pablo Neruda (with James Wright), Madison, Minnesota: The Sixties Press, 1968.

Forty Poems of Juan Ramon Jimenez, Madison, Minnesota: The Sixties Press, 1969.

Robert Bly lives on a farm in Minnesota where he edits *The Seventies* (formerly *The Fifties* and later *The Sixties*) and manages The Seventies Press (formerly The Sixties Press), which he founded. He graduated from Harvard and, though he hates to admit it, later did graduate work at the University of Iowa's Writers Workshop. In 1966 with David Ray he founded American Writers Against the Vietnam War, and in 1967 he won the National Book Award.

Among his contemporaries, Robert Bly is one of the few poets who has written a substantial amount of criticism, including essays for *Choice* and *The Nation,* and critical essays on the work of contemporary American poets for *The Fifties* and *The Sixties.* He has also translated Scandinavian fiction, Selma Lagerlof's *The Story of Gosta Berling* (1962) and Knut Hamsun's *Hunger* (1967), and he has edited and published various small anthologies, including *A Poetry Reading Against the Vietnam War* (1966).

Influenced by the thought of the 17th century German theosophist, Jacob Boehme, and the techniques of such 20th century Spanish surrealists as Lorca and Neruda, Bly's poems tend to be almost purely phenomenological. Revolting against the rationalism and empiricism of his century, Boehme emphasized an intuitive perception of the outer tangible world of men and things as being a symbol of the corresponding and truer inner spiritual world. The outward man is asleep, Boehme wrote; he is only the husk of the real inner man. Like Emerson, he insisted that men do not see nor respond to that inner spiritual world because "the wise of this world . . . have shut and locked us up in their art and their rationality, so that we have had to see with their eyes."

Bly himself has written that American poetry took a wrong turn, moving in "a destructive motion outward" rather than "plunge inward, trying for a great (spiritual and imaginative) intensity." In his revolt against Eliot's theory of the "objective correlative" and Pound's practice in the *Cantos* ("eating up more and more of the outer world, with less and less life at the center"), Bly has fashioned his poems after the work of the Spanish surrealists. In them he seems to have found a poetics which corresponds to Boehme's mysticism, enabling him to plunge beneath the phenomenology of surface and find images and words to suggest the inner reality and intensity of both the simple rural experience and international events.

GWENDOLYN BROOKS (1917)

Poetry

A Street in Bronzeville, New York: Harper & Brothers, Publishers, 1945.
Annie Allen, New York: Harper & Brothers, Publishers, 1949.
The Bean Eaters, New York: Harper & Brothers, Publishers, 1960.
Selected Poems, New York: Harper & Row, Publishers, 1963.
In the Mecca, New York: Harper & Row, Publishers, 1968.
Riot, Detroit: Broadside Press, 1969.

A graduate of Wilson Junior College in Chicago, Gwendolyn Brooks began her professional writing career in 1941 with Inez Stark Boulton's poetry workshop at the South Side Community Art Center in Chicago. In 1950 she won the Pulitzer Prize for her second book of poems, and in 1953 she published a novel, *Maud Martha*.

Gwendolyn Brooks' poems are often marked by a directness and boldness of social observation and language which precedes, indeed foreshadows, much of the "Black poetry" written by younger poets and the later poetry of LeRoi Jones. Her Negro hero's assertion: "I helped to save them . . . / Even if I had to kick their law into their teeth in order to do that for them," might well have been written in the 60's rather than in the 40's. In those poems addressed specifically to the horror of the Black experience in America, she is also capable of a range of emotions: brutal anger, wry satire and visionary serenity.

Informed by the range of the Negro experience and her own emotional objectivity, some of Gwendolyn Brooks' poems are also marked by the simplicity, quiet and gentility of a woman's sensibilities. And yet, in a poem like "The Mother," she also demonstrates the kind of fierce emotion which other women poets like Sylvia Plath and Anne Sexton have displayed in more consciously personal poems. But gentle or fierce, personal or social, her poems consistently affirm the common denominator of human experience in poetry and the community of men.

ROBERT CREELEY (1926)

Poetry

For Love, New York: Charles Scribner's Sons, 1962.
Words, New York: Charles Scribner's Sons, 1967.
The Charm, San Francisco: Four Seasons Foundation, 1969.
Pieces, New York: Charles Scribner's Sons, 1969.

Criticism

A Quick Graph, San Francisco: Four Seasons Foundation, 1970.

A New Englander by birth and perhaps sensibility, Robert Creeley was educated at Harvard, Black Mountain College and the University of New Mexico. He has traveled extensively and has taught at the University of New Mexico and Black Mountain College, where he also edited the influential journal, *Black Mountain Review.* Besides some 15 books of poems, he has also published a novel, *The Island* (1963) and a collection of short stories, *The Gold Diggers & Other Stories* (1965). He is currently teaching at the University of Buffalo.

In his poems Creeley often comes through as hung-up but cool, a kind of hip Puritan, Emily Dickinson's nephew, one-eyed, unvirginal and pot smoking. Creeley *is* hung-up: "I think I grow tensions/ like flowers. . . ." Pain is central to his work, a sharp, stinging pain evoked in such images as "I can/ feel my eye breaking." But even more crucial is love: "But I love you./ Do you love me./ What to say/ when you see me" might be a summary of his central concern. Indeed, Creeley has written some of the most lyrical love poems of the past two decades.

No essay or statement reveals Creeley's poetics as precisely as his own poems, especially "The Language" and "The Window." In the former he states simply: "Locate *I*. . . ." and in the latter he writes: "Position is where you put it, where it is. . . ." The position of the I, as locus, as viewer and speaker largely determines the form and direction of the poem. The position of words on the page results from the location of this I, who, by putting it where it is, speaks not only in grammatical units, but also in linear units. In other words, Creeley's poems evolve on both a sequential grammatical level and on a cumulative linear level, with each individual line reaffirming and/or modifying the sense of the sentence and of the poem.

JAMES DICKEY (1923)

Poetry

Into the Stone and Other Poems, New York: Charles Scribner's Sons, 1960.
Drowning with Others, Middletown: Wesleyan University Press, 1962.
Helmets, Middletown: Wesleyan University Press, 1964.
Buckdancer's Choice, Middletown: Wesleyan University Press, 1965.
Poems 1957–1967, Middletown: Wesleyan University Press, 1967.
The Eye-Beaters, Blood, Victory, Madness, Buckhead and Mercy, New York: Doubleday and Co., Inc., 1970.

Criticism

The Suspect in Poetry, Madison, Minnesota: The Sixties Press, 1964.
Babel to Byzantium, Poets & Poetry Now, New York: Farrar, Straus & Giroux, 1968.

James Dickey received his B.A. and M.A. from Vanderbilt University. He was a night fighter pilot during World War II and the Korean War and an advertising executive in Atlanta and New York. He has taught at Reed College, San Fernando Valley State and the University of Wisconsin. In 1966 he won the National Book Award, and between 1966 and 1968 he served as Consultant in Poetry to the Library of Congress. In 1970 he published a novel, *Deliverance.*

One of the less ostensibly 'academic' poets of his generation, Dickey's poems are marked by an exuberant language and a primal energy, passion and ritual. Probing to the most elemental in man, Dickey's poems often trace man's mythic subconscious and paradoxical evolution to a primitive level where men and animals become brothers and mates in the same irrational but holy species. From this viewpoint his poems are often reminiscent of Whitman's.

Simultaneously many of Dickey's poems are also marked by a Southern Puritanism. His characters are grotesque, physically or spiritually wounded. They are violent creatures; their brutal sexual love is immersed in pain and death. And they move about in a world churning with violence and profound evil that is as much inherent in the human condition as it is man-made. In other words, men and beasts are also brothers and mates in the same irrational and damned species. Dickey's vision, then, includes the polarities of light and grace, darkness and sin. The total impact of his poems is often the drama of Adam shimmering with primal light, awakening to guilt and finding it magical.

ALAN DUGAN (1923)

Poetry

Poems, New Haven: Yale University Press, 1961.
Poems 2, New Haven: Yale University Press, 1963.
Poems 3, New Haven: Yale University Press, 1967.
Collected Poems, New Haven: Yale University Press, 1969.

Born in Brooklyn and a graduate of Mexico City College, Alan Dugan is married to the daughter of the late Ben Shahn. His first book won the Yale Series of Younger Poets Award, the Pulitzer Prize and the National Book Award.

Although Dugan's work can be humorous, lyrical or cerebral, his most effective poems are tough, brutal and ugly. For William J. Martz' *The Distinctive Voice,* he wrote about his voice as a poet: "[I] am trying to say what is hardest to say; that is, words wrung out of intense experience and not constructed." This attempt has also resulted in hard poems. Moreover, as Richard Howard has said, in Dugan's poetry one senses that "the act of writing poetry is, precisely, an invocation of destruction, a luring of language to its wreck. . . . [He] is too honest . . . for the consolation of some visionary transcendence of language. . . ."

In many of his poems Dugan talks about the least public experiences in a language also generally considered the least public. Moreover, he refuses to burden his subject or language with any redeeming mystical, magical or Great Social impact. He tells it like it is, and, rather than be offensive (as one vaguely and uneasily wishes they were), his poems emerge as the product of a fierce honesty generating words that burn like acid through all pretense.

LAWRENCE FERLINGHETTI (1919)

Poetry

Pictures of the Gone World, San Francisco: City Lights Books, 1955.
A Coney Island of the Mind, New York: New Directions, 1958.
Starting from San Francisco, New York: New Directions, 1961; enlarged edition 1966.
The Secret Meaning of Things, New York: New Directions, 1969.
Tyrannus Nix, New York: New Directions, 1969.

Translations

Selections from Paroles by Jacques Prévert, San Francisco: City Lights Books, 1958.

Lawrence Ferlinghetti received an A. B. from the University of North Carolina, an M. A. from Columbia and a Doctorat de L'Université from the Sorbonne. He is the owner and manager of City Lights Books, the paperback bookstore and publishing house in San Francisco. His writings include fiction, *Her* (1960), and drama, *Unfair Arguments with Existence* (1963) and *Routines* (1964).

In a "Note on Poetry in San Francisco" (1958), Ferlinghetti wrote: "the kind of poetry which has been making the most noise here . . . is what should be called street poetry. For it amounts to getting the poet out of the inner esthetic sanctum where he has too long been contemplating his complicated navel. It amounts to getting poetry back into the street where it once was, out of the classroom, out of the speech department, and—in fact—off the printed page. The printed word has made poetry so silent." Ferlinghetti's own poems are often conceived as "oral messages," designed primarily for their oral impact and often sharing the characteristics of popular songs. Intended to be understood by the ear, not by the eye, they often lack the density and complexity of the printed poem. For the same reason, they often depend on the (literary) cliché which serves much the same function as the formula in ancient oral poetry.

Like Hart Crane, Ferlinghetti sees the poet as "a charleychaplin man," and with a measure of self-directed irony which Crane never could quite muster, he admits that the poet is "constantly risking absurdity." Thus in his poems, while engaging in slapstick and often corny humor, aimed at socio-cultural evils and absurdities, he pokes fun at the world, himself, seeks moments of tenderness, sometimes succumbs to sentimentality, and occasionally discovers moments of terror.

ALLEN GINSBERG (1926)

Poetry

Howl and Other Poems, San Francisco: City Lights Books, 1956.
Empty Mirror: Early Poems, New York: Totem Books, 1961.
Kaddish and Other Poems, 1958–1960, San Francisco: City Lights Books, 1961.
Reality Sandwiches, San Francisco: City Lights Books, 1963.
T. V. Baby Poems, London: Cape Goliard, 1967.
Airplane Dreams, Toronto: Anansis Press, 1968.
Ankor Wat, London: Fulcrum Press, 1968.
Planet News, 1961–1967, San Francisco: City Lights Books, 1968.
Indian Journals, San Francisco: Dave Haselwood Books, 1969.

Correspondence

The Yage Letters (with William Burroughs), San Francisco: City Lights Books, 1963.

Biographical and Critical Studies

Ehrlich, J. W. E. *Howl of the Censor,* San Francisco: Nourse Publishing Co., 1956.
Kramer, Jane. *Allen Ginsberg in America,* New York: Random House Inc., 1969.
Merrill, Thomas F. *Allen Ginsberg,* New York: Twayne Publishers, Inc., 1969.

Born in Newark, New Jersey, Allen Ginsberg attended Columbia University, was dismissed, returned and received his B. A. in 1949. Poet, guru, world traveller, prophet of the Beat Generation and visionary Uncle Sam of the Flower-Acid-Rock Generation, Ginsberg may well be the planet's most renowned poet.

To date Allen Ginsberg's notoriety as socio-cultural *enfant terrible* has obscured his power as a poet. Nevertheless, he is recognized by his contemporaries as one of the most influential post-War poets, whose first major poem, "Howl," is a milestone of the generation, perhaps as significant a poem and document as Eliot's "Wasteland," and whose entire work may eventually achieve the stature of *Leaves of Grass*.

At once intimate and prophetic, hilarious and terrifying, profoundly religious and, at times, outrageously queer, Ginsberg's poetry encompasses a myriad of experiences ranging over the full spectrum of human life on this planet, and, like the poetry of Whitman, is a combination of incredible power and drivel. But clearly in technique, scope and intent, Whitman is Ginsberg's model and mentor; like him, Ginsberg is attempting to recreate not only the world, but also the full dimensions of a man's physical and spiritual odyssey through a given moment in history, with the crucial difference that Whitman's poems were hefty songs and Ginsberg's are often reverberating lamentations.

Part of Ginsberg's impact and strength results from his prophetic stance as a man and as a poet, sustained by the vital presence and spirit of William Blake and the prophets of the Old Testament. A modern-day Isaiah, Ginsberg is the public conscience of the nation, if not of the species, lamenting the imponderable evil man has perpetrated against life. But like Isaias, Blake and Whitman, he is also moved by a profound belief in the holiness of life and by a vision of a new Jerusalem, a new world.

LEROI JONES (1934)

Poetry

Preface to a Twenty Volume Suicide Note, New York: Totem-Corinth Books, 1961.
The Dead Lecturer, New York: Grove Press, 1964.
Black Magic: Poetry 1961–1967, Indianapolis: The Bobbs-Merril Company, 1969.

Born in Newark, LeRoi Jones holds degrees from Howard, Columbia and the New School for Social Research. He has taught at the New School, Columbia and Buffalo. The founder of Totem Press, Jones has also written a novel, *The System of Dante's Hell* (1965), three books of essays, including *Home: Social Essays* (1966), and several plays which have been published and produced. He has received various awards and fellowships, including a Guggenheim fellowship (1965–1966).

Admitting the influence of Pound, Williams and Charles Olson's concept of "projective verse," in Donald M. Allen's *The New American Poetry,* Jones said: "MY POETRY is whatever I think I am. . . . I CAN BE ANYTHING I CAN. I make poetry with what I feel is useful & can be saved out of all the garbage of our lives. What I see, am touched by (CAN HEAR) . . . wives, gardens, jobs, cement yards where cats pee, all my interminable artifacts . . . ALL are poetry. . . ." Some of his early poems also reflect Jones' affiliation with Frank O'Hara and other New York poets.

Jones has also said: "I have always thought of writing as a moral art; that is, basically, I think of the artist as a moralist, as demanding a moral construct of the world, as asking for a cleaner vision of society. . . ." Since his participation in the Black Nationalist movement, Jones' vision and poetics have been unmistakably moral, perhaps didactic. In his introduction to *Black Magic* Jones wrote: "We are spiritual, and we must force this issue, we must see our selves again, as black men, as the strength of the planet, and rise to rebuild what is actually spiritual, what is actually good. . . ." As he makes clear in "Black Art," the function of poetry in this vision is not aesthetic, but rather social, a political gesture, a medium for revolution: "we want 'poems that kill.'/ Assassin poems, Poems that shoot/guns."

Like much of the political and anti-war poetry written during the sixties and much of the Black poetry published to date, Jones' later verse, often powerful and moving, challenges many basic assumptions about the nature and function of poetry. Thus his poems are aesthetic and critical, as well as social and moral challenges.

KENNETH KOCH (1925)

Poetry

Poems, New York: Tibor de Nagy Gallery, 1953.
Ko, or a Season on Earth, New York: Grove Press, 1959.
Permanently, New York: Tiber Press, 1960.
Thank You and Other Poems, New York: Grove Press, 1962.
Poems from 1952 and 1953, New York: Black Sparrow Press, 1968.
The Pleasures of Peace, New York: Grove Press, 1969.
When the Sun Tries to Go On, New York: Black Sparrow Press, 1969.

Born in Cincinnati, Ohio, Kenneth Koch has degrees from Harvard and Columbia. He has lived in Italy and France and now teaches at Columbia and conducts a poetry workshop at the New School. The author of plays produced off-Broadway, a collection of plays, *Bertha and Other Plays* (1966), and a mock-epic poem, *Ko,* he has also received Fulbright and Guggenheim grants.

Kenneth Koch is generally recognized as one of the finest comic poets of his generation. But Koch's humor, as Paul Carroll has rightfully observed, is not a cerebral, metaphysical wit à *la* Auden or Stevens. For Donald M. Allen's *The New American Poetry,* Koch wrote that while in France he became very excited by French poetry. "I began to try to get the same incomprehensible excitement into my own work . . . to recreate the excitement I had felt." That excitement is present in the humor of his poems which, though unmistakably literate and sophisticated, are marked by a genuine spontaneity and exuberance.

The incomprehensible is equally central to Koch's poems. Although funny, they are also often macabre, as in the last stanza of his spoof on William Carlos Williams' poem: "I was clumsy and/ I wanted you here in the wards, where I am the doctor!" Moreover, one senses that the poet is trapped in an absurd situation, the victim of "an absolute and total misunderstanding (but not fatal)." Koch's poems are the kind Kafka might have written if he'd had a greater sense of humor.

DENISE LEVERTOV (1923)

Poetry

With Eyes at the Back of Our Heads, New York: New Directions, 1959.
The Jacob's Ladder, New York: New Directions, 1962.
O Taste and See, New York: New Directions, 1964.
The Sorrow Dance, New York: New Directions, 1966.
Relearning the Alphabet, New York: New Directions, 1970.

Translations

Selected Poems of Guillevic, New York: New Directions, 1969.

Critical Study

Wagner, Linda Welshimer. *Denise Levertov,* New York: Twayne Publishers, Inc., 1967.

Denise Levertov was born in England and privately educated. She is married to the novelist Mitchell Goodman. She has been Poetry Editor for *The Nation*, she has taught at Vassar, Drew and the YMHA Poetry Center and has been a Guggenheim Fellow, a Scholar of the Radcliffe Institute for Independent Study, and a recipient of a grant from the National Institute of Arts and Letters. During the past few years especially she and her husband have been active participants in the anti-war movement in this country.

Influenced by William Carlos Williams and the Black Mountain Poets, the poems of Denise Levertov nevertheless are charged by a distinctive voice. Clearly this is a woman's voice, capable of gentility and warm, though intense, lyricism; at the same time, without being brutal or hysterical, this voice is also capable of being direct and tough. But her poems are not simply spoken by a woman; they also fully explore and, with assurance and pleasure, celebrate the multi-faceted female psyche and experience.

In "Art" Denise Levertov says: "The best work is made/ from hard, strong materials,/ obstinately precise. . . ." Her poems repeatedly assert that the most obstinate and hard materials are not onyx and steel, but rather, the small, at times elusive materials of daily human life. And an anti-war poem like "The Altars in the Street" affirms the inestimable power of the human gesture over "the frenzy of weapons, their impudent power."

JOHN LOGAN (1923)

Poetry

Cycle for Mother Cabrini, New York: Grove Press, 1955.
Ghosts of the Heart, Chicago: University of Chicago Press, 1960.
Spring of the Thief, Poems 1960–1962, New York: A. A. Knopf, 1963.
The Zig-Zag Walk, Poems 1963–1968, New York: E. P. Dutton & Co., Inc., 1969.

Born in Red Oak, Iowa, John Logan received his B. A. in zoology from Coe College and his M. A. in English from the University of Iowa. He has also done graduate work in philosophy at Georgetown, Notre Dame and Berkeley, and he has taught at Notre Dame, San Francisco State and the University of Buffalo. He served as Poetry Editor for *The Nation* and with Aaron Siskind has been editing *Choice*—a magazine of poetry and photography which he founded. His work also includes critical essays, short stories, and children's literature.

Although John Logan's poems are often personal, they differ considerably from the work of other personal poets. Logan's are far less confessional: he spares us the brutal details of failure, guilt and deterioration and suggests them rather, not asking the reader to be father confessor. At his best Logan's poems are genuinely personal and natural, determined neither by thematic nor structural formula. They succeed in sounding as natural as breathing, beginning simply and growing in intensity and power out of their own necessity, as the breath of a man in battle or in love, rising to a discovery of personal epiphanies. They are as "unpredictable as grace."

Perhaps because he began his career as a scientist, Logan's poems are also constructed out of the most minute details from the world around him, and such lines as "I let the rain/ move its audible little hands/ gently on my skin" suggest the thrilling sensuousness of his language. He lingers on things and their words, delighting in their sound and texture. In Logan's poetry suffering does not negate the fact of beauty or the possibility of celebration. Pain and guilt do not negate the alternatives of joy and grace. His poems repeatedly affirm that "there is a freshness/ nothing can destroy in us—/ not even we ourselves."

ROBERT LOWELL (1917)

Poetry

Land of Unlikeness, Cambridge: The Cummington Press, 1944.
Lord Weary's Castle, New York: Harcourt, Brace & Co., 1946.
The Mills of the Kavanaughs, New York: Harcourt, Brace & Co., 1951.
Life Studies, New York: Farrar, Straus & Cudahy, 1959.
Imitations, New York: Farrar, Straus & Cudahy, 1961.
For the Union Dead, New York: Farrar, Straus & Giroux, 1964.
Near the Ocean, New York: Farrar, Straus & Giroux, 1964.
Notebook 1967–1968, New York: Farrar, Straus & Giroux, 1969.

Translations

Phaedra, New York: Farrar, Straus & Cudahy, 1961.
The Voyage & Other Versions of Poems by Baudelaire, New York: Farrar, Straus & Giroux, 1968.

Bibliography

Mazzaro, Jerome. *The Achievement of Robert Lowell, 1939–1959*, Detroit: University of Detroit Press, 1960.

Critical Studies

London, Michael and Robert Boyers, eds. *Robert Lowell: A Portrait of the Artist in His Time*, New York: David Lewis Publishers, Inc., 1970.
Mazzaro, Jerome. *The Poetic Themes of Robert Lowell*, Ann Arbor: University of Michigan Press, 1965.
Parkinson, Thomas, ed. *Robert Lowell*, Englewood Cliffs: Prentice-Hall, Inc., 1968.
Staples, Hugh B. *Robert Lowell: The First Twenty Years*, New York: Farrar, Straus & Cudahy, 1962.

Robert Lowell attended Harvard and graduated from Kenyon College in 1940. During World War II, after trying to enlist in the armed forces and being rejected, he was drafted. Convinced that the saturation bombing raids against enemy civilians were not justifiable, he refused to serve and spent several months in jail as a conscientious objector. He has taught at various colleges and universities, including Harvard, the University of Iowa, and Boston University. He served as Poetry Consultant to the Library of Congress in 1947, and his many awards include the Pulitzer Prize (1947) and the National Book Award (1960).

To date Lowell has shaped his career in three stages. His early poems, written under the tutelage of John Crowe Ransom and Allen Tate, were intricately wrought and complex, clearly reflecting the dictates of new criticism. Evolving out of a Christian spiritual tradition, an English poetic tradition and a New England historical and ethical tradition, they were poems written by a young man whose sensibilities and talent began to mature at a time when T. S. Eliot was an overpowering presence in American poetry.

In *Life Studies*, perhaps his most brilliant and significant book, Lowell implicitly renounced many of the new critics' formal demands and Eliot's later cultural and spiritual vision. His poems were less consciously wrought and extremely intimate. As M. L. Rosenthal has observed, the orchestration of *Life Studies* asserted and traced the deterioration of Western tradition and civilization, the U. S. republic, his family and his self. In the powerful concluding poem, "Skunk Hour," Lowell asserted "The season's ill . . . My mind's not right." And in this cultural and personal wasteland there was no kingfisher, no Christ diving in fire.

"I am tired. Everyone's tired of my turmoil," Lowell wrote in *For* the *Union Dead,* and this affirmation seems to mark the beginning of the third phase of his career. His more recent poems have been serenely formal, less intricate still, and surely less hysterical. In *Near the Ocean* he turns to muted couplets and his *Notebook* is in effect a sonnet sequence. Although his central theme of the desolation and deterioration of man and his world remains, Lowell is able to view that drama with a measure of objectivity, distance and at times profound detachment.

W. S. MERWIN (1927)

Poetry

A Mask for Janus, New Haven: Yale University Press, 1952.
The Dancing Bears, New Haven: Yale University Press, 1954.
Green with Beasts, New York: A. A. Knopf, 1956.
The Drunk in the Furnace, New York: The Macmillan Co., 1960.
The Moving Target, New York: Atheneum, 1963.
The Lice, New York: Atheneum, 1967.
Animae, San Francisco: Kayak Books Inc., 1969.

Translations

The Satires of Persius, Bloomington: Indiana University Press, 1961.
The Poem of the Cid, New York: New American Library, 1962.
Lazarillo de Tormes, New York: Doubleday & Co., Inc., 1963.
Spanish Ballads, New York: Doubleday & Co., Inc., 1963.
Selected Translations, New York: Atheneum, 1968.
Voices (Antonio Porchia), Chicago: Follett Publishing Co., 1969.
Products of the Perfected Civilization (Chamfort), New York: The Macmillan Co., 1969.
Transparence of the World (Jean Follain), New York: Atheneum, 1969.
Twenty Poems of Love and A Song of Despair (Pablo Neruda), London: Cape Editions, 1969.

Born in New York City and a graduate of Princeton, W. S. Merwin has been poetry Editor for *The Nation* and has worked as a tutor in France, Portugal and Spain. Since 1951 he has devoted most of his time to writing, giving poetry readings and translating from French, Spanish, Latin and Portugese. He has lived in the United States and England and currently lives in the South of France.

Among contemporary poets whose talents were shaped by new criticism, Merwin is also one whose style has undergone a radical change in the course of his career. His early poems were elegant, controlled, symmetrical, informed by expected myth and archetype. *The Drunk in the Furnace,* however, suggested a dissatisfaction with old techniques. His forms were looser; his language less contrived, closer to the spoken word; and like other poets of the moment he too turned to family history and individual human suffering. But his new and most exciting style broke through only in *The Moving Target.* Open, terse, these surrealistic poems are controlled not as much by a craftsman's delicate hand as by a powerful imagination and rising out of the depths of necessity.

Throughout his career one of Merwin's dominant concerns has been death—especially extinction. Coupled with the journey motif which critics have recognized, in Merwin's poetry all life is a motion toward death. In the later poems this concern becomes more immediate, more personal, more intense. For he sees and anticipates not only the extinction of certain forms of life, but indeed the annihilation of all life. Moreover, Merwin seems to agree with Berryman that man has undertaken the biggest job of all: *son fin.*

FRANK O'HARA (1926–1966)

Poetry

Meditations in an Emergency, New York: Grove Press, 1957.
Second Avenue, New York: Corinth Books, 1960.
Odes, New York: The Tiber Press, 1960.
Lunch Poems, San Francisco: City Lights Books, 1964.

Before his untimely death, Frank O'Hara was Editorial Associate for *Art News* and Associate Curator of the Department of Paintings and Sculptures at the Museum of Modern Art. A graduate of Harvard and the University of Michigan, he received the Avery Hopwood Award for poetry, and his work includes not only poetry but also plays and art criticism.

Like the work of his contemporaries in the graphic arts, Frank O'Hara's poetry is marked by a spontaneity, exuberance and wit. Light and chatty, his often seem to be anti-poems, the product of a pop-camp imagination. In 1959 O'Hara wrote, "I am mainly preoccupied with the world as I experience it. . . ." That world consists primarily of New

York city streets and apartments, and his poems, like the paintings of Warhol and Oldenburg, focus on the obvious, every-day things of this world: hamburgers, malts, cigarettes, instant coffee.

Looming above this world, however, are its own immortals and gods, Lichtenstein's supra-human heroes of the comic strips and O'Hara's movie stars. Their mythic proportions in fiction and in real life are the dimensions of contemporary man's fantasies and dreams. Thus beneath the adolescent awe and excitement in O'Hara's poems there crackles a stinging, if somewhat hysterical, comment on the quality of contemporary man's experience.

SYLVIA PLATH (1932–1963)

Poetry

The Colossus, New York: A. A. Knopf, 1962.
Uncollected Poems (a pamphlet), London: Turret Books, 1965.
Ariel, New York: Harper & Row, Publishers, 1966.

Critical Study

Newman, Charles, ed. *The Art of Sylvia Plath,* Bloomington: Indiana University Press, 1970.

A native of Boston and a graduate of Smith College, in 1955 Sylvia Plath won a Fulbright Scholarship to Newnham College, Cambridge. While in England she met and married the British poet, Ted Hughes. After a year of teaching at Smith, the Hugheses returned to England. In 1962, under the pseudonym of Victoria Lucas, she published a novel, *The Bell Jar.* On February 11, 1963, Sylvia Plath committed suicide.

A friend of Anne Sexton and Robert Lowell's student, Sylvia Plath wrote poems that are not only brutally personal, but also almost unbearably painful. Moreover, the poems are not merely *about* acute mental and emotional suffering; their very structure—the flow of images, the insistent appositive—draws the reader fully into that suffering. So frightfully honest and painfully personal are her later poems that some critics have argued that after writing them her suicide was perhaps inevitable. She seemed engaged in "a murderous art."

However, Sylvia Plath's poems are not distinguished only by suffering and honesty. In poems like "Cut" and "Lady Lazarus" there is also a strong measure of wit and humor—albeit somewhat black—often conveyed through resuscitated clichés which manage to rescue the poems from pathos. But even more important, the success of her poems rests largely on the precision of her imagination (the onion simile in "Cut" which not only accurately describes the swirls of a thumb print, but also serves as the entire poem's controlling metaphor) and on the mastery of her craftsmanship.

On more than one occasion Sylvia Plath insisted that even the most personal poetry could not be merely a *cris de coeur;* it had to be informed by and participate in a greater historical drama. Her own poems participate fully in the vibrant Puritan tradition, not only through her preoccupation with evil, but also through her metaphysical and emblematic technique. They also occur against a constant historical drama, especially the contemporary phenomenon of Nazi Germany in which she discovers (or fabricates) a modern myth. In short, the pain, the suffering, the edge of madness—all are ultimately controlled by the fine hand of genius.

ANNE SEXTON (1928)

Poetry

To Bedlam and Part Way Back, Boston: Houghton Mifflin Co., 1960.
All My Pretty Ones, Boston: Houghton Mifflin Co., 1962.
Live or Die, Boston: Houghton Mifflin Co., 1966.
Love Poems, Boston: Houghton Mifflin Co., 1969.

Born in Newton, Massachusetts, according to a short autobiographical note she wrote for *A Controversy of Poets,* Anne Sexton received "no visible education." However, with Sylvia Plath and George Starbuck she did study under Robert Lowell at Boston University. Her many awards include fellowships from the American Academy of Arts and Letters, the Radcliffe Institute for Independent Study and the Ford Foundation. In 1967 she received the Pulitzer Prize and in 1968 she was elected a Fellow of the Royal Society of Literature in London.

As an inscription for her second book, Anne Sexton chose an excerpt from one of Kafka's letters in which he wrote that the kind of books we need are those that "make us feel as though we were on the verge of suicide." "A book," Kafka added, "should serve as the ax for the frozen sea within us." If Mrs. Sexton's poems slash at our emotional complacency, they do so because she consistently focuses on the most intimate and private details of her life and recreates the seemingly factual and emotional dimensions of each experience with unabashed, at times embarrassing honesty.

Someone once facetiously remarked that Anne Sexton has written about every physical and emotional trauma a middle-aged woman could conceivably experience. Closer to the truth, however, is Ralph J. Mills' observation that few poets "have attempted to convey the feeling of the continuity of a single life" as has Anne Sexton. It does seem possible to trace her progress from the hysteria of a young woman's breakdown to the more stable intensity of a vibrant middle-aged woman's encounter with human life.

However, in an interview with Patricia Marx, Mrs. Sexton warned against the lie of fabrication. Truth, even the most brutal, in a poem is sifted and remolded by the imagination's energy and the craftsman's hand. So that what evolves in Anne Sexton's poems is a fabricated, and not a wholly factual life.

W. D. SNODGRASS (1926)

Poetry

Heart's Needle, New York: A. A. Knopf, 1959.
After Experience, New York: Harper & Row, Publishers, 1968.

Translations

Gallows Songs (Hans Morgenstern), Ann Arbor: University of Michigan Press, 1967.

W. D. Snodgrass was educated at Geneva College and the University of Iowa. In 1958 he was the Hudson Review Fellow in Poetry and in 1960 his first book won the Pulitzer Prize. He has taught at Cornell University, the University of Rochester, Wayne State University and Syracuse University.

As Paul Carroll notes, Snodgrass writes a kind of "down-home" personal poetry. Unlike Lowell, Plath and Sexton, Snodgrass makes poetry, not out of madness and sensationally violent suffering, but rather out of the daily neuroses and everyday failures of a man, husband, father and teacher. Moreover, Snodgrass sees this domestic suffering as occurring against a backdrop of a more universal suffering and tragedy, a suffering which is inherent in the whole of man's experience, in the universe itself. In "Heart's Needle," he demonstrates and says: "We need the landscape to repeat us."

Although noted for their candor, Snodgrass' poems are nevertheless controlled by an unmistakable sense of irony, directed by a highly literate and organic imagination shaped by the New Critics, and organized by a consciously formal craftsmanship. Never intensely or vehemently personal, Snodgrass has achieved a measure of distance between himself as subject and himself as object. Thus the speaker of a Snodgrass poem often sounds like a personal-confessional persona.

With a number of his contemporaries Snodgrass shares that fundamental concern of the generation which Albert Camus announced: "There is but one truly serious philosophical problem, and that is suicide." In "April Inventory" he writes: "I have not learned how often I/ Can win, can love, but choose to die." And in "Heart's Needle" he says: "Of all things, only we/ have power to choose that we should die. . . ."

GARY SNYDER (1930)

Poetry

Myths & Texts, New York, Totem-Corinth Books, 1960.
Six Sections from Mountains and Rivers without End, San Francisco: Four Seasons Foundation, 1965.
The Back Country, New York: New Directions, 1968.
Riprap & Cold Mountain Poems, San Francisco: Four Seasons Foundation, 1969.

Essays

Earth House Hold, Technical Notes & Queries To Fellow Dharma Revolutionaries, New York: New Directions, 1969.

Born in San Francisco, Gary Snyder received his B. A. in Literature and Anthropology from Reed College. He did further study in Oriental Languages at Berkeley and later studied Zen in a monastery in Kyoto, Japan. He has worked as a seaman, logger and forester and has taught at Berkeley.

In *Six San Francisco Poets,* David Kherdian quotes Snyder as saying: "As much as the books I've read, the jobs I've had have been significant in shaping me. My sense of body and language and the knowledge that intelligence and insight, sensitivity, awareness, and brilliance are not limited to educated people, or anything like it." Among his contemporaries Gary Snyder perhaps has been most successful in writing what might be called a poetry of and for the common man. Marked by an elemental reverence for life, many of his poems are simple and direct, salvaging poetry from the most basic human experience.

The simplicity, however, is not simplistic, for it reflects the profound influence of Zen on Snyder's sensibility and thought. As Snyder has said: "A poet faces two directions: one is to the world of people and language and society, and the other is the nonhuman, nonverbal world, which is nature as nature is itself; and the world of human nature—the inner world, as it is itself, before language, before custom, before culture. There's no words in that realm."

Snyder's participation in the response to both the inner and outer worlds has resulted in a primitive identification with nature and a contemporary concern for the ecological consequences of progress and civilization. "As a poet," Snyder has said, "I hold the most archaic values on earth. They go back to the late Paleolithic: the fertility of the soil, the magic of animals, the power-vision in solitude, the terrifying initiation and rebirth, the love and ecstasy of the dance, the common work of the tribe. I try to hold both history and wilderness in mind, that my poems may approach the true measure of things and stand against the unbalance and ignorance of our times."

RICHARD WILBUR (1921)

Poetry

The Beautiful Changes and Other Poems, New York: Reynal & Hitchcock, 1947.

Ceremony and Other Poems, New York: Harcourt, Brace & Co., 1950.

Things of This World: Poems by Richard Wilbur, New York: Harcourt, Brace, & Co., 1956.

Advice to a Prophet and Other Poems, New York: Harcourt, Brace & World, 1961.

The Poems of Richard Wilbur, New York: Harcourt, Brace & World, 1963.

Walking to Sleep, New York: Harcourt, Brace & World, 1969.

Translations

The Misanthrope, New York: Harcourt, Brace & Co., 1955.

Tartuffe, New York: Harcourt, Brace & World, 1963.

Critical Study

Hill, Donald. *Richard Wilbur*, New York: Twayne Publishers, Inc., 1967.

A graduate of Amherst and Harvard, Richard Wilbur has taught at Harvard and Wellesley and is now Professor of English at Wesleyan University where he is also an editor of the Wesleyan University Press poetry series. His many prizes and honors include the Pulitzer Prize and the National Book Award (both in 1957), a Guggenheim Fellowship, the Prix de Rome and a Ford Fellowship. His work includes an operetta, *Candide* (1957) with Lillian Hellman, and several collections, including *A Bestiary* (1955).

Among contemporary poets whose sensibilities were shaped by the New Critics, Wilbur is the consummate artist. His poetry is marked by grace, wit and a masterful craftsmanship. In his statement for John Ciardi's *Mid-Century American Poets,* Wilbur affirmed the poet's need for form, for "artistry," saying that "limitation makes for power: the strength of the genie comes of his being confined in a bottle." Elsewhere he has also stated that the poet must move "to attempt a maximum range" and to do so "without apparent strain." At his best Wilbur's mastery of language and form is not merely without strain—it is dazzling and breathtaking.

The precision of sensuous detail and the verbal *entrechats* in Wilbur's poems are formal affirmations of his profound humanism, his belief in man's potential natural grace in this "world of sensible objects." In an era which has traced the deterioration of the social and psychic fabric and has proclaimed man and his world to be absurd, Wilbur has consistently sought for "a reconciliation between joy and pleasure, between acceptance and transcendence." By so doing he has found the possibility of beauty and grace.

JAMES WRIGHT (1927)

Poetry

The Green Wall, New Haven: Yale University Press, 1957.
Saint Judas, Middletown: Wesleyan University Press, 1959.
The Lion's Tail and Eyes, Poems Written Out of Laziness and Silence (with Robert Bly and William Duffy), Madison, Minnesota: The Sixties Press, 1962.

The Branch Will Not Break, Middletown: Wesleyan University Press, 1963.

Shall We Gather at the River, Middletown: Wesleyan University Press, 1968.

Translations

Twenty Poems of Georg Trakl (with Robert Bly), Madison, Minnesota: The Sixties Press, 1963.

Twenty Poems of Cesar Vallejo (with Robert Bly and John Knoepfle), Madison, Minnesota: The Sixties Press, 1964.

Twenty Poems of Pablo Neruda (with Robert Bly), Madison, Minnesota: The Sixties Press, 1967.

James Wright received his B.A. from Kenyon College, his M.A. and Ph.D. from the University of Washington, and he attended the University of Vienna as a Fulbright Scholar. The recipient of several grants and fellowships, he has taught at the University of Washington, Macalester College and is currently with the English Department at Hunter College.

Like many other poets of his generation, James Wright's style has undergone a radical change in the course of his career. With the publication of his first book, Wright stated that he "wanted to make [his] poems say something humanly important" and that he'd "tried very hard to write in the mode of Robert Frost and Edwin Arlington Robinson." After his second book, however, he asserted: "Whatever I write from now on will be entirely different."

According to Robert Bly, Wright's decision to a great extent was the result of his having read the German poet, Georg Trakl, a contemporary of Goethe. "In Trakl," Bly writes, "a series of images makes a series of events. Because these events appear out of their 'natural' order, without the connection we have learned to expect from reading newspapers, doors silently open into unused parts of the brain." In Wright's poems the doors often open to startling images, strange but emotionally precise.

In his early poems such as "In Shame and Humiliation," Wright was primarily concerned with his response to the life and suffering of others. His later poems are more personal, more inward, discovering in his own subconscious and imagination the secret pools of human fear and joy. The poems themselves rise, evolving quietly through layers of images, up until they surface with the quick thrust of a striking final image and epiphany.

Contemporary American Poetry:
The Radical Tradition

American poetry since 1945 may be viewed as the product of the dialectics of generations. A recurrent phenomenon in literary (as well as in much of human) history, the pattern of one generation's revolt against another is familiar indeed. That rebellion, however, is usually not so much against the generation as against its excesses: principle atrophied into prejudice, freshness of thought and sensibility petrified into cliché, discipline forged into tyranny. The revolution also doesn't always succeed in realizing a clean break with the immediate or distant past; the blood, the genes remain camouflaged by a radical façade.

Emphasizing the freshness of contemporary poetry, poets and critics have argued that it reflects a violent break with modernist poetry, if not with all of tradition. In the Introduction to his anthology of contemporary American poetry (1962), Donald Hall announced that the orthodoxy of T. S. Eliot and the New Critics had ceased: "In modern art anarchy has proved preferable to the restrictions of a benevolent tyranny." The modern artist, Hall wrote, "has acted as if restlessness were a conviction and has destroyed his own past in order to create a future." In *The Poem In Its Skin* (1968), Paul Carroll argues that today's poets have attempted "to write poems either alien or hostile to the poem as defined and explored by Eliot and leading writers dominating the scene ten or fifteen years ago." Later he asserts: "this generation of American poets is on the high, happy adventure of creating and innovating a complex of new ways in which to view our common condition—an adventure which in its abundance, freshness and originality is . . . as interesting as any since the Olympians of 1917."

That the adventure of today's poets is somewhat anarchic but abundantly fresh is unquestionable. That it has produced poems entirely alien to modernist poetry is open to much debate. But the notion that the contemporary poet has destroyed his own past, for whatever reasons, is hogwash. Admittedly, T. S. Eliot may have been poetically, temperamentally and constitutionally incapable of writing a poem like Sylvia Plath's "Daddy" or Frank O'Hara's campy poem to Lana Turner. And the New Critics may not quite know what to make of such poems. (When confronted by the poems in *Life Studies*, Allen Tate reportedly turned to Lowell and agonizingly blurted "But, *Cal*, it's not *poetry!*")

Nevertheless, although the dicta of the New Critics have not been regarded as sacred commandments by contemporary poets, they haven't been ignored altogether either. Nor have the older and more profound Whitman and Puritan traditions; they are still active and vital, influencing the formal and thematic directions of much contemporary poetry. If today's poets have achieved a unique vitality, they have done so by making full use of the past, immediate and distant, personal and communal, while simultaneously contributing new and exciting elements of their own.

The characteristics of the modernist poem are obviously vital elements in the work of such poets as Richard Wilbur, John Berryman and Robert Lowell, the younger poets of the modernist generation whose sensibilities were shaped by new criticism. Commenting on his own poetry in *Poets on Poetry,* Wilbur said: "Most American poets of my generation were taught to admire the English Metaphysical poets of the seventeenth century and such contemporary masters of irony as John Crowe Ransom. We were led by our teachers and by the critics whom we read to feel that the most adequate and convincing poetry is that which accommodates mixed feelings, clashing ideas and incongruous images. Poetry could not be honest, we thought, unless it began by acknowledging the full discordancy of modern life and consciousness. I still believe that to be a true view of poetry. . . ." Written under the tutelage of John Crowe Ransom and Allen Tate, Robert Lowell's early work was immediately hailed as a model of what the modernist poem should and could be. And even for his recent monumental series of dream songs, John Berryman clearly employed the basic techniques of modernist poetry, including inventing a multi-dimensional persona, Henry Pussycat.

The major difference between modernist and contemporary poetry is that the latter is more intimate and personal. The elements of the modernist poem worked toward assuring a distance between the poet and his subject, the poet and his poem. From persona to tradition, each was a formal, emotional and intellectual means for the poet's objectification of his subject, emotion and medium. The unique personality of the poet, his more intimate experiences and emotions were not only absent, indeed they were virtually taboo, and in the hands of lesser poets such an attitude resulted in a depersonalized and inhuman versification.

In contemporary poetry, although means of objectification remain, the person is more vibrant than the persona; "he" is replaced by "I." The speaker of the poem and the poet are often one in the same person, and his subjects are his own personal, at times intimate experiences. Full appreciation of some contemporary poems hinges on the reader's knowledge of biographical information about the poet's life:

Robert Lowell was in fact jailed as a C.O., as he says in "Memories of West Street and Lepke"; Sylvia Plath's father was a German emigrant and, reputedly, "Pure Aryan, pure Nazi," as she implies in "Daddy." With the poet's private self as both subject and speaker of the poem, the interaction between the work of art and the reader becomes proportionately more intimate: the poet speaks directly to the reader, as if he were father confessor, psychiatrist, intimate friend or lover.

The personalization of poetry has evolved in various ways. In the work of Robert Bly, James Wright, and W. S. Merwin a personal poetry occurs as a result of the exploration of and response to the most inner reaches of the poet's self below the rational and conscious levels. Poems grow out of images discovered in the depths of human darkness; they are spoken by the voice of that most profound silence in a man. The poems of Allen Ginsberg and Frank O'Hara, on the other hand, although they contain moments of private joy and grief, depend primarily on the self's discovery of the outer world and response to it. The reader hears with O'Hara's ears or touches with Ginsberg's hands.

The personalization of poetry is most obvious in the work of those poets who reveal elements of their personality, events in their personal lives usually considered intimate, private or confidential. When the sexual deviance of some of this century's great poets remains among the best kept secrets in literary history, Allen Ginsberg's repeated avowal of his own deviance can be somewhat startling, albeit refreshing. Illness, madness, failure, a propensity for self-destruction—these are some of the re-occurring subjects of personal-confessional poets like Lowell, Plath, Sexton and Snodgrass.

Today's poets, then, have succeeded in making poetry often radically personal; but under closer scrutiny factors come into focus to temper that judgment. Subject and voice paradoxically work toward making even the most intimate poetry less personal than it first seems and toward erecting another kind of persona, i.e., that part of the poet's private self which he wishes to make public. Because they have been primarily concerned with physical and psychic limitations, the personal-confessional poets have written a poetry which to a large extent reveals only the deteriorating self speaking in a chosen voice, ranging from the modulated whine of W. D. Snodgrass to the near hysteria of Sylvia Plath. Moreover, in the work of some poets, technique and craftsmanship cause more doubt as to just how personal poetry can be; for by drawing formal attention, even the most personal poem reminds the reader that it is a fabrication. Like any art, personal poetry is a selective, calculated and public gesture, a formal utterance for which the poet selects a voice, one which is as approximate to his own as is manageable.

Irony and paradox are also present in the work of today's poets.

Confronted by the quality of our common condition, the sensitive and mature human being may not survive without a strong ironic sense; for although irony may thwart all genuine emotion, its absence also makes genuine emotion virtually impossible. The range and uses of irony in contemporary poetry can be seen in the work of two rather different poets: Sylvia Plath and Frank O'Hara. In Sylvia Plath's poetry, especially her later poems, the presence of irony serves to temper the intensity of emotion and suffering by under-cutting the vehement and often near-gothic imagery and emotion. Indeed, many of Sylvia Plath's more intense poems survive *as poems* because her sharp ironic sense is also at play. For example, "Lady Lazarus" is protected from bathos by the ironic sense of humor which not only views the would-be suicide as "The big strip tease" in a three-ring circus of horrors, but also through intonation and line break which begin the poem by suggesting that it is spoken by some rich Jewish lady coming out of a beauty spa like Maine Chance.

The irony in Frank O'Hara's poems may be more implicit—a broad and pervasive sense in the impetus of most of his poems; nevertheless, it is present and crucial. In the poem to Lana Turner, for example, especially in the effusive emotion of the last line, as well as in much of "To the Film Industry in Crisis," an ironic sensibility functions in an opposite manner to that in Plath's poetry: it undercuts the humor by suggesting the emptiness, if not the decadence, of the emotion. In other words, in O'Hara's poems one recognizes the peculiar contemporary phenomenon of camp irony.

Because contemporary poetry is intensely personal, it is also generally direct and transparent; but the essential complexity of emotion, the richness of words and the potential of form make ambiguity inescapable. For example, today's reader cannot avoid the basic *double entendre* in the opening lines of John Logan's "Love Poem": "Last night you would not come,/ and you have been gone so long." John Ashbery's use of wide open form and broken syntax in a poem like "Leaving the Atocha Station" often demands that the reader invent interpretation. Robert Creeley's poems depend largely on structural ambiguity—the emotional and thematic tension between the linear unit and the syntactical unit—for their introverted effect. By eliminating punctuation in his more recent poems, W. S. Merwin succeeds in creating an additional level of ambiguity, and John Berryman achieves still another level through a manipulation of pronouns referring to his schizoid persona.

The characteristic of the modernist poem which seems less prevalent than others in today's poetry is wit, especially as the word is used to refer to a kind of intellectual humor. A measure of this cerebral wit still can be found, but today's verse is generally marked by a humor which is broader, often a buffoonish or slapstick comedy. In his dream songs Berryman consciously uses minstrel comedy, situation comedy, as well as other techniques, including a kind of verbal double-take. Kenneth Koch is the academic and symbolist Red Skelton of his generation, the innocent clown bumbling through an absurd, though sophisticated universe. And, especially when he reads his poems, Lawrence Ferlinghetti, as Paul Carroll has observed, sounds like a hip Will Rogers. Moreover, in contemporary poetry the comedy often belies the poet's intent: humor verges on hysteria, laughter camouflages horror: Pagliacci facing a firing squad.

The reader of modern poetry has come to expect allusion as part and parcel of a poem. T. S. Eliot's "The Waste Land" is the archetype of the poem as footnote. However, contemporary poets, as Ferlinghetti has said, have consciously avoided the excesses of literary allusion which resulted in a "poetry about poetry." Although most post-War poets are university graduates and professional academicians, their poems do not obviously wear their erudition on their sleeves. The reasons are varied and complex. The scarcity of allusion in part is the result of the democratization of poetry and of the strong influence of Walt Whitman and William Carlos Williams on the Americanization of language and rhythm. Moreover, as mentioned above, contemporary poetry is often intensely personal, the poet responding to experience in a visceral rather than intellectual fashion. His response is not filtered or controlled by his knowledge or formal education nor shaped by his conscious sense of the formal tradition. That this is an age when the individual, the self is threatened by the dehumanization of a technocratic society and by the overwhelming sense of imminent atomic or ecological annihilation has long been a journalistic cliché. But the phenomenon is real and has resulted in the poet's vehement affirmation of his individual self and in an equally intense effort to respond fully and directly to experience both as a person and as an artist. This kind of Emersonian self-reliance (with absolute stakes) is an implicit refusal of the practice of Eliot's theory of tradition and the individual talent, because of contemporary man's profound fear of that history, culture and tradition which are ultimately responsible for the deterioration of the modern self.

Compared with the Eliot school of poetry, then, today's poetry is noticeably mean in allusion. However, as Susan Sontag has written, "language is the most impure, the most contaminated, the most exhausted of all materials out of which art is made. . . . It's scarcely possible for the artist to write a word (or render an image or make a gesture) that doesn't remind him of something already achieved." Consequently, because language is contaminated, because history shackles, and the post-War poet simply cannot escape his own ruthless memory, allusion, conscious or not, persists and is found in both expected and unexpected ways and places.

The more obvious examples of allusion may be found in the early work of Lowell and such poems as Snodgrass' "April Inventory," which can be read as a retelling of an academic Prufrock's story, with intermittent references to Shakespeare's Sonnet 73, Hopkins' "God's Grandeur," Edward Taylor's Meditation Six, First Series, and echoes of Thoreau and Camus. Ferlinghetti's "I Am Waiting," in spite of his renunciation of "poetry about poetry," relies heavily on obvious and well known literary phrases. In Ashbery's "Leaving the Atocha Station" Paul Carroll has ferreted out mangled echoes of Pound, Eliot, Hopkins and others. And as critics have noted, James Dickey's famous "The Heaven of Animals" is derivative of and perhaps consciously fashioned after Edwin Muir's "The Animals," and his poem, "Encounter in Cage Country," clearly calls to mind Rilke's "The Panther."

The burden of language and the grasp of memory result in other kinds of allusion. For example, the presence of Rilke is also felt in the concluding statement of James Wright's "Lying in a Hammock . . ." The position, tone and emotional impact of Wright's line ("I have wasted my life") is much the same and indeed echoes the concluding line of Rilke's "Torso of an Archaic Apollo" which C. F. MacIntyre has translated as "You must change your life." The imagery, tone and effect of Robert Bly's "Come with Me" make the poem sound like a verse rendition of part of Pablo Neruda's brief prose statement, "Toward Impure Poetry."

On the other hand, the personal and existential quality of today's poetry results in allusion to specific people, places and experiences in the poet's personal life: Wichita, Missoula, Pine Island, William Duffy, Dean Rusk, Lyndon Johnson, et al. Contemporary arts, especially the popular arts and performers, also become points of reference: movies, folk-rock, Lana Turner, Bob Dylan, Joan Baez. Contemporary poetry, then, is very much the poetry of today, the poetry of the day, requiring from the reader as much full consciousness of the present as of the past, of the banal as of the sublime.

If the contemporary poet is more drawn toward existential experience, he is also less inclined to use what Eliot called "the mythical method" to organize and present his experience. Indeed, myth, except as a sub-conscious, elemental and perhaps inevitable ritualistic pattern of human response, is virtually absent from the work of post-War poets. However, if the traditional mythic method at this moment in history is not viable, the mythical vision and the need for it remains an active force in contemporary poetry. Poets increasingly sense the necessity to be not simply myth users, but myth makers. Both as persons and as poets they reflect "the instinct that their work-a-day world is interpenetrated with a super-rational or extra-rational activity in which they can and do share." If the pattern of such more-than-human activity is not immediately accessible, then they must dig it out of the accumulation of their experience and create myths that are closer to the contemporary experience than those inherited from myth makers of the past.

In the poetry of W. D. Snodgrass there emerges a rather clear pattern of extra-rational activity against which the action of the poem takes place and in which the speaker senses inevitable participation. As he says in "Heart's Needle": "We need the landscape to repeat us." That pattern is quite simply Darwin's law of the survival of the fittest. Snodgrass may not be pleased to find himself participating in that brutal dialectic; but he recognizes its energy as one of the major determinants in human activity. He makes this clear in "After Experience," where he juxtaposes the rules for survival as spoken softly by Spinoza and shouted by a military instructor. The concern for survival is also the energy generating "April Inventory" in which case those who seem most fit to survive are the "solid scholars" who get "the degrees, the jobs, the dollars." The extent to which Darwin's law of evolution is the extra-rational pattern interpenetrating the poet's diurnal world is unmistakably clear in "Heart's Needle," especially in Part Nine when the speaker of the poem walks through the museum and recognizes that his experience with his estranged wife is similar to the gesture of primitive conflict in which the animals on display are engaged. Rather than turn to a fabricated myth construct of a pre-scientific age, Snodgrass has recognized and used a scientific law as a more cogent drama and myth for this age of science.

Other poets have discovered myth in other contemporary dramas and figures. For an age of violence Sylvia Plath has turned away from ancient mythology (the Colossus of Rhodes) and toward more recent history (Hiroshima and Hitler's concentration camps) for the mythic background against and in which her personal suffering occurs. For an age of media Frank O'Hara has recognized the mythic dimensions of those "stars" whose personal and public lives determine the rhythm and quality of this civilization just as surely and profoundly as did the fabricated gods of other mythologies. In Henry Pussycat Berryman has erected a myth out of and for the tortured and suffering, middle-aged, white "human American man." But throughout contemporary poetry one also senses that the isolated self, the multi-faceted and complex "I" rises above communal, historical and extra-rational events and assumes mythic proportions of its own. The collective impact of contemporary poetry seems to say: I am my own myth.

The blood and genes inherited by contemporary poetry, however, are not merely the formal demands of new criticism, but the full tradition of American (and British) poetry. Muted, modified, transformed— nonetheless, the spirit and energy of that tradition continue as vital forces in today's poetry. And it is not simply an aesthetic heritage, but a complex of formal and thematic (moral) stances which constitute the polarities, not only of our art, but also of our national psychic and mythic life. The polarized stances (toward man, his history and his art) constituting the mainstream of American poetry are the Puritan tradition and the Whitman tradition. Of course, other less powerful currents, occasional springs and pools have also contributed to the evolution of American poetry. But the life and energy of American poetry, especially in the twentieth century, springs primarily from the tension, balance and occasional reconciliation between the microcosmic and macrocosmic vision and art of the Puritans and, for lack of a more felicitous term, the Whitmanians.

Whether written by Edward Taylor or Robert Lowell, Puritan poetry arises out of the fundamental view of man as the heir of and participant in the specific history of the fallen Adam. It views man as essentially corrupt, seeking the contours of his life in an equally corrupt universe, incapable of personal salvation. Characteristically intellectual and highly personal, seeking the speaker's place in history, it focuses primarily on his spiritual and physical limitations and deterioration. Its structure is usually complex, emblematic and metaphysical, the texture of its language intricate. Because contemporary Puritan poets have rejected the possibility of the traditional concept of Christian salvation, that one thread of light which sustained the original Puritan, sin is symbolically replaced by mental and emotional imbalance and, lacking the hope of salvation, the poet is threatened by madness and tempted to self-destruction. Robert Lowell's "Skunk Hour" and Sylvia Plath's "Lady Lazarus" are among the best examples of the Puritan tradition in contemporary American poetry.

The Whitman tradition stands in stark contrast to its predecessor. Refusing to submit man to the bonds of history, sacred or secular, it asserts the holiness of the Adamic man, inside and out, and celebrates the grace of purely human and physical activity in an equally holy universe. Impatient with and often scornful of intellectualization, it focuses on the unique and separate self's place and role in the day and points to that self's limitless potential for transcendence. Open, loose, often the product of emotion rather than of intellect and conscious craftsmanship, its language also tends to be more recognizably "American" and earthy. However, because the tradition is more specifically "literary," Whitman the *poet*, his vision and his poems often serve as the basis for lament; and the contemporary poet decries the betrayal of history since Whitman's prophetic songs. Allen Ginsberg's "Howl" and Lawrence Ferlinghetti's "Starting from San Francisco" are rather obvious examples.

As critics have noted, however, American poetry has also experienced a large measure of internationalization and reflects the presence of other traditions. The influence of the French symbolists persists. Pound's "discovery" of the East is expanded through the influence of Zen Buddhism and Japanese poetry on the work of Gary Snyder, and Spanish surrealists have had a profound effect on the poetry of such poets as Robert Bly and W. S. Merwin.

Clearly, then, the vitality of contemporary American poetry depends in large part on its full participation in and transformation of a broad and rich tradition of poetry. And yet, after having posited this participation, one must also recognize the contemporary poets' measure of dissatisfaction and restlessness—not only with that tradition, but also with their specific art and medium—which also accounts for the vitality and diversity of today's poetry.

The poets' restlessness with their medium is largely evident in the number of those who for various reasons have changed their styles radically in the course of their careers; these stylistic transformations in turn reflect equally radical shifts in their basic assumptions about the nature and function of their art. From compact and tripplingly anapestic poems dealing with somewhat private experience, James Dickey's poems have grown more expansive, looser, public, and charged by a kind of revivalist energy. On the other hand, W. S. Merwin's poems have moved from technical and structural complexity toward an imaginative and emotional density which is almost hermetic. At times savagely personal, Merwin's poems seem to refuse all further human contact. For reasons which ultimately may not be far removed from Merwin's, LeRoi Jones' style and attitude have also undergone a radical shift, moving from a projectivist (literary) poetics informed by a sense of the Black heritage and an awareness of the political situation toward a more emphatic and indeed ethnic and political poetics of activism. Other poets have shown their restlessness with their medium in other ways by attempting the techniques of other media. Some of John Ashbery's poems, for example, clearly reflect the influence of action painting, while Lawrence Ferlinghetti's poems explore the possibilities of poetry as jazz. Underlying these stylistic transformations and experiments, however, is not merely an obsession with originality, but rather the more profound need of the poet to shape the structures and rhythms and to explore the timbre of the voice of the individual man and his day.

Each age discovers or fabricates one or two encompassing metaphors for the quality of human experience which it affords or seeks. It was T. S. Eliot, of course, who fabricated the first encompassing metaphor for the twentieth century: the waste land was the image of man's spiritual and cultural sterility, an image which, after Hiroshima and Nagasaki, proved to be frighteningly precise in its prophetic implications. To date no single poet seems to have fabricated the central metaphor for the quality of our experience since World War II. However, this is what seems to have happened. "The Waste Land" was a powerful *mise en scène* of the modern situation, but to a large extent its characters were composite ghosts, unreal men and women in an unreal city. Eliot was describing "the human condition" and not the individual condition. In other words, Eliot set the scene, but contemporary poets have peopled that waste land, mostly with themselves. They have described the deterioration and sterility of the individual self and, having done so, have fabricated a cumulative metaphor for our own age.

The language of that metaphor is as stark, brutal and familiar as the experience. More often than not it is the language of experience and emotion—and not recollected in tranquillity. The brutalized self responds neither in pentameters nor in euphemisms, nor, at times, even in metaphor. In the midst of unbearable suffering, Sylvia Plath, as do most of us, utters clichés. At the peak of emotion and frustration John Logan utters obscenities at "this fucking war." And the language in LeRoi Jones' later poems not only reflects the poet's fierce emotion but indeed brutalizes the reader. In differing ways, today's poets have followed the advice and example of Walt Whitman and later William Carlos Williams and agree with George Starbuck's remark: "We've got language we haven't yet used." And it is the language of today's poetry which immediately strikes us as vitally contemporary and fresh. By making poetry out of the full range of everyday speech, including obscenity, vulgarity and slang, contemporary poets have returned to poetry a richness of expression and experience which has been lacking probably since the Renaissance.

A healthy respect for the living language of the tribe and for its potential is in part responsible for an equally healthy respect for the full spectrum of that tribe's experiences. Perhaps just the opposite is truer. At any rate, contemporary poets have managed to reinstate in poetry a directness and honesty toward that tribe's sexual experience and all its ramifications. The range is broad: menstruation, masturbation, love making, adultery, homosexuality, sodomy, abortion. Moreover, whether the cause for celebration or lamentation or both, sexuality in today's poetry is neither a programmatic metaphor, a consciously Freudian exploration, or a mystical Lawrencian-Victorianism. Although clearly an essential element of the poet's theme, first and foremost it is an existential human experience, capable of being simultaneously ugly and the source of grace, tender and brutal, and, as John Berryman suggests, lyrical and vulgar: "like the memory of a lovely fuck."

An imagination of commitment which recognizes and responds directly, honestly and morally to everyday political realities is also one of the distinguishing elements of today's poetry. The political climate has become a crucial arena within which contemporary poets have exercised their talents, and the conflict in Viet Nam has generated an enormous amount of anti-war poetry which reflects the contemporary poets' belief in poetry engagé. The political consciousness of the contemporary poets has returned poetry to a long and vital tradition in the life of poetry. That tradition was virtually ignored during the first half of this century, especially when the notion of art for art's sake virtually prohibited poetry from being anything but hermetic, when political concern had to be masked with myth, clothed with wit and moved by indirection. But the contemporary poet agrees with Sartre and Camus that art must be committed if it is to survive. As Ferlinghetti said: "Only the dead are disengaged."

Commitment, however, does not necessitate "head-line" poetry. In a statement for The London Magazine (1962), Sylvia Plath said: "The issues of our time which preoccupy me at the moment are the incalculable genetic effects of fallout and . . . the terrifying, mad, omnipotent marriage of big business and the military in America. . . . (But) my poems do not turn out to be about Hiroshima, but about a child forming itself finger by finger in the dark. They are not about the terrors of mass extinction, but about the bleakness of the moon over a yew tree in a neighborhood graveyard."

The imagination of commitment is reflected in at least three obvious, though by no means exclusive, ways. The first includes poems informed by a general and sometimes indirect socio-political consciousness. Plath's preoccupation with the "incalculable genetic effects of fallout" is reflected in "Nick and the Candlestick" when, addressing her young, perhaps unborn child, she suggests the end of the world and of the universe in two stanzas also reflecting the scientific quality of her imagination:

> Let the stars
> Plummet to their dark address,
>
> Let the mercuric
> Atoms that cripple drip
> Into the terrible well. . . .

The possible destruction of the world through a nuclear holocaust is also the immediate occasion for Wilbur's "Advice to a Prophet." Snodgrass' " 'After Experience Taught Me . . .' " suggests not only the horror inherent in any system of ideas or values carried to its logical conclusion, but also that terrifying brotherhood of men, the seeming inevitability of the military-industrial-university complex. Merwin's "I Live Up Here" rejects the surreal quality and the meanness of the democratic process: "For I see/ What my votes the mice are accomplishing." And a poem like Ginsberg's "Howl" is a full scale indictment of the quality of American life and the recent history which has contributed to that experience.

In the second group, recent historical events inform the poets' imaginations. The soldiers, battle-fields and truce in Snodgrass' "Heart's Needle" are references to events during the Korean conflict. Elsewhere, poets are responding directly to recent historico-political events: Wright's "Eisenhower's Visit to Franco," Levertov's "The Peachtree" from "During the Eichman Trial." These poems, as well as others, are an indication that the imagination of commitment in contemporary poetry has not been challenged exclusively by the war in Viet Nam.

However, that war has occasioned the greatest number of poems, perhaps more than any other single event since World War I. To date at least three collections of anti-war poetry have been published. And the poets' opposition to the war and to the political figures responsible for it is clear, not only in the more obvious poems by Bly, Levertov, Merwin and Ginsberg, but also indirectly in poems like Dugan's "American Against Solitude" and Wilbur's "A Miltonic Sonnet for Mr. Johnson. . . ." Each of these reflects a profound moral outrage against the fact and quality of this nation's participation in and support of the war in Viet Nam and the depth of frustration that continued involvement has generated. Implicit in each of these poems is a silent echo of Ginsberg's courageous but ultimately disillusioning prophecy:

> I lift my voice aloud
>> make Mantra of American language now,
>> pronounce the words beginning my own Millenium—
>> I here declare the end of the war!

Political or moral questions aside, contemporary anti-war poetry does raise important questions about the art, the most obvious of which is: Where does poetry leave off and propaganda begin? And that raises the equally important question: Can propagandistic poetry be good? (Dryden's "MacFlecknoe" probably sets a precedent.) Moreover, contemporary anti-war poetry is the result of a peculiar set of circumstances, for unlike the poetry that emerged out of World Wars I and II, it has been written primarily by individuals who are non-combatants or who haven't even been in the embattled country. (One is reminded of the shocking contrast between Wilfred Owen's trench poems and Rupert Brooke's chauvinistic sonnets written in the comfort of his precious university circle.) Thus the anti-war poetry of the 60's is based not on the reality of direct experience, but on the removed reality of the media; often it is a poetry not about the victims of war, but about the perpetrators of war; not about the blood of war, but about the language of war; not about the pity of war, but about the policy of war. If it is imperfect as poetry, as it sometimes is, it nevertheless testifies to today's poets' full and human involvement in and commitment to the quality of their fellow creatures' lives.

The poets' moral stance against the war is only part of their more inclusive ethical and spiritual concerns. Although to date none has publicly proclaimed allegiance to any formal ethical or religious system, and although some have been members of the Catholic Church, for example, and later quietly left it, nevertheless there is a diversity of profound religious experience in the work of most of them. In some of Richard Wilbur's poems ("A Dubious Night," for example) the existence of God is at best irrelevant, at worst a handicap to the discovery of that more profound salvation found through human activity. The ending of Lawrence Ferlinghetti's "Sometime during eternity" affirms (but implicitly laments) the contemporary theological stance that God is dead, while "I Am Waiting" humorously reveals the poet's quest for and anticipation of a measure of salvation. His profound mystical sense is also acutely felt in "Assassination Raga," as is Allen Ginsberg's in "Wichita Vortex Sutra." In "Medusa" Sylvia Plath rejects the formal religion of the Vatican, and yet in "Mary's Song" she sees the cycle of Christian salvation present in contemporary history's need for sacrificial victims. Moreover, in much of her poetry one senses the ancient mysticism which affirms salvation through suffering: "The fire makes it precious." And whereas the existence of God or the possibility of human grace seems either irrelevant or impossible in most of Merwin's poems, "Lemuel's Blessing" is probably the most powerful prayer-poem of the century.

To a large extent, then, most contemporary poets, like many of their modern predecessors, view traditional, formal and established religious belief and experience as impossible. Rather, they affirm a personal and vital religious or mystical or spiritual sense. John Berryman is one of the few who use the traditional Judaic-Christian mythology, complete with God, Saint Peter and Satan, as at least a potentially legitimate (and, in his poems, credible) framework for religious experience. However, the work of John Logan, perhaps one of the most truly religious poets of the generation, is more exemplary of the contemporary poet's evolution from a formal and established to a personal religious affirmation. Logan's early work, such as "On a Prize Crucifix by a Student Sculptor," relied primarily on what James Dickey called an "orthodox symbology" and religious sense. His more recent work, however, having shed the formal accoutrements of religion, has also gained intensity of fervor tempered by a greater human complexity. The mystery of salvation is its human incarnation. Grace is discovered and given and received specifically through human and incarnate acts. Thus, "The White Pass Ski Patrol" is a secular and sporty account of the ascension. The member of the ski patrol continually rises and then caroms down—speeding, dancing, balancing, taking all human risks and ministering to others, even in danger. And he rises again, "vanishes in air!" But only after he has come down, after he has learned what the body can do, what grace the body can realize on its own. And finally, like Teilhard de Chardin's fully evolved man, he moves through the final process into pure light.

Politics, sex and religion, the outdated taboos of polite conversation, are only a few of the many concerns to which today's poets have addressed themselves. They are also only a few of the themes which contribute to the freshness and especially the "relevance" of contemporary poetry. Alive with the blood and genes of the immediate and distant tradition of poetry, rebelling against all that is petrified and dead in that heritage, and affirming their fierce personal response to all that is demanded of a human being at this moment of history, contemporary American poets repeatedly affirm with Louis Simpson that American poetry,

> Whatever it is, . . . must have
> A stomach that can digest
> Rubber, coal, uranium, moons, poems. . . .
>
> It must swim for miles through the desert
> Uttering cries that are almost human.

Criticism
A Selected Bibliography

Most of the following books and pamphlets contain substantial discussions of contemporary American poets, especially those represented in this book. A few, however, are primarily concerned with pre-1945 poetry and some contain critical essays by the poets. Since Norman Friedman's series of essays is the only one of its kind and rather substantial, I have included it in this bibliography. Those entries marked by an asterisk (*) should be particularly useful to readers of this book.

Cambon, Glauco. *Recent American Poetry,* Minneapolis: University of Minnesota Press, 1962.

*Carroll, Paul. *The Poem In Its Skin,* Chicago: Follett Publishing Co., 1968.

Deutsch, Babette. *Poetry In Our Time,* New York: Doubleday & Co., Inc., 1963.

*Dickey, James. *Babel to Byzantium, Poets & Poetry Now,* New York: Farrar, Straus & Giroux, 1968.

*Friedman, Norman. "The Wesleyan Poets I–IV," *Chicago Review,* Volume 18, Numbers 3 and 4; Volume 19, Numbers 1, 2, 3, 1966–1967.

Hamilton, Ian, ed. *On The Modern Poet,* New York: Horizon Press, 1969.

*Hungerford, Edward B., ed. *Poets in Progress,* Evanston: Northwestern University Press, 1967.

*Howard, Richard. *Alone with America: Studies in the Art of Poetry in the United States since World War II,* New York: Atheneum, 1969.

Jarrell, Randall. *Poetry and the Age,* New York: A. A. Knopf, 1955.

Kherdian, David. *Six San Francisco Poets,* Fresno: The Giligian Press, 1969.

*Mills, Ralph J., Jr. *Contemporary American Poetry,* New York: Random House, 1965.

Mills, Ralph J., Jr. *Creation's Very Self: On the Personal Element in Recent American Poetry,* Fort Worth: Texas Christian University Press, 1969.

*Nemerov, Howard, ed. *Poets on Poetry,* New York: Basic Books, 1961.

*Ossman, David. *The Sullen Art: Interviews by David Ossman with Modern American Poets,* New York: Corinth Books, 1963.

Ostroff, Anthony, ed. *The Contemporary Poet as Artist and Critic*, Boston: Little, Brown and Co., 1964.

Poulin, A., Jr., *Making In All Its Forms: Contemporary American Poetics and Criticism*, New York: E. P. Dutton and Co., Inc., 1970.

Rosenthal, M. L. *The Modern Poets, A Critical Introduction*, New York: Oxford University Press, 1962.

*Rosenthal, M. L. *The New Poets, American and British Poetry Since World War II*, New York: Oxford University Press, 1967.

*Stepanchev, Stephen. *American Poetry Since 1945*, New York: Harper & Row, Publishers, 1965.

Waggoner, Hyatt H. *American Poetry from the Puritans to the Present*, Boston: Houghton Mifflin Co., 1968.